Wittgenstein: to Follow a Rule

International Library of Philosophy

Editor: Ted Honderich

A catalogue of books already published in the
International Library of Philosophy
will be found at the end of this volume

Wittgenstein: to Follow a Rule

Edited by
Steven H. Holtzman
and
Christopher M. Leich

ROUTLEDGE & KEGAN PAUL
London, Boston and Henley

First published in 1981
by Routledge & Kegan Paul Ltd
39 Store Street, London WC1E 7DD
9 Park Street, Boston, Mass. 02108, USA and
Broadway House, Newtown Road,
Henley-on-Thames, Oxon RG9 1EN
Set in 10/12 pt Times by Input Typesetting Ltd, London
and printed in Great Britain by
Page Bros (Norwich) Ltd
Norwich and London
Introductory Essay and editorial matter
Copyright © Steven H. Holtzman and
Christopher M. Leich 1981
Text © Routledge & Kegan Paul 1981

British Library Cataloguing in Publication Data

Wittgenstein: to follow a rule.
– (International library of philosophy)
I. Holtzman, Steven H.
II. Leich, Christopher M.
192   B3376.W564   80–42299

ISBN 0–7100–0760–4

To the memory of Gareth Evans

CONTENTS

Contents

NOTES ON THE CONTRIBUTORS

Gordon Baker is a Fellow of St John's College, Oxford.

Christopher Peacocke is a Fellow of New College, Oxford.

Crispin Wright is Professor of Logic and Metaphysics in the University of St Andrews.

Gareth Evans was Wilde Reader in Mental Philosophy in the University of Oxford, and a Fellow of University College.

John McDowell is a Fellow of University College, Oxford.

Simon Blackburn is a Fellow of Pembroke College, Oxford.

Charles Taylor is Chichele Professor of Social and Political Theory in the University of Oxford, and a Fellow of All Souls College.

Philip Pettit is Professor of Philosophy in the University of Bradford.

Steven H. Holtzman (ed.) is a Graduate Student at Corpus Christi College, Oxford.

Christopher M. Leich (ed.) is an Assistant Professor of Philosophy at Georgetown University.

ABBREVIATIONS

Unless otherwise indicated, all references are to Ludwig Wittgenstein, *Philosophical Investigations*, Blackwell, Oxford, 1953. References to Part I are by section number, and to Part II by page number.

The following abbreviations are used in references to other works by Wittgenstein:

BB   *The Blue and Brown Books*, Blackwell, Oxford, 1958. Followed by page number.

'BT'   '*Big Typescript*', Manuscript no. 213 in von Wright catalogue.

LFM   *Lectures on the Foundations of Mathematics*, Harvester Press, Hassocks, 1976. Followed by page number.

OC   *On Certainty*, Blackwell, Oxford, 1969. Followed by paragraph number.

PG   *Philosophical Grammar*, Blackwell, Oxford, 1975. Followed by page number.

PR   *Philosophical Remarks*, Blackwell, Oxford, 1975. Followed by page number.

RFM   *Remarks on the Foundations of Mathematics*, revised 3rd edition, Blackwell, Oxford, 1978. Followed by part and section numbers.

WWK   *Ludwig Wittgenstein und der Wiener Kreis*, shorthand notes of F. Waismann, McGuinness (ed.), Blackwell, Oxford, 1967. Followed by page number.

Z   *Zettel*, Blackwell, Oxford, 1967. Followed by section number.

The abbreviation 'PLP' stands for F. Waismann, *The Principles of Linguistic Philosophy*, R. Harre (ed.), Macmillan, London, 1965. Followed by page number.

PREFACE

The essays and replies in this volume represent, with some modifications, the proceedings of a colloquium held in Oxford in Trinity Term, 1979. A few points concerning the goals of and participants in this colloquium deserve explanation at the outset.

With occasional notable exceptions, critical response to the *Philosophical Investigations* in the two decades following its publication tended to focus on a fairly limited range of topics, suggested by certain especially striking series of remarks of Wittgenstein's – e.g. the idea of 'family resemblance', the conception of philosophy as therapy, the 'private language argument' and so on – and to treat these topics piecemeal, in isolation from one another. An apparently unsystematic book was discussed in a genuinely unsystematic fashion; even the remarks about the connection between meaning and use that Wittgenstein wove into nearly every corner of Part I of the *Investigations* were regarded as having a quite limited application, usually to problems of pragmatics in the philosophy of language. The assessment of Wittgenstein's contribution to philosophy thus varied from one interpreter to the next; on one account, he would seem best conceived as centrally concerned with the philosophy of mind, while on another, his principal interest would appear to lie in exploring the varieties of illocutionary force.

The last decade, however, has witnessed a mounting dissatisfaction with this general pattern of interpretation. A different approach has surfaced, one that interprets those apparently disconnected discussions of Wittgenstein's as united by a single underlying set of powerful arguments. The hallmark of this new approach has been its interest in a set of remarks that have hitherto received little critical attention outside the philosophy of mathematics, though they appear at the very centre of the *Investigations*, §§ 139–242, and recur with a minimum of variation throughout Wittgenstein's later manuscripts, in a wide variety of contexts. In these passages, it is held, Wittgenstein articulates a series of considerations about rules and understanding upon which the other, more celebrated discussions of privacy, philosophy, reference and the like are best conceived as consequential. And the philosophical concerns that emerge from these considerations are, according to this new approach, entirely general ones, not in the order of specific contributions to the philosophy of mind or speech-act theory, but rather attempts to deal with global issues in metaphysics and epistemology.

Though it would be unwise to suggest that there are clear areas of general agreement, we believe that several of the contributors to this volume give expression, in various ways, to something like this new approach. But though the idea of this new approach played a central role in our planning of the colloquium, we did not aim solely to provide a forum for it – or even, for that matter, to focus exclusively on interpretations of Wittgenstein. Thus, while some of the contributors are well known as scholars of Wittgenstein, others are not, and some of the essays scarcely treat at all of Wittgenstein's own work. This is so because the principal aim of the colloquium was as much to explore the kinds of impact that Wittgenstein's work has had on a cross-section of current Anglo-American philosophy, as to explore his work itself. In particular, we sought contributors whose responses, we hoped, would help to confront Wittgenstein's work with traditions and problems from which it has lately become estranged.

Among the traditions, 'analytical' philosophy seemed of special interest. In the last decade, developments in linguistics, cognitive psychology and formal semantics have occasioned the flowering of a new, especially close relationship between the 'analytical' tradition and these disciplines. It would be fair to say that, regardless of its intent, an effect of the formation of this new community of scholarship has often been a diminution of interest in, and indeed a quite general alienation from, Wittgenstein and his interpreters. A sense of intellectual responsibility demands an attempt to understand and evaluate this situation.

Among the problems, issues in moral philosophy and, though to a considerably lesser extent, the philosophy of the social sciences have traditionally been thought to be of only peripheral interest when it comes to assessing Wittgenstein. To be sure, there is one obvious explanation of this fact; in his later work, Wittgenstein almost totally neglects problems of morals and politics. But only a little reflection on the *Investigations* rapidly leads one to conclude that it would be surprising if Wittgenstein's philosophical work in other areas did not have important ramifications for such problems; and perhaps it is not too much to hope that investigation of those ramifications will eventually help to explain that neglect – surely one of the single most striking differences between his earlier and later works.

The contributors who, we believe, subscribe in various ways to what we have called the 'new approach' themselves help to confront some of these traditions and problems. But other problems and other traditions are considered as well; and the reactions are various. Taken together the contributions provide, we hope, a set of soundings genuinely revelatory of the spirit of a broad area of current Anglo-American philosophical work; one that will perhaps help us to see how, in taking the measure of Wittgenstein, we ourselves are measured.

POSTSCRIPT

Shortly before going to press, we learned that in August 1980, Gareth Evans died. To some of the contributors to this book he was a personal friend; to all of us he was a deeply admired colleague. We should like to dedicate the book to the memory of this brilliant man.

S.H.H.
C.M.L.

INTRODUCTORY ESSAY: COMMUNAL AGREEMENT AND OBJECTIVITY

Christopher M. Leich and
Steven H. Holtzman

In this essay we shall take up certain questions raised by recent discussions of Wittgenstein's *Investigations*. These questions revolve around the notion of *objectivity*. As the contributions to this volume testify, there is certainly a good deal of disagreement about how to capture the fundamental purposes and conclusions of the central sections of the text, §§ 139–242. Nevertheless, there does seem to be something approaching a majority view; a view which holds that §§ 139–242 are best conceived as addressing questions of objectivity, and in a predominantly negative fashion. If sound, according to this view, these arguments, in which Wittgenstein addresses the concepts of rules and understanding and their relation, would entail that certain very influential philosophical conceptions of and in some cases claims to objectivity lose much of their appeal.

It will hardly be possible to do justice to all, or indeed any, of the salient issues that arise in this connection. But we should like very briefly to take up the two topics that seem to us most plainly relevant to the contributions to this volume, as well as of considerable independent importance. One concerns the relationship between §§ 139–242 and the sections that immediately follow them (the 'private language argument'); this topic is central to the first two sets of essays and replies. The second topic concerns the bearing of §§ 139–242 on problems about specifically *moral* objectivity, and it is the focus of the second pair of essays and replies. Our intention is not to express a position common to all the contributors. In outlining our own particular view, we hope

1

only to provide a unified argumentative context for the papers which follow.

I

Objectivity, on one well-established use of the term, is located in the distinction between appearance and reality; to maintain that it is an objective matter whether or not a certain speaker's claim is true is, on this use, to maintain that there is a clear difference between the claim's merely seeming to be true to the speaker, and its actually being true. This makes it understandable why Wittgenstein's treatment of privacy might be thought to involve some views about objectivity; if it is not the only sector of his later work that makes play with the relation between how things seem and how they really are, it is at any rate the one that appears most obviously to do so. This fact is recorded in the amount of critical attention long paid to the striking sentences that conclude § 258: 'But in the present case I have no criterion of correctness. One would like to say: whatever is going to seem right to me is right. And that only means that here we can't talk about "right".'

Hitherto the appropriate context in which to discuss § 258 was considered to commence at § 243, and little time was spent enquiring into the relationship between the criticism of the wish for a private language that begins there and the immediately preceding sections. But, as noted, the character of this attention has lately undergone something of a change. Although no one could deny that § 243 marks the start of a new phase in Wittgenstein's discussion, several commentators have held that this change in phase does not introduce a fundamentally new set of ideas of Wittgenstein's, but rather develops, in slightly sharpened focus, a set of ideas rooted in §§ 139–242. They thus hold that the significance of such discussion of objectivity as there is in the 'private language argument' will be missed if it is conceived as self-contained, rather than largely consequential upon the earlier passages.

On purely textual grounds, such a view has an obvious merit. If § 258 involves a dismissal of a claim to objectivity, this dismissal is certainly anticipated clearly, if tersely, at § 202:

And hence also 'obeying a rule' is a practice. And to *think*

2

one is obeying a rule is not to obey a rule. Hence it is not possible to obey a rule 'privately': otherwise thinking one was obeying a rule would be the same thing as obeying it.

But the crucial question is as to the nature of the link that this anticipation signals. In particular, what are we to learn from the juxtaposition of the dictum that 'obeying a rule is a practice' with the reference to privacy?

Several answers might be given, but one seems worth special attention. It is an answer which, we believe, is not so very far from the thinking of some of the proponents of the 'new approach', including some of the contributors to this volume. However, we shall make no effort to support its attribution to any specific philosopher here; even if no one actually would subscribe to it, it would still be worth considering by way of contrast.

According to this answer, what that juxtaposition registers is the fact that Wittgenstein's repudiation of 'private objectivity' is one part of a larger argument, which has as its conclusion the claim that there is a very close connection between objectivity and agreement. Specifically, we learn, according to this account, that that repudiation, together with certain other thoughts, leads Wittgenstein to the view that, given any natural language, there is bound to be a wide class of claims formulated in that language which are such that a speaker can coherently be held to be wrong in making them only in so far as, in making them, he diverges from the verdict of the majority of the speakers of the language. That is, Wittgenstein is committed (on this interpretation) to maintaining that for such claims the only coherent notion of an individual's error is one that can be analysed as consisting in disagreement with the majority. Hence there is no coherent sense in which the majority of the speakers of a given language can be supposed to be wrong in making their verdicts on such claims; when it comes to such claims, the majority is, on this interpretation, in roughly the position of the private linguist described at § 258. Lacking any larger community, the majority lacks a criterion of correctness; hence 'whatever is going to seem right [to them] is right.'

This account of Wittgenstein – we shall call it the 'majoritarian account' – is not without considerable *prima facie* appeal. Nevertheless it is, we believe, mistaken. We shall attempt to show why in detail below, when we consider what arguments might be offered on its behalf. But it may help to state now what we take to be the central difficulty with it. In essence, this difficulty is a familiar one; it is that the account takes Wittgenstein to be denying that a language which is only, so to speak, *contingently* private, is not capable of objectivity, whereas Wittgenstein's repudiation of objectivity in § 258 is directed against a language that is supposed to be *necessarily* private. If the majoritarian account is correct, Wittgenstein is committed to holding that if I *happen to be* the sole speaker of a certain language, i.e. if I happen to constitute a majority of one, then 'whatever is going to seem right to me is right.' But, as many commentators have stressed, the wish for a private language with which § 258 is concerned is a wish for a language which no more than one speaker *could* in principle understand. So much is made explicit at § 243, where the notion of a private language is first introduced: 'The individual words of this language are to refer to what can only be known to the person speaking; to his immediate private sensations. So another person cannot understand the language.' This makes it look as though the majoritarian account is too ambitious. For to deny that a language which is necessarily private is capable of objectivity is not yet, or anyway not obviously, to deny that a language which is contingently private is not capable of objectivity.

By itself, however, this difficulty will probably not seem very impressive to a proponent of the majoritarian account. It is, as stressed above, a hallmark of his approach to Wittgenstein's treatment of privacy that the majoritarian pays attention not simply to § 243 ff., but also to §§ 139–242. And in these passages, he will now very likely reply, we find evidence meeting this difficulty, evidence which links Wittgenstein's repudiation of objectivity in a necessarily private language to a more global repudiation of objectivity in a contingently private language.

But now, what exactly is this evidence? To begin with, it will be suggested, we should focus on § 242: 'If language is to be a means of communication there must be agreement not only in definitions but also (queer as this may sound) in judgments. This seems to abolish logic, but does not do so.'

This passage, it might be argued, registers Wittgenstein's view that the role played by agreement in judgments in a language is, in some sense, a *constitutive* one: it is *essential*, if we are to share

4

a common language, that we agree in certain judgments. Hence, one might continue, § 242 shows that in Wittgenstein's view, in any given language L, there is a large class of judgments such that, if an individual speaker of L disagrees with the majority of L-speakers over them, this only shows that he does not attach to the relevant words the same meaning as the majority does. But that, one might conclude, just implies that there is no clear sense in which the majority of speakers of a given language can be said to be *wrong*, in making any one of this large class of judgments. For, surely, the only sense in which they could be wrong, by the foregoing, is if they spoke, in some sense, the wrong language. But clearly, the 'right' language, for a given group of speakers, is the one determined by the majority; there is no other sense in which a language can be right or wrong. Hence, it seems, Wittgenstein is properly interpreted by the majoritarian account.

This argument needs unpacking. In the first place, it is important to grasp that the argument contains a genuine insight into Wittgenstein. For it is clear enough that the role accorded in the *Investigations* to agreement of judgments in communication is, in some sense, a constitutive one. One might interpret § 242 as making only the rather banal claim that, in order for me to find out that you mean by a given sign what I do, I have no option but to look at a broad class of the judgments you make using that sign; these are, as it were, my only *evidence* for your meaning the same. Such an interpretation would not, to be sure, have to render Wittgenstein's thought *totally* banal; it could at least be claimed to have the merit of understanding him as drawing attention to the fact that a surprisingly wide class of judgments has to be taken into consideration in establishing identity of meaning, because any small class is open to too large a number of alternative interpretations. Thus, it could be said, Wittgenstein is exposing a remarkably far-reaching indeterminacy in the evidence employed in settling ascriptions of meaning and belief.

But it is natural to think that Wittgenstein meant something more ambitious than this, something that would really seem to 'abolish logic'. Specifically, it is natural to suppose that he meant to claim that one's applications of a particular sign are not merely evidential, but actually in some sense *constitutive* of what one means by the sign. So much certainly seems to be suggested by his insistence (e.g. at § 146) that one's applications of an expression are 'criteria' of one's understanding of it. Whatever exactly 'criterion' means in Wittgenstein's usage, criteria are apparently to be contrasted with merely evidential 'symptoms'; criteria belong to grammar, and grammar expresses essence (§ 371). But if this is so, then it must seem as though Wittgenstein's view is that for at least a large class of cases, our agreement in applications of a word determines, or is part of the essence of, our meaning the same by it.

To be sure, this insight needs considerable elaboration; one would like to have a much clearer idea of the notion of constitution in play here. But we shall not attempt to investigate this question now. For it seems clear that *however* the notion of constitution is interpreted, the majoritarian account does not follow from this insight alone. Let it be granted that, in Wittgenstein's view, if you and I are to mean the same by our words, then it is (in whatever sense one likes) essential that we agree on a wide class of judgments; it still does not follow, in the way suggested by the argument above, that in Wittgenstein's view there is no clear sense in which the majority of speakers in a given linguistic community cannot be wrong about a large class of their common judgments.

In order to make this clear, we should stress first that we agree that if the insight just sketched is correct – if Wittgenstein held that agreement in a large class of judgments is constitutive of sharing a common language – then it does indeed follow that there is, in his view *one* way in which the majority of speakers of a given language *cannot* go wrong in any one of a large class of their common judgments. For if (to take a very crude example), asserting S in certain circumstances is constitutive of meaning by S whatever a given speaker means by it, then it follows that it is wrong, in those circumstances, to assert S, only if it is wrong to mean by S whatever that speaker means. Hence, if asserting S is constitutive of meaning whatever the majority means, it cannot be both wrong for the majority to claim that S holds, and yet right for them to mean what they do. We might try to sum this up by saying that Wittgenstein is committed to holding that, for a large class of their judgments, the majority of speakers of a given language cannot be (simply) mistaken; instead, if they are wrong, they must *misunderstand*. For it cannot turn out that they are right to mean what they do – that they have a correct understanding – and yet they are wrong to judge as they do, i.e. be simply mistaken.

This much, we agree, seems sound enough. But now, it is crucial to appreciate that such pressure as this conclusion puts on the idea of objectivity in connection with the majority's judgments is not, by itself, enough to sustain the majoritarian account. If what we have just seen is right, then Wittgenstein is committed to agreeing that the majority of the speakers of a given language cannot, in the sense sketched, be *mistaken* in any one of a large class of their judgments. But it does not yet follow from this that in Wittgenstein's view there is no *other* way in which the majority might go wrong; being 'mistaken', as characterized above, is surely only one species of error. Yet the majoritarian account maintains that in Wittgenstein's view there is *no* sense in which the majority of speakers of a given language can go wrong in such judgments; for them, appearance and reality are not distinguishable.

So the majoritarian must take some further steps; and it is crucial to appreciate just how large these steps are. One might imagine that the majoritarian needs only a little. What he needs, one might say, is only to credit Wittgenstein with recognition of the fact that what a word means, in a given language, is determined solely by what the majority of speakers of that language mean by it. For, one might argue, granted this fact, it follows from what we just agreed to be Wittgenstein's view that there is in fact *no* sense in which the majority can be wrong to make any one of a large class of their judgments. We just agreed that Wittgenstein is committed to maintaining that if the majority is *wrong* to make one of a large class of its judgments, this cannot be because the majority is (simply) mistaken; instead, their error must lie in their understanding. But clearly, (one might say), talk of 'misunderstanding' a given word makes sense only relative to a particular language; one can be said to misunderstand S only in so far as one does not mean by S what S means in some language, viz. the language one is trying to speak. So if the majority of speakers of a given language is trying to speak its own language, then it can misunderstand its words only if those words mean in that language something other than what the majority means by them. But this, we have just agreed, is impossible. So it looks as though the majority cannot go wrong in any sense.

But now, this makes the task of the advocate of the majoritarian account seem much easier than it really is. For the reasoning just given does not commit Wittgenstein only to the assumption that what a word means in a given language is determined solely by what the majority of the speakers of that language mean by it; this reasoning also commits Wittgenstein, without supporting argument, to the assumption that there is no sense in which a given word of a given language can mean the *wrong* thing. Without this further assumption, there will be room for the idea of a speaker's going wrong in his judgments, though he is not mistaken, in the sense sketched earlier, and though he means by his words what they mean in the language that he wishes to speak. And so, by the same token, there will be room for the idea of the majority of the speakers of a given language going wrong in this way; despite the fact that what they mean by their words is definitive of what those words mean in their language.

Now it may be felt that this is not really a further assumption; it is, rather, an obvious truism that there is no sense in which a word can mean the wrong thing. Wittgenstein could hardly have said anything to the contrary. But, in fact, such an appraisal seems hasty. So much becomes clear when one reflects on the possibility of a word's meaning *nothing whatsoever*. It is, surely, at least arguable that a speaker might use a word, thinking that he means something by it, whereas in fact he means nothing whatsoever by it. That is, he might be under the impression that he has given the word a perfectly clear meaning, whereas he has in fact given it no meaning at all. But now, if that is a possibility, then it is presumably one that could be realized by the majority of the speakers of a given language; they might all be under the impression that they had given some word of their language a perfectly definite meaning, while in fact they had given it no meaning at all (and hence the word meant nothing in their language). Yet if that is correct, then there is certainly room for Wittgenstein to maintain, consistently with what we have admitted that he does maintain, that the majority of the speakers of a given language can go wrong in certain of their judgments, though those judgments are constitutive of their meaning what they do mean. For they might mean nothing whatsoever; their making those judgments might be constitutive of their meaning nothing. Admitting this possibility is certainly consistent with admitting that the meaning of a word in a language is determined solely by what the majority of the speakers of the language mean by it. In this case, their judgments would show that the word means nothing.

It might be replied that the possibility is nevertheless not a live one: it is in reality impossible that someone should think he means something quite definite by a word, and yet fail to do so. But clearly, this stands in need of a great deal more argument; we need a strong *reason*, now, for thinking that Wittgenstein accepted it.

But now, it might be felt that we do not have to seek far for such a reason. For, one might argue, if we explore the motivation underlying Wittgenstein's claim that how one applies a word is constitutive of what one means by it, we find him committed to denying that it is possible that I should think that I mean something by a word, though I fail to do so. To begin with, we should notice that Wittgenstein's commitment to that constitutive claim must involve him in rejecting the thought that one has a *privileged* access to one's own understanding of a word, an access that does not rely on observation of one's own applications of the word, and is indeed more dependable than the access afforded by such observation. The thought that one has such an access is, after all, surely the most powerful factor militating against the idea that agreement in judgments plays a constitutive role. If one really has such an access, then one's applications of a word must seem not to be *criteria*, but rather merely evidential symptoms. Now it is well known that Wittgenstein does indeed mount an attack against this notion of privileged access, and indeed that the dismissal of the claim to objectivity in § 258 plays a crucial role in it. But, one might say, when we take a closer look at the actual shape of this attack, we find some comfort for the majoritarian account. For it begins to seem as though Wittgenstein is prepared to conclude, on the strength of his discussion of the private language, that 'whatever is going to seem right to me is right' applies not only to the private linguist's use of 'S', but also, with equal justice, to a wide variety of natural-linguistic expressions, including, especially, avowals; and this without much auxiliary argument. That is, it looks as though Wittgenstein is prepared to say that sentences of the form 'Ø(I)' lack objectivity, in just the way the private linguist's use of 'S' does. Yet if this really is his view, then one might conclude the majoritarian account is after all well-founded. For the only objection brought above against this account was that it failed to establish that Wittgenstein is committed to denying that it is possible for the majority of speakers of a given language to go wrong because it seems to them that they mean something quite definite by their words though in fact they do not. But if sentences of the form 'Ø(I)' lack objectivity, then presumably he is committed to denying that possibility; for, 'I mean that p by S', is of the form, 'Ø(I)'. Hence in Wittgenstein's view its seeming to me that I mean that p by S must be tantamount to my meaning that p by S; and so I cannot go wrong because I think that I mean something (p) by my words and yet in fact fail to. But, what goes for me presumably goes for the majority as well.

Though immensely appealing, this argument is not, we believe, satisfactory. But it reveals a second important insight underlying the majoritarian account. The insight is that Wittgenstein was prepared to maintain that at least certain uses of natural-linguistic expressions lack objectivity in just the way that the private linguist's use of 'S' does. Now one might imagine that Wittgenstein cannot have held any such thing; for how, if this is correct, can the repudiation of objectivity at § 258 be conceived as a *criticism* of the wish for a private language? If, as alleged, 'whatever is going to seem . . .' can be said with equal justice, in Wittgenstein's view, of certain fragments of natural language, how can it help to show that the private language is not fully imaginable? Whatever else it is, after all, natural language is imaginable.

But this worry rests on a misapprehension. The wish for a private language is explicitly formulated in § 243 as a wish for a means of 'referring' to one's 'immediate, private sensations'. This means that there is room to agree *both* that the repudiation of the idea of objectivity for such a 'private' language constitutes a criticism of the wish for it, and also that the same repudiation can be applied to certain fragments of natural language. One need only hold that the fragments of natural language in question are not more referential than is the private linguist's 'S'. And this, as is no doubt familiar, seems to be exactly what Wittgenstein is prepared to do:

> if we construe the grammar of the expression of sensation on the model of 'object and designation' the object drops out of consideration as irrelevant (§ 293).

'Joy' designates nothing at all. Neither an inward thing nor any outward thing (Z, § 487).

These passages, of course, treat only of words for emotion and sensations. But it is clear that Wittgenstein is prepared to extend his claims of non-referentiality to 'I' as well; § 404 makes the point succinctly:

'When I say "I am in pain," I do not point to a person who is in pain, since in a certain sense I have no idea *who* is.' And this can be given a justification. For the main point is: I did not say that such-and-such a person was in pain, but 'I am . . .' Now in saying this I don't name any person. Just as I don't name anyone when I *groan* with pain. Though someone else sees who is in pain from the groaning.

We agree, then, that Wittgenstein would be prepared to maintain that at least some uses of 'I mean that p by S' state nothing objective. Many more passages might be cited to support this interpretation. But we shall not attempt to canvass them here, for we are already in a position to explain why, even though this interpretation is sound, the argument sketched above on behalf of the majoritarian account is misguided. The argument assumes that if Wittgenstein is willing to declare that a speaker's 'I mean that p by S' states nothing objective, then he must also agree that it is in no sense an objective matter whether the speaker does mean that p by S. But this assumption, it seems to us, rests on a profound misunderstanding of Wittgenstein.

That it is mistaken is, in fact, suggested by what we have just seen. For if it is true, as we noted, that the critical power of the private language argument can be squared with a denial that certain natural-language expressions state anything objective only at the expense of denying that those expressions state (refer to) anything at all, then it follows that Wittgenstein could afford to maintain that 'I mean that p by S' states nothing objective only at the expense of maintaining that it states nothing at all. That is, Wittgenstein is required to agree that if 'I mean that p by S' states anything objective it cannot be taken to imply that it is not an objective matter whether a certain speaker – the speaker I am – means that p by S. For that would assume that the utterance

11

stated *something*. Instead Wittgenstein must hold, as Miss Anscombe puts it, that 'I am X' is not an identity proposition.[1]

It might be replied that this is unsatisfactory. For surely, one might complain, Wittgenstein must have recognized that one could always use one's own name in place of 'I' – indeed, some very young children do just that. But if this is possible, then (one might argue), what it shows is that if 'I am Ø' states nothing objective, so can 'X is Ø' where 'X' is my name; and if that is true, then indeed it follows from the fact that 'I am Ø' states nothing objective, that 'X is Ø' does not either – or, as one might say, that it is not an objective matter whether X is Ø. And so, from the fact that, 'I mean that p by S', states nothing objective it follows that there must be a clear sense in which it is not an objective matter whether the speaker I am means that p by S.

But this reply obviously will not serve. It is certainly true that I can use my own name in place of 'I', and so it follows that, in Wittgenstein's view, my utterances of 'X is Ø' could state nothing objective. But it does not follow that it would never be an objective matter whether X – the speaker I am – is Ø, for 'X' might have, and indeed it is natural to suppose that it would have, another (referential) use. Indeed, Wittgenstein held that 'I' itself has exactly such a double use. At BB, p. 66, he distinguishes an 'objective' and a 'subjective' use of 'I'. The 'subjective' use is not based on observation, and it simply *expresses* how things are with the speaker, much as a dumb animal's whines express how things are with it. It is this use which fails to be referential. But there is another use of 'I' as well, the 'objective' one: this use *is* based on observation, and would normally be exemplified in an utterance like 'I have a bump on my forehead.'[2] Often, the syntactical form of a sentence will not be sufficient to distinguish which use is at stake: 'I am standing up' for example will normally contain a subjective use, but not always – it *can* be based on observation.[3]

To be sure, the two uses of 'I' are not unconnected. On the contrary, their coincidence is constitutive of self-consciousness. If my subjective use comes adrift from what I believe observationally, true of me – if, for example, I know on the basis of observation that I (objectively) have fallen, and I do not know that I (subjectively) have fallen, e.g. I say, 'I think it was I who fell' – then my self-consciousness is gone. But self-consciousness does not, in Wittgenstein's view, consist in mastery of an identity, an identity between something to which 'I' refers, when used subjectively, and a person who is visible to others. If it did consist in mastery of such an identity, then either someone else could, as it were, express my situation for me; or I would have grasped an identity that no one else could possibly comprehend. But neither alternative, in Wittgenstein's view, is a respectable one. You cannot express my situation for me, because then you would have become me; that is one of the seeds of the wish for a private language. But neither can I grasp an identity which no one else could possibly comprehend; it makes sense to speak of my grasping an identity only where it makes sense to suppose that someone else should grasp it. (Which is not to say, of course, that I do grasp an identity only if others actually do so as well. That, it will be remembered, required further argument.)

The majoritarian account, then, is not supported by Wittgenstein's views on self-knowledge. Indeed, the account must seem not just to go beyond those views, but actually, in a sense, to reverse them. The majoritarian holds that according to Wittgenstein it is not possible for the majority of the speakers of a given language to fail, unintentionally, to mean something by their words. But now, surely one way to sum up Wittgenstein's conclusions about the subjective use of 'I' – and expressive uses of words generally – is to say that, for him, such uses *mean* nothing, in the sense that mastery of them does not reside in mastery of referential relations. This is what is signalled by their failure to state anything objective. But then it must, in Wittgenstein's view, be a necessary condition of our intending to make them *more* than expressive that the possibility is not foreclosed of our uses going awry, of their failing to refer. The foreclosure of that possibility ensures our correctness only at the price of depriving finally our words of referential power. As it were, what we have to fear is the position of the private linguist.[4]

To be sure, this conclusion raises almost as many questions as it answers. In particular, no interpreter of Wittgenstein can rest content with dismissing the majoritarian account unless he tackles the possibility left open by the account's demise: the possibility of the majority of the speakers of a given language unintentionally failing to mean anything by their words. Two issues seem especially crucial in this connection. One concerns *recognition* of the possibility's being realized. Because there is an objective use of

'I', it is possible for me to grasp that I (objectively) meant nothing by a word, though I thought that I (subjectively or objectively) meant something by it. But it is unclear that my coming to grasp this, if in fact I do succeed in grasping it, can be conceived as a process of recognition; rather, it appears that I will have to have undergone a conceptual change. A further exploration of this matter would, we believe, yield valuable insights into Wittgenstein's later views on necessity.

But there is another, perhaps more urgent reason, for investigating Wittgenstein's views on the possibility of meaninglessness. Part of the appeal of the majoritarian account lies, no doubt, in its promise to explain Wittgenstein's attitude towards a generalized epistemological scepticism. That he was deeply concerned with such scepticism seems clear enough from his later work, and it might be felt that unless the majoritarian account, or something very like it, is correct, we shall have no explanation of how Wittgenstein might have taken himself to have *refuted* scepticism. That impression seems to us wholly correct; without the majoritarian account, or something like it, Wittgenstein cannot seem to have been attempting to refute scepticism. But what this implies, in our view, is that it is a mistake to look, in the later work, for such an attempt. Wittgenstein's treatment of scepticism is of an entirely different order. This is not to say that he embraced scepticism; there are more options in philosophy than endorsement or refutation.[5]

We shall not, however, attempt to pursue this issue here. For other questions about Wittgenstein's conception of objectivity have been raised elsewhere, from a different perspective from the one adopted here. It is time now to turn our attention to these.

II

We mentioned at the beginning that recent discussions of the *Investigations* have been led to examine the impact of §§ 139–242 on debates about objectivity in one especially crucial area, ethics. In the remainder of this introductory essay we should like to take up this question, albeit in a rather limited fashion. Once again, it is our view that Wittgenstein's discussion does have an important bearing on these matters. But, once again, we feel that it is imperative first to recognize the limitations of that discussion, limitations that parallel the ones just sketched.

In order to effect as close a connection as possible with our earlier remarks, let us begin by singling out a class of utterances that might be called First-Personal Utterances of Pure Taste/Desire: paradigmatically, utterances of the form 'I like x', 'I want you to do x'. Like 'I am in pain', utterances of these syntactic types seem capable of two distinct uses:

1 *Expressive uses*, in which 'I like x' or 'I want you to do x' simply express, non-observationally, the utterer's affection or desire. In such uses, 'I want you to do x' performs the same role as what one might call a Pure Demand: an utterance of the form 'Do x!' that simply expresses the utterer's desire;

2 *Descriptive uses*, in which 'I like x' and 'I want you to do x' describe, on the basis of observation, the fact that the person who the utterer in fact is has a certain affection or desire.

This distinction between kinds of use obviously parallels Wittgenstein's distinction between subjective and objective uses of 'I', introduced earlier; the susceptibility of these utterances to this distinction suggests that most of the central points made in our recent discussion of 'I mean that p by S' could have been cast in terms of them.

Now it is little secret that analytic philosophers of a non-cognitivist or anti-naturalist bent in this century have felt that the study of the logical form of First-Personal Utterances of Pure Taste/Desire (and Pure Demands) can help to elucidate the nature of critical moral assessment. Nor should this seem very surprising; the appeal of an assimilation of critical moral assessments to these paradigms must not be undersold. For such an assimilation accommodates at least the striking connection between critical moral assessments and action. All things being equal, a sincere utterance of 'I like x' presumably will normally be followed by attempts to secure x, or something relevantly similar; and a sincere 'I want you to do x' (or 'Do x!') presumably will normally be followed by (or partially constitute) attempts to get the person to whom the utterance is addressed to perform x. Analogously, a sincere utterance of, e.g., 'X is the just thing to do here' will (all other things being equal) be followed by a performance of x, and attempts to get others to perform x when they are in the same circumstances.

But, given the discussion in the preceding section, we should be prepared for confusion to arise if attention is not paid to which *use* of the relevant paradigm utterances is appropriate to the non-cognitivist's assimilation. And, in fact, just such a confusion has its place in the history of ethics. It arises because the non-cognitivist is thought to be comparing utterances of the form 'x is good' to 'I like x' used *descriptively* – used, that is, to report observationally the affection of the person who is speaking. Now in the first place, it should seem a little odd to call such a position non-cognitivist, for descriptive uses of 'I like x' are on any account fully cognitive, observationally based reports. But the position might seem non-cognitivist nevertheless, because it is, in a straightforward sense, anti-objectivist. For the property that the speaker would be cognizing and reporting in 'x is good' would be a state of himself or a subjective relation in which he stands to x; namely a relation of affection or desire.

Such a position, which might be called subjectivism, has a clear weakness: it renders moral disagreement inexplicable. For how can you and I even *seem* to disagree about whether x is just, if our respective utterances ('It is!', 'It isn't!') merely describe different things – our respective attitudes towards x? But now, one must be careful about what inferences to draw from this. Noting this absurd consequence of subjectivism, many genuine moral objectivists or cognitivists have been prompted to deny altogether the non-cognitivist's assimilation of moral assessments to First-Personal Utterances of Pure Taste/Desire. And indeed, if one imagines that the non-cognitivist is committed by that assimilation to the idea that 'x is just' simply describes the speaker's attitude, the appeal of the analogy rapidly seeps away. But the non-cognitivist will protest that this is a crude misunderstanding of his position, based on a failure to apprehend the distinction noted above between expressive and descriptive uses. The relevant analogy, he will say, is between 'x is just' and *expressive* uses of 'I like x'; for it is only in that use that the internal connection of utterance to action, the very feature that made the analogy attractive in the first place, remains intact. Our attitudes towards an object can certainly conflict, the non-cognitivist will say, because the actions

16

that express them can conflict; and since the claim is that critical moral assessments express attitudes, not that they describe them, it is clear how disagreement over whether x is just can be real enough. The point is simply that such disagreement amounts, as it were, to no more than a disagreement *between people* – a conflict of attitudes with attitudes. So it is as expressions, according to the non-cognitivist, that critical moral assessments are not the right candidates for objectivity.

Now it might appear as though anyone who disagrees with the non-cognitivist must deny that moral assessments so much as *express* personal attitudes. Rather, one might say, the objectivist will have to claim that moral assessments are purely descriptive of non-personal properties of actions and objects. We should like to stress, however, that this is not so. An objectivist may maintain that moral assessments, like the paradigm utterances with which we began, do express personal attitudes, so long as he is prepared to maintain that, unlike those paradigms, moral assessments make in addition a further descriptive or cognitive claim.

To be sure, such a moral objectivism will need careful handling. In particular, it must not be confused with a position which attempted to wed subjectivism and the non-cognitivism just distinguished. Such a position would combine the features of 'privileged access' and internal-connectedness to action, characteristic of the expressive use, with the feature of objective self-description, characteristic of the descriptive use. Thus, 'x is good' would be claimed both to express *and* describe the speaker's attitude towards x. Now it should be clear why, at least in Wittgenstein's view, any such position must be avoided. It suffers, in effect, from just the difficulties that beset the private linguist; by attempting to secure referentiality for expressive uses of words, it threatens to abolish expression altogether.

But the moral objectivist need not, we suggest, violate Wittgenstein's insights. He can maintain that moral assessments do express personal attitudes, and hence stand in an internal relation to action, while maintaining that they make a further cognitive claim, if this claim is understood as a claim to being justified in having the attitude which he expresses. This would not be to say that the speaker claims to be justified in *expressing* that attitude; that he has, as it were, looked into himself to see whether the attitude that he proposes to express is the one he actually has.

That is just the combination of ideas Wittgenstein makes untenable. Rather, the objectivist's contention would be that the claim of justification carried by a moral assessment is with respect to *having* the attitude. In the objectivist's view, to refuse to attempt to justify having one's attitudes is to refuse to engage in moral discourse. One is left merely expressing one's immediately felt (dis)approval or desire, the efficacy of which will be a function solely of one's position of power. In moral discourse, by contrast, features of an action are cited as providing compelling reasons for the attitudes held and expressed and the recommendations made. It is to this conception of an expressive use functioning in a field of discourse which imparts a cognitive claim that the objectivist may subscribe, in a spirit entirely friendly to Wittgenstein.

To be sure, few non-cognitivists, at least nowadays, would endorse the idea that moral assessments are best conceived as *strictly* assimilable to those paradigmatic utterances with which we began. Rather, it is quite generally conceded that such assessments, at least at a superficial level, must be conceived roughly as the objectivist just sketched would recommend; 'x is just' is, it is generally conceded, best understood as bipartite, the sum of an expression of an attitude and the claim that the attitude is justified.[6] Recognition of this point is marked in numerous ways in recent analytic writings on morality; e.g., moral argument is held to be a reason-giving activity, moral assessments are seen as involving appeals to standards, etc. But the agreement between objectivist and non-cognitivist is only a limited one. The non-cognitivist grants that 'x is just' makes an appeal to standards, but he calls the objectivity of the standards themselves into question. It is here, he maintains, that we come down to what is purely expressive; although a limited class of moral assessments can be understood as making a genuinely cognitive appeal, that to which they appeal cannot itself be justified.

One example of this position, call it non-cognitivism$_1$, is the view that whether the attitude expressed by a particular moral assessment is justified depends solely on whether the person making the assessment is also willing to affirm a universalized version, one containing no singular referring terms, of his particular assessment.[7] This universalized assessment counts as the 'standard' for the justification of, or the 'reason' for, the particular assessment, because the former is claimed to support deductively an inference to the latter. What distinguishes moral evaluations and prescriptions, according to this view, is their reliance on such universalized assessments, a reliance that 'I like x' and 'I want x', as distinguished earlier, do not share. But, while such a reliance (perhaps) secures the rationality of moral assessments, it does not secure their objectivity, for the universalized assessment, the 'reason' remains ineluctably a matter of what the individual making the assessment finds himself able to will. That is, the 'standard' by which the particular moral appraisal is justified is itself just an *expression* of a speaker's attitude, albeit an attitude towards a more universalized matter. It lays no claim to objective justification itself.

Non-cognitivism₁ has been found wanting by anti-non-cognitivists on several counts. One criticism, of particular relevance to Wittgenstein, but which cannot be taken up in full here, would focus on the logical relations that obtain between expressive uses of language. Non-cognitivism₁ has two salient features: (i) it construes both the universalized and the particular assessments as expressive (herein lies the non-cognitive/anti-objectivist aspect), while (ii) claiming that the former deductively supports the latter (herein lies the *reason*-giving status of the universalized assessment). Suppose (i) is correct. Then (ii) straightforwardly depends on construing one expressive use of language (the universalized assessment) as the universal generalization of another expressive use (the particular assessment) – and it is anything but obvious to us that expressive uses of language, syntactic appearances to the contrary, are so straightforwardly related.

A second criticism might well be thought to elicit some sympathy, or even receive its impetus, from Wittgenstein. This is the idea that whether a certain consideration constitutes a reason – be it for action, for believing a proposition, for doubting, for holding an attitude – is a matter of the nature of the practice of argumentation in which such considerations are cited. In Wittgensteinian terms, it is a matter of the *grammar* of the field of discourse. This is not to claim that in any such practice all relevant considerations and their roles must be fixed. That may be true of specialized argumentative practices, e.g. those we find in games. But, as Wittgenstein stresses, it is no objection to the idea that a criterion is part of grammar that there is some fluctuation between criteria and symptoms (cf. § 354). The central point is that *gram-*

mar, and thus what grammatically constitutes a reason for an attitude, is not a matter of personal decision or individual will. On these grounds alone, non-cognitivism$_1$ can be seen to be inadequate.[8]

If this second criticism is correct, then the problem with non-cognitivism$_1$ is that it neglects the role that a communal practice determinative of the grammar of a field of discourse plays in an elucidation of the nature of reasons or standards. Now, we agree that that certainly is a lesson to be learned from Wittgenstein's discussion in §§ 139–242. Nevertheless, there might seem to be room for another position, call it non-cognitivism$_2$, which can absorb this lesson from Wittgenstein yet still maintain that moral standards are not proper candidates for objectivity. For, recall the paradigmatic utterances with which we began. Their lesson is that purely expressive utterances are not candidates for objectivity. If moral assessments are to be such candidates, then the standards, appeal to which distinguishes the grammar of moral assessments from the grammar of the pure paradigms, cannot themselves be merely expressive. Concede that what constitutes a standard or reason cannot be simply the expression of an *individual's* will or attitudes; non-cognitivism$_2$ will maintain that these standards are nothing but *expressions* of attitudes which are *de facto* shared in a community. And now it seems that non-cognitivism$_2$ can rightfully conclude that the standards are still essentially expressive – being shared cannot alter that fact – and thus are not candidates for objectivity.

A standard of rational argumentation which is nothing but the expression of a communally shared attitude is not objective – that is, as we shall argue, a point well worth taking from non-cognitivism$_2$. However, this reflection will support an anti-objectivism about specifically *moral* assessments only in conjunction with some means by which to draw a contrast between the foundations of the standards employed in our practices of critical moral assessment and the foundations of those employed in our other, paradigmatically objective, forms of rational assessment, e.g. mathematics. In other words, the argument will not afford a special claim about ethics if it equally condemns our 'reasons' for, or the 'standards' by which we justify, standard mathematical and logical inferences as 'mere expressions' of shared attitudes.

A proponent of non-cognitivism$_2$ will no doubt wish to reply that there is a salient difference, inasmuch as practices of ethical argumentation depend on shared attitudes in a way that other kinds of argumentative practices (e.g. mathematics) do not. But this reply looks dubious in the light of Wittgenstein's discussion. Much of the opening movement of §§ 139–242 serves precisely to illustrate the extent to which mastery of mathematics depends on possession of a complex cluster of attitudes – senses of what is important, relevant, even senses of what constitutes a good reason for drawing a particular inference. In the face of these points, it is exceedingly difficult to find a clear sense in which the practice of moral assessment depends on attitudes in a way that mathematical practice does not – and in such a way as to rob it, but not mathematics, of objectivity.

One might imagine, for example, that a moral disagreement must differ from mathematical disagreement inasmuch as the latter must be assessed as the product of one of the disputants' involvement in self-contradiction or plain error or deviant understanding, whereas a moral dispute may be the product of some fourth option; one not equivalent to these others, perhaps rightly called a (mere) difference in attitudes. But the appeal of such an idea is bound to diminish when one reflects on, e.g. Wittgenstein's example of the wood-sellers (RFM I, 143–152), which appears to be designed precisely to show how someone, or some community, may diverge from us in mathematics though we cannot convict him or them of a mistake, self-contradiction or a disagreement in meaning, at least in the sense that it is indifferent what we choose to mean by a word, so long as we are consistent. If we therefore say that Wittgenstein's wood-sellers 'merely differ in attitudes' from us, does that rob *our* mathematics of objectivity? If not, why should parallel reflections on, for instance, the differing value systems of foreign cultures force that conclusion on us in the case of our standards of moral assessment?

For the moment, and with deliberate vagueness, let us say that what emerges from Wittgenstein's discussion in §§ 139–242, particularly those sections which stress the importance of attitudes and the notion of a form of life, is the *anthropocentric* nature of even our most objective practices of understanding, such as mathematics. Put this way, the problem with non-cognitivism$_2$ is that the standard of objectivity which it claims moral assessments fall short of is of such a nature that mathematics *must* fall short of it as well. It is an illusory standard which places an illusory demand on human knowledge, whose failure to satisfy it can only issue forth in a generalized scepticism. In denying the anthropocentricity of practices of objective understanding, non-cognitivism$_2$ makes all rational assessment merely expressive. But this just means that it has lost the contrast between morals and, e.g., mathematics, upon which it depended.

To be sure, if Wittgenstein's ideas about anthropocentricity are accepted, non-cognitivism$_2$ is not the only position that will be found wanting. For those ideas presumably must have at least this much content: an appeal to a shared form of life in part constituted by shared attitudes is held to have a role to play in the elucidation of any practice of objective understanding. This is, in effect, a more generalized version of the claim that we discussed in the preceding section: our agreement in our applications of our words is constitutive of our meaning the same by them. But now, if that is so, an appeal to shared meanings (or shared universals) cannot help, in Wittgenstein's view, to explain such agreement. So if moral intuitionism, particularly in a form which invokes the notion of a cognitive 'moral sense', is fairly characterized as employing moral universals in just such an explanatory manner, then clearly it is a form of moral objectivism which an objectivist sympathetic to Wittgenstein cannot endorse. Put figuratively, if the cognitivist response under consideration functions by humanizing mathematics, bringing it down from an illusory status, it cannot be a form of moral objectivism which would leave our conception of mathematics intact while elevating moral assessments to the same illusory status.

This is fine as far as it goes. But Wittgenstein's lesson of the anthropocentricity of objective understanding needs considerable filling in if it is to support moral cognitivism. In the final part of the preceding section we suggested one way in which Wittgenstein alters our understanding of objectivity, humanizes it. But we also discussed a *misinterpretation* of Wittgenstein's discussion, one which has its parallel in the case of morals. According to this reading of Wittgenstein, the lesson of anthropocentricity is taken to be that objectivity, be it in the case of morals or mathematics, amounts to nothing more than *de facto* shared attitudes. If this were the correct way to interpret Wittgenstein, then, though some sense could be given to the idea of a particular speaker's possess-

22

ing the wrong attitudes, namely by reference to his divergence in holding them from a particular community, no sense could be given to the idea that most of the members of the community hold wrong attitudes; those attitudes are prior to, and are the basis of, any meaningful criticism. 'Objectivity' therefore exists wherever we find a practice of assessment marked by a modicum of agreement. And, arguably, this is the case with morals.

The claim that agreement constitutes objective correctness in the realm of meaning becomes, in the realm of morals, totalitarian majoritarianism, with its highly conservative implications. An analogous view in the social sciences would amount to cultural relativism.

However, this moral position is a product of a wholly general interpretation of §§ 139–242, one which, in our parallel discussion in the case of meaning, we have argued is not rightfully attributed to Wittgenstein. To approach the source of that misinterpretation differently, consider once again non-cognitivism$_2$. Its failure lay in erecting a standard of objectivity which threatened to make objectivity transcendent of all practices of human understanding, threatened to issue in a generalized scepticism by making all practices of understanding merely expressive. The moral cognitivism we are presently considering interprets Wittgenstein's lesson of 'anthropocentricity' as suggesting that, in an odd sense, all understanding *is* indeed merely expressive. This, however, is not seen as issuing in scepticism, about either morals or mathematics, because there is nothing else, at least nothing non-illusory, for practices of objective understanding to be. As far as the form of cognitivism under consideration is concerned, the existence of a shared practice becomes the *only* feature relevant to the issue of objectivity. *This* is taken to be Wittgenstein's response to the sceptic; and, if we grant that there is sufficient agreement present, the response extends to a defeat of moral non-cognitivism – in effect, moral scepticism – as well.

But while we see §§ 139–242 as integral to Wittgenstein's response to scepticism, and further agree that, correctly interpreted, the anthropocentricity of objective understanding is at the heart of that response, we again see no grounds for burdening Wittgenstein's discussion with this 'majoritarian' construction of objectivity. A philosophically coherent notion of the lone reformer who can with justification repudiate the practice of his community, yet go forever unrecognized, is if anything more urgently required in the case of ethics than in the case of mathematics.

Furthermore, the important and correct claim of non-cognitivism$_2$ becomes salient here; viz. that a standard of argumentation which is essentially expressive of an attitude is not objective, and does not become so merely in virtue of being *de facto* shared. We distinguish practices of assessment which, though they may be different from our own due to their cultural and historical settings, are objective from other differing practices which we label as prejudices or claim to be founded merely in tradition, superstition or fanatic blindness – characterizations intended to signal the lack of objectivity of such practices. Wittgenstein's discussion of the anthropocentricity of even our most objective practices of understanding cannot obliterate these distinctions. If anything, his work should prompt us to take a closer look at the practices themselves, to determine how they are related, how distinct, to examine the nature and function of these different practices in order to determine when the standards employed by particular communities attain, or fail to attain, objectivity.

Wittgenstein's arguments, then, do not decisively settle the dispute in morality in favour of the moral objectivist. At best, they show that there is no straightforward way, of the sort envisaged by non-cognitivism$_1$ or non-cognitivism$_2$, of differentiating moral standards from other alleged paradigms of objectivity, e.g. mathematical standards. But this negative thesis can hardly satisfy a reflective moral cognitivist. For there remains the brute fact that when it comes to recognizing genuine moral reformers we lack all but a fraction of the confidence we possess in our parallel mathematical capacity. The thought that *all* forms of action-oriented understanding (moral and otherwise) are in the end nothing but the masked expression of particular interests – of an individual or a class – is far from foreign to twentieth-century intellectual and political life. And that thought, all too manifestly true throughout history, is enough to revive a form of non-cognitivism which avoids the pitfalls of both varieties so far examined. This means that the onus is on the cognitivist to outline and justify some account of the conditions under which moral assessments can be claimed to be based in an objective understanding of man – an account not susceptible either to the charge that it is ideological or to rejection

Introductory Essay

as nothing more than a convoluted expression of personal
attitudes.

But that lack of confidence must trouble the revived non-cognitivist as well. The heart of his position – as it has been since the
opening discussion of the Pure Paradigms (Expressions of Taste/
Desire) – is that no understanding of human action with intrinsic
practical import can be objective; this allows him to escape the
majoritarian consequences of the form of cognitivism recently
dismissed. This central thesis is set forth as a *philosophical* claim,
one which purports to be *objective*. But, at bottom, this surely
seems to amount to the position that the final basis of choice for
moral standards can only be an individual's agreement with, or
admiration for, the attitudes which the standards express. And
this 'philosophical' claim must begin to look suspiciously like a
very particular *moral* position: an understanding of man, with
intrinsic practical (including political) import, that might deserve
the title of liberal individualism. To vindicate himself, the non-
cognitivist must restore the gap between *philosophical* and *moral*
conceptions of man which his position at once presupposes yet
threatens to annihilate. A gap which, one might add, a cognitivist
can by now quite happily repudiate.

And Wittgenstein? Has he a contribution to make to this debate? One central concern of his, manifest in both §§ 139–242 and
the sections that succeed it, was with the manner in which repres-
sion of the natural expression of the human being alienates the
repressed individual(s) not only from others, but from himself
(themselves) as well; it leaves him (them) without self-knowledge.
Perhaps a moral objectivist position which attempted to synthesize
this concern with another Wittgensteinian theme, the role of community and practice in concept formation, in the form of reflections on the societal conditions under which the language that
men employ to record themselves and their interrelations can be
truly expressive of their needs, might deservedly lay claim to
sharing the spirit of Wittgenstein's later work.[9]

NOTES

1 See G. E. M. Anscombe, 'The first person', in *Mind and Language*,
  ed. Guttenplan, Oxford University Press, 1975.

25

2 A similar duality of use is, presumably, discernible, in Wittgenstein's view, in 'joy', 'pain', '. . . mean p by S'. These nouns and predicates have an objective use, mastery of which consists in mastery of referential relations, or at any rate grasp of the contribution made to the truth-conditions of whole sentences in which they may occur. But they also have a subjective use, mastery of which does not consist in grasping a sense at all (except in so far as, if one is self-conscious, the two uses must be acquired together: see next text paragraph).

3 It may be protested that this account of Wittgenstein saddles him with maintaining, implausibly, a plethora of ambiguities in natural language, and moreover with denying the possibility of a truth-conditional semantics for natural language.

There is much to be said in reply to this protest. Two preliminary points are worth making here.

(i) Philosophers of this century, and especially Wittgenstein, came to be interested in the study of language not as an end in itself, but as a means to resolving traditional metaphysical and epistemological disputes. Claims about semantic identity and difference are thus made in a particular kind of context. If it seems implausible to suggest that 'I' – and other expressions of natural language – are ambiguous, in that they have two uses, perhaps it will seem less implausible to maintain that self-consciousness is not continuous with, or reducible to, a form of consciousness of the objects to which we refer in our normal commerce with the world. This latter claim is, we believe, a central theme of *Investigations*.

(ii) If a particular interpretation of Wittgenstein commits him to looking askance at the project of constructing a truth-conditional semantics for natural language, this is not, perhaps, a point against it. It is worth reminding oneself that the author of the *Tractatus* presented such a systematic truth-conditional semantics; that a major concern of Wittgenstein's middle and later periods was the inadequacy of the *Tractatus*'s treatment of the self; and that the *Investigations* stresses the importance of different *kinds* of use of expressions in natural language.

4 This is not, we believe, the only way in which the majoritarian account is actually inconsistent with Wittgenstein's views. His philosophy of mathematics, in particular, seems to require him to recognize the possibility of a word's meaning the wrong thing in a language – and not just because it means nothing. But we cannot explore this issue here.

5 See Stanley Cavell's profound discussions of scepticism and the *Investigations* in *The Claim of Reason*, Oxford University Press, 1979.

6 For those familiar with the literature, the claim here is *not* the same as Hare's claim that moral words have a bipartite nature: the sum of a descriptive and prescriptive component (see e.g. Hare, *Freedom and Reason*, Clarendon Press, Oxford, 1963, Chapter 2). Rather, the element in Hare's work which corresponds, albeit in an attenuated sense, to the claim that the attitude expressed in a moral assessment must be

justified, is his demand for a universalized prescription to deductively support the particular assessment. See below.

7 The model for non-cognitivism₁ is, of course, Hare's work. See Hare, *op. cit.*

8 In fairness, it should be pointed out that Hare's later work, in which universal prescriptivism becomes indistinguishable from a form of utilitarianism, is, at least on one reading, immune to this criticism.

9 We should like to thank Lindsay Judson and Simon Blackburn for comments, both philosophical and stylistic, on an earlier draft of this introduction.

PART ONE

FOLLOWING A RULE: THE BASIC THEMES

I

FOLLOWING WITTGENSTEIN: SOME SIGNPOSTS FOR *PHILOSOPHICAL INVESTIGATIONS* §§ 143–242[1]

Gordon Baker

Long ago I was asked to start the ball rolling for this symposium. My brief was a modest one. I was to lay out a detailed exegesis of *Philosophical Investigations* §§ 185–242 and to complement this with an analysis of §§ 143–84, a synopsis of the private language argument (§§ 243–315), and a systematic comparison with the related material published as *Remarks on the Foundations of Mathematics*, Parts I and II. *En passant* I was to give a critical examination of existing expositions of Wittgenstein's account of rule-following, at the very least discussing the interpretations presented by Saul Kripke and Crispin Wright.[2] Finally, I was to round off the whole composition with a coda demonstrating whether or not the *Philosophical Investigations* proves the impossibility of constructing a theory of meaning for a language on the lines suggested by such philosophers as Donald Davidson and Michael Dummett. Hardly enough grist here to keep the millstones from grinding each other to splinters!

Alas, in this case, as so often, the finished edifice has only the remotest resemblance to the specifications issued to the architect by the client. Like any well-trained architect, I shall excuse my performance by the twin pleas of 'force of circumstances' and 'the logic of the building'.

1 The original invitation and my acceptance of it both presupposed that I would be in a position to deliver the goods contracted for. This rested on the expectation of progress in completing the

31

relevant parts of the commentary on the *Philosophical Investigations* which I am writing jointly with Peter Hacker. In the event, the first volume terminated after § 184, and detailed research on the subsequent remarks has yet to begin. Hence there is no question of giving an authoritative exegesis of this material or a fully informed account of the development of Wittgenstein's thinking about rules and rule-following. Much of this paper is programmatic and provisional. Many comments, in spite of their surface form, should be understood as incorporating the problematic mood in their depth structure.

2   My original brief also presupposed the feasibility of at least the central part of the programme. The central remarks on rule-following (§§ 185–242) are the keystone of the argumentative structure of the *Investigations*, Part I. They have multiple logical connections with preceding and subsequent remarks, and they are themselves dense with argument. They cover such major topics as necessity and possibility, identity and difference, the autonomy of grammar, avowals, criteria and the distinctions explanation/training, cause/reason, and rules/regularities/hypotheses. Light will bathe the phenomena of rule-following only after dawn has broken over a vast terrain. The difficulty of giving an illuminating and systematic analysis of this material is obvious. A vague optimism disguised from me the impossibility of this task. What seemed impossible would just take a little while. It seemed reasonable to expect something to turn up which would act as a nucleus for crystallizing out Wittgenstein's diffused ideas. All this is a pernicious illusion. Clarity about rules and rule-following will not miraculously emerge from some artful reshuffling of the pieces in the jig-saw of §§ 185–242. What stands in the way of our grasping these remarks is the same thing that blocks our understanding of the phenomena of rule-following, namely the desire to discern some simple pattern in the midst of what seems superficially chaotic. The profundity of Wittgenstein's reflections depends precisely on his avoiding the oversimplifications that generate our perplexity. To the extent that his method is appropriate for investigating what it is to follow rules, any concise systematic synopsis of rule-following is impossible. Moreover, to the extent that his remarks conform to his method, there is no hope of forcing them into a single pattern that will embody the bulk of their insights. Any quick survey of *Investigations* §§ 185–242 must be an im-

pressionistic sketch of a few aspects of Wittgenstein's thought. Though self-conscious simplification may foster insight, *unacknowledged* simplification is falsification.

For these two reasons the finished product falls far short of the original specifications. Instead of definitive answers to important questions, there is little more than an outline of the proper approach to elaborating correct answers together with some clarification of a few of the most pressing questions. Though somewhat disappointing, this is not an altogether trivial harvest. It is a precondition of any lasting satisfaction of our more ambitious aspirations for achieving an understanding either of Wittgenstein's remarks or of the phenomena of rule-following that he investigated. Even if there is no gold and little enough ore laid up here, this fact will ensure a dramatic contrast between this paper and the rest of the contributions to this symposium.

1 METHODOLOGICAL ORIENTATION

An initial question, as obvious as it is fundamental, is what is the point or purpose of the discussion of rule-following in *Investigations* §§ 185–242. A natural response is to plead for postponement of this issue. Is it not reasonable to answer this question only at the end of a detailed analysis of this set of remarks? This general consideration might be reinforced in this case by the contention that the *Investigations* consists of a string of remarks most of which are at best only loosely related even to their immediate neighbours, and many of which have an epigrammatic style that positively invites us to interpret each one in isolation from the rest. Wittgenstein castigated all forms of theory-construction in philosophy. He is alleged to have secured his own later reflections from this vice by writing self-contained remarks the totality of which displays no more structure than the molecules of a gas. The conclusion to be drawn must be that it is *in principle* mistaken to begin an examination of §§ 185–242 from any consideration of Wittgenstein's strategy, at least to the extent that his own remarks conform to his conception of proper method in philosophizing.

This approach is widespread. It is sanctioned by both the theory and the practice of most exegeses of Wittgenstein's writings. It justifies eclecticism as the appropriate procedure of interpretation.

But, however natural and expedient, it is profoundly misguided. From the very outset we should take a wider look around §§ 185–242. Not to discern the contours of some hidden theory, but to clarify Wittgenstein's strategic purpose in locating these remarks where they occur. Only in this way can detailed scrutiny bear sound fruit. To ignore the context of his remarks is to throw away the key to understanding what he meant to convey.

It would be a lengthy and intricate undertaking to demonstrate the truth of the general claim that context is of paramount importance for proper understanding of Wittgenstein's remarks. But before applying this principle to the interpretation of §§ 185–242, I must at least marshal three reasons in support of the heresy.

1 In the 'Preface', Wittgenstein stressed the importance that he attached to the ordering of his remarks. The principal source of his dissatisfaction with the various versions of the *Investigations* was the feeling that he had not found a way so to organize the remarks 'that the thoughts should proceed from one subject to another in a natural order and without breaks'. He ultimately despaired of achieving this goal. But this retreat manifests a continued recognition of the relevance of different remarks to each other. The upshot was not complete chaos, but chains of remarks that criss-crossed at many points. Linearity was sacrificed, but not order. The history of the composition of the text of the *Investigations* suggests that §§ 1–421 are a structured, complex, and many-pronged campaign of argument. The remarks up to § 189 are a stable nucleus. From his papers we can still identify at least three distinct continuations. A rearrangement of the first was published as Part I of the *Remarks on the Foundations of Mathematics*. The second serves as the backbone of the third, which is the published version up to § 421. The fact that Wittgenstein made repeated attempts to weld together remarks on the nature of rules and rule-following is of crucial importance. It suggests that especially here we ignore at our peril what so preoccupied him, namely the foreign relations among his separately numbered remarks.

2 In practice, attention to argumentative context allows an authoritative solution of many mysteries and a definitive resolution of many controversies about remarks in *Investigations* §§ 1–421. Conspicuous examples are § 79 on proper names and § 22 (together with p. 11n.) on Frege's conception of assertion and supposition (*Annahme*). Ripped from their contexts and truncat-

ed, these have filled the heads of philosophers with many ideas, the most celebrated of which, the cluster theory of proper names and the analysis of sentences into mood operators plus sentence-radicals, are commonly ascribed to Wittgenstein even though demonstrably antithetical to his thought.[3] A parallel blindness to context supports the widespread idea that §§ 65–88 argue for the importance of vagueness in constructing a theory of meaning, and suggest some initial steps towards the construction of a semantics for vague predicates.[4] As if the main error in Frege and in logical atomism had been to treat language as being definite and precise![5] The prevalence of such caricatures among reputable interpretations of the *Investigations* should recommend adherence to the principle that a philosophical remark has significance only in the context of an argument. In particular, we should be alert to the possibility that current interpretations of §§ 185–242 may be very wide of the mark. To perceive in Wittgenstein's remarks concern with a form of scepticism or a denial of the objectivity of judgments about rule-following may be to parody his thought by directing attention to matters peripheral or even altogether alien to his line of argument.

3   Most of the remarks of *Investigations* §§ 1–421 do not occur only in this setting, but rather are repetitions or reformulations of remarks occurring in various earlier texts. A proper study of argumentative context should therefore include a close examination of these texts, with particular attention to the integration of the recurring remark into the chain of reasoning. Taking a wider look around requires detailed scrutiny of texts other than the *Investigations*. Used with due caution, this method too clarifies many obscurities. Typically the printed text was arrived at by many stages of sifting out and pruning remarks from manuscript notebooks and earlier typescripts. 'Scissors and paste' is close to a literal description of Wittgenstein's procedure. His passion for succinct and pithy expression, together with a tendency to impatience about detailed explanations of his ideas, often led to radical truncation of a remark and drastic excisions of material connecting remarks. Restoring what has been sifted out or pruned away can yield definitive solutions to problems of interpretation. In the *Investigations*, this method is conspicuously successful in clarifying many of the dicta about philosophy (§§ 89–133).[6] It is, of course, subject to two major caveats. First, the same remark

may occur in different contexts of argument in different texts, and hence establishing its significance in one text does not *eo ipso* settle its significance in another. This point is of great importance in practice, for it is not generally recognized how substantial the evolution of ideas is within what is called 'Wittgenstein's later philosophy'.[7] The second caveat is that Wittgenstein may have failed to modify a remark to fit it properly into a new sequence of remarks, and therefore expressions that apparently explicitly link one remark with an immediate predecessor or successor (e.g. 'hence', 'therefore', 'consider this example') may sometimes be misleading.[8] Textual modifications sometimes get out of step with argumentative deletions and accretions. In spite of these caveats the study of parallel texts promises to be especially important for the interpretation of §§ 185–242, because of Wittgenstein's repeated attempts to treat the topic of rule-following. An appreciation of his strategy in the *Investigations* might be the product of trying to map out some of this tract of seemingly alien territory.

These three reasons indicate the fundamental importance of the question 'What is the purpose of *Investigations* §§ 185–242?'; i.e. the question 'To what campaign of argument do these remarks on rule-following belong?' At the same time, these reasons also point towards methods for arriving at a satisfactory answer to this question; i.e. methods for coming to see these remarks aright. Much of the answer that I will now start to sketch is certainly tentative. Only part of it is grounded in a rigorous application of these methods to the *Investigations* and other parallel texts. But even if my answer is implausible or grotesque, this fact should not distract attention from the importance of the question and from the delineation of the methods appropriate to answering this question.

2   *ÜBERSICHT* OF *INVESTIGATIONS* §§ 1–421

The first task is to locate the chain of remarks on rule-following (§§ 143–242) in the grand strategy of Part I of the *Investigations*. Since the text was presumably designed to be read from the beginning, the main guide to correct identification of the argumentative setting of these remarks must be the campaign expressly initiated in the preceding remarks (§§ 1–142). If we were to fail to fathom it, or later to lose sight of it, we might react to §§ 143–242 as unpercipiently as somebody who guffaws throughout *Othello* under the erroneous impression that he is witnessing the performance of a farce.

The strategic purpose of §§ 1–142 is transparent, being explicitly stated at the outset. Wittgenstein cited a quotation from Augustine to introduce a critical discussion of what he called 'Augustine's picture of language'.[9] The core of this picture is a pair of theses: all words are names, and all sentences are combinations of names. In a more developed form, the first thesis is expressed by the claim that every word has a meaning which is the object with which this word is correlated and for which it stands. The leading ideas of Augustine's picture of language were frequently associated in earlier texts with the pair of theses that ostensive definition is the basic form of explanation (the foundation of language) and that all sentences are really descriptions. Naming and describing are conceived to be the essence of language. The importance of Augustine's picture for Wittgenstein is not that it represents one theory of language among others, but that it is a proto-theory or *Urbild* that shapes a vast range of philosophers' theorizing about language, like what Kuhn calls a scientific paradigm. Russell's account of language and the *Tractatus* both obviously fit within this framework. Frege's semantics is arguably just a more baroque version of the same underlying paradigm.[10] Hence, in confronting Augustine's picture of language, Wittgenstein did not see himself as tilting at a windmill. Rather he meant to engage the combined forces mustered by the most advanced philosophers of the modern era, and he did so by addressing himself to the deep presuppositions held in common by what appear to be very different theories of meaning. This purpose dictated a strategy of indirect attack instead of frontal assault. For the most part, direct criticism of an articulated thesis belonging to a developed theory of language like the *Tractatus* encounters a well-defended position, so that the momentum of the criticism is spent in manoeuvring around hosts of qualifications thrown up in defence of what is attacked. Moreover, even if successful, direct criticisms lead to victories only in isolated skirmishes. The opposing forces escape substantially unscathed, ready to dig in to defend other positions or even to open new fronts. Though less dramatic,

Wittgenstein's indirect attack on Frege and the logical atomism of Russell and the *Tractatus* was intended to be more conclusive.

§§ 1–27 open the offensive. After a delineation of the Augustinian *Urbild*, there is a preliminary criticism of each of its main components. The theses that all words are names and that all sentences are descriptions are criticized as masking all the important differences among expressions under a uniform, and hence misleading, form of representation. Unless the term 'name' is vacuous, it is patently false that all words are names (cf. §§ 10–5). A similar absurdity results from classing all sentences as descriptions (cf. § 24).

§§ 28–64 focus on ostensive definition, thereby attacking one of the pillars supporting the Augustinian picture. The purpose is to undermine the notion that ostensive definitions provide the foundations of language. In contrast to 'verbal' definitions, which seem to be intralinguistic, ostensive definitions seem to many philosophers to supply extralinguistic anchors, tying language to reality. This exaggerates their importance and distorts their role. They typically correlate words with samples. These are best conceived of as (concrete) symbols or instruments of language, for then ostensive definitions appear in the guise of rules for the substitution of symbols in place of other symbols.[11] Seen as rules for the transformation of symbols, they shed the appearance of being a uniquely privileged form of explanation which is immune from the possibility of being misinterpreted or misunderstood. Wittgenstein's aim is not, as so often supposed, to show that ostensive definitions are peculiarly defective forms of explanation, but merely to dethrone them from the misguidedly exalted position assigned to them in the Augustinian *Urbild*.

§§ 65–88 concentrate on the correlative notion of analysis or definition. According to a venerable tradition, a proper explanation of any expression not defined by ostension must take the form of a statement of the conditions necessary and sufficient for its correct application. In the case of a concept-word, a 'verbal' definition standardly must specify the properties common to all objects to which the word is applicable. Wittgenstein points out that this dogma does not square with our actual practice of explaining words. We do explain such terms as 'game' or 'number' by giving paradigmatic examples. To say 'chess, tennis, patience, cricket, and so on are games' is typically to give a correct explanation and to satisfy a criterion for understanding the word 'game'. The discussion of family resemblance concepts is not meant to be the foundation of a fresh theory of meaning to replace traditional analysis, but simply to cast down a philosophical dogma.[12]

To explode this dogma necessitates sapping the defences readily available to the forces of orthodoxy. It might be claimed that actual explanations of expressions are typically rough and ready, designed for merely practical purposes of facilitating communication; they must be condemned as inexact and incomplete when measured against the exacting standards appropriate for constructing rigorous scientific definitions in a theory of meaning. Although giving an explanation of 'number' by examples is treated as evidence of understanding this word, it is strictly speaking only inductive evidence, hence not a criterion but a mere symptom of understanding. To understand an expression is to be able to use it correctly over a whole range of standard contexts. A complete description of what it is to have such an ability typically is *far* more complex than anything contained in the everyday practice of explaining a word. Understanding would seem to go far beyond what is contained in explanations (cf. § 209), perhaps even beyond what can be stated at all (cf. § 70). This idea might rehabilitate the dogma of analysis by construing it as an account of understanding. For, although we cannot *define* every concept-word by specifying properties common to everything to which it is applicable, we can *understand* any concept-word only by grasping the common properties of things falling under it (cf. §§ 71–4). When suitably generalized to other kinds of expression, this idea supports the claim that in uttering a sentence and *meaning* or *understanding* it we are in fact operating a calculus according to definite rules (§ 81). Frege's specifications of the senses of number-words were an attempt to expose such rules laid up in the medium of our understanding. The programme of logical atomism was to exhibit the whole of the intelligent use of language as the unconscious operation of an elaborate calculus of meaning-rules.

Wittgenstein does not tackle this defensive manoeuvre in §§ 65–88. He hinted at a strategy of counter-attack, but did not carry it out. The idea that the use of language is a rule-governed activity is perfectly correct. Explanations of meaning are rules for the use of expressions. Philosophers go wrong in putting an absurd interpretation on what it is for an activity to be rule-governed. They are obsessed with the idea that a complete set of rules, each of which is perfectly precise, would dictate verdicts in any conceivable case of its application. By this standard, ordinary explanations are clearly defective (cf. §§ 79–80). Dazzled by this ideal of completeness, philosophers come to doubt whether explanations suffice to make speaking a language a rule-governed activity at all (cf. § 100). Such doubt can be allayed only by refining and completing in unheard-of ways our system of rules for the use of our words (cf. § 133). Philosophers therefore seek to disclose the strict and clear rules of meaning that they suppose must lie in the background, undergirding our understanding of language (cf. § 102). Mythology is here piled on misconception. The initial movement of thought rests on a distorted understanding of what it is for an activity to be rule-governed (cf. §§ 82–3). As a corrective we must consider what it is for a rule to be exact or precise and what it is for a system of rules to be complete (§§ 84–9, cf. § 213). The subsequent myth-making misconceives the connection of explanation with meaning and understanding. The meaning of a word is what is explained in *explaining* its meaning, not something over and above this. Explanations are not means to bring about understanding; rather what is understood is the very same thing as what is explained. Hence explanations by examples are not mere 'hocus-pocus' (PG, 273) or an '*indirect* means of explaining – in default of a better' (§ 71). Instead, my understanding of an expression is *completely* expressed in the explanations that I could give (§ 75, cf. § 210). My understanding of 'game' is therefore expressed by my giving an explanation by examples and intending these examples to be used in a certain way (§ 71, cf. § 208). Refusing to acknowledge as genuine any explanation not laying down necessary and sufficient conditions for the correct application of an expression (in every conceivable case) manifests the tendency of philosophers to sublime the notion of explanation.[13] This either distorts the concept of understanding or cuts off specifications of sense (proper 'semantic' definitions) from an account what it is to understand expressions.

Wittgenstein's observations in §§ 65–88 are only a tentative exploration of this line of argument. Individual remarks are quite liable to be misconstrued by philosophers defending the legitimacy of exhibiting language as a calculus of meaning-rules. The phrase 'to mean examples to be taken in a particular way' (§ 71) may be cashed by appeal to an epistemically private mental event, and the suggestion that 'we are not equipped with rules for every possible application' of a word (§ 80) might suggest that the expressions of ordinary language are ineradicably 'open-textured'.[14] Wittgenstein did not ward off these errors. Still worse, he did not secure the line of argument in §§ 65–88 from global misinterpretation. To many philosophers, his quarry appears to be a misconception about precision or exactness. The principal defect of Frege's semantics and of logical atomism was allegedly an exaggeration of the precision of meaning-rules. If this gratuitous demand is dropped, the general enterprise of philosophical analysis can proceed substantially unaltered. The target, according to this interpretation, is not the very idea of language as a calculus of meaning-rules, but the optional extra of conceiving these rules to be absolutely precise or definite. Wittgenstein, however, did not argue that an appreciation of the vagueness of ordinary language is indispensable merely for executing the programme of constructing a theory of meaning, but rather that misconceptions about exactness and definiteness, both of language and of systems of rules, provide the entire rationale for the programme itself (cf. BB, 25f.). A correct perspective on vagueness is inseparable from a proper account of understanding.[15] That is why the discussion of §§ 65–88 'can only appear in the right light when one has attained greater clarity about the concepts of understanding, meaning, and thinking' (§ 81). Here Wittgenstein left a major and *explicit* loose-end in the web of the argument up to § 88.

§§ 89–133 are correlative to §§ 65–88, being addressed to the idea that the task of philosophy is to deepen our understanding by penetrating to the essence of concepts through disclosure of the properties common to things falling under them. As a model of this procedure Wittgenstein took the account of the general propositional form in the *Tractatus*. This conception of philosophy rests on a mistaken assimilation of philosophy to science. Against it Wittgenstein advanced certain well-known slogans: philosophy must contain no explanations, hypotheses or theses (§§ 109, 128), it must not seek to provide a foundation for language (§ 124), and it must be purely descriptive (§§ 109, 124, 496). The visible support of these claims is not substantial. They are readily and commonly treated as mere dogmas, betraying ignorance and insensitivity to the achievements of science, mathematics and formal logic. Yet Wittgenstein's slogans are immediate corollaries of fundamental components of his thought. He held that philosophy was essentially concerned with *understanding*. In so far as paradoxes and conceptual perplexities arise from how we use language, the only means for dissolving or removing them is to attain a proper understanding of the expressions that we use. Since what is understood in understanding a word is just what is explained in explaining it, we typically stand in need of nothing more recondite than a bird's-eye view (*Übersicht*)[16] of our practice of explaining (and using) certain expressions (§§ 122–5). How we explain expressions is not something hidden from view and awaiting discovery by a science of language (§ 126). At worst, it is something of which we have lost sight and need to be reminded (§ 127). Wittgenstein's conception of philosophy is the visible fruit of his picture of the relations of meaning, understanding and explanation.

§§ 134–42 constitute a bridge-passage linking the discussion of §§ 65–133 with the argument of § 143–242. These remarks cover the topics of the general propositional form and the derivation of the application of a concept-word from a mental picture.

A retrospect over §§ 1–142 discloses a clear and explicit argumentative setting for the subsequent discussion of rules and rule-following. These later remarks have every appearance of being a continuation and development of the campaign against the Augustinian picture of language. Wittgenstein aimed at a smooth transition between §§ 1–142 and §§ 143–242, and he achieved it to the extent that the exact articulation of §§ 134–42 and their grouping with preceding and subsequent remarks is itself open to controversy. Continuity here is conceptual as well as stylistic. The tentative explorations of §§ 65–88 are in fact resumed. In particular, backing is supplied for the blank cheque earlier drawn on the attainment of greater clarity about the concepts of understanding, meaning and thinking (§ 81). The maximum of seamlessness in the web of Wittgenstein's argument is obtained by treating §§ 143–242 as a criticism of the notion that anyone who utters a sentence and *means* or *understands* it is operating a calculus according to definite rules (§ 81). As is to be expected, the attack is *indirect*. The myth of language as a calculus of meaning-rules is undermined by a careful scrutiny of what rules are and what it is to calculate and to follow a rule. The goal is to render transparently ridiculous the idea of a hidden or unconscious *following* of a *rule*. If successful, the general argument would reduce to absurdity the thesis that the intelligent use of language is grounded in our following, unbeknownst to ourselves, a complex set of uniform meaning-rules. This does not entail, of course, that in speaking we do not follow rules or that language is not a rule-governed activity. Explanations of meaning do function as norms for the use of words; we do indeed follow these rules. But explanations take many different forms, they are a *motley*, quite dissimilar to the axioms of a calculus. Moreover, many different activities constitute instances of following such rules; many of them are far removed from paradigms of calculating. Wittgenstein's target is a philosophers' myth, not the innocuous everyday conception of language as a rule-governed activity. Only a hair's breadth separates platitude from absurdity. The strategic purpose of §§ 143–242 is to clarify this boundary, and thereby to demolish one of the main obstacles to seeing understanding aright.

An interpretation of the strategic purpose of §§ 143–242 is strengthened to the extent that it meets certain conditions other than coherence with the preceding remarks of the *Investigations*. Three such conditions are obvious. First, it should fit smoothly with the drift of subsequent material in the *Investigations*, especially with §§ 243–421. Second, it should show how these central sections of the *Investigations* grow out of the central preoccupations of Wittgenstein's work from 1929 to 1945; ideally, it should exhibit these remarks as the culmination of developments in his thought about meaning and language. Third, it should maximize the forcefulness and cogency of the arguments in §§ 143–242 against the wider background of his investigations of rules and rule-following; *ceteris paribus*, it should not make sense of these remarks at the price of rendering them ineffectual, lop-sided or riddled with fallacies when viewed from his perspective. The minimal interpretation that emerges naturally from §§ 1–142 satisfies all three requirements to a conspicuous degree.

First, construing §§ 143–242 as an extension of the earlier critical onslaught on the Augustinian picture of language makes excellent sense of the contours of the subsequent remarks. On a narrow front, it connects the celebrated argument against the possibility of a private language with what has gone before. That argument, far from being an autonomous critical theory, is an application of certain morals drawn from consideration of rules and rule-following to a particularly seductive realization of the Augustinian picture. For Russell's logical atomism, and arguably Wittgenstein's too, had tried to secure the foundations of language by means of private assignments of meaning to primitive indefinables through mental ostensive definitions correlating words with 'objects'. The point of the private language argument is not to demonstrate a theory about language acquisition, nor is it to speculate about the inhabitants of desert islands. Rather, Wittgenstein sought to make clear that there is no such thing as a private explanation of meaning. Something that *could not* function as a criterion of correctness for the use of an expression cannot coherently be characterized as a rule, and therefore cannot count as an explanation at all. This disqualifies private ostensive definitions from playing any role whatever in accounting for the meanings of expressions. On a wider front, too, the proposed global interpretation of §§ 143–242 conforms to a perceptible change of climate in Part I of the *Investigations*. What begins as a discussion of certain topics in the philosophy of language is gradually transformed into a consideration of issues in the philosophy of mind. This might seem to indicate at least one fundamental discontinuity in the chain of reasoning. But this conclusion is unwarranted. By emphasizing the links of meaning and explanation with understanding, Wittgenstein revealed the relevance of basic issues in the philosophy of mind for assessments of theories of meaning. The Augustinian picture is a caricature of language, but recognizing this presupposes a clarification of the concepts of understanding, meaning and thinking (cf. § 81). Separation of the logical from the psychological is a programme with certain merits, but it led Frege and the *Tractatus* into a basic misconception that it was the business of the *Investigations* to expose.

Second, the proposed interpretation of §§ 143–242 does exhibit these important remarks as the outgrowth of some major developments in Wittgenstein's thought.

1 Whereas Wittgenstein had originally exploited the idea that language was a calculus, he later became critical of it. This is visible, particularly, in his terminology and choice of slogans. The notion of a calculus is replaced by the concept of a language-game.[17] For the earlier slogan 'The meaning of a word is its place (or role) in the calculus' (PR, 178; PG, 63, 67; cf. PG, 70, 312;

WWK, 178f.) is substituted the slogan 'The meaning of a word is its role (or use) in the language (or language-game)' (§ 43; PG, 59f.; BB, 102f.). Parallel changes are the disappearances of the concept of *Satzsystem* (WWK, 63ff., 89ff.) and of concrete representations of rules of grammar (e.g. the colour octahedron, PR, 51f.). It would be mistaken to dismiss these transformations as mere shifts of expository style.

2 The critical examination of philosophers' myths about rules and rule-following in the *Investigations* is a direct development from Wittgenstein's earliest criticism of logical atomism. That particular realization of the Augustinian picture of language was committed to a mythology of meaning-bodies (*Bedeutungskörper*). The rules for the correct use of a word must somehow follow from the nature of the object correlated with this word as its meaning. Only thus can its meaning determine its use, given that the meaning of a name is the object named. Wittgenstein attacked this conception, arguing that the idea of meaning-bodies is an absurd bit of fiction (§ 559; PG, 54ff.; PLP, 234ff.). To salvage anything from the Augustinian picture requires a programme of demythologization. The 'objects' that mysteriously determine the uses of words must be cancelled out of the picture. This leaves the meaning of a word as the totality of rules for its use. The meaning of a word is analogous to the powers of a chess piece, which are determined by the rules for the game of chess (cf. PG, 67). Identifying the meaning of a word with the totality of rules for its use is an immediate protective response to an attack on the model of meaning-bodies embedded in the Augustinian picture.[18] Wittgenstein made this manoeuvre in response to his own criticism of the *Tractatus* (WWK, 41ff.). This conception informed his adoption of the *Leitmotiv* that the meaning of a word is its role in the calculus, and it explained the attractiveness of the chess analogy in his reflections on language. Yet this conception itself replaces one form of mythology with another: myths about 'objects' become myths about rules. Where previously there were mechanical relations among objects, now there are interacting fields of force. In unmasking this fresh form of mythology about meaning, Wittgenstein was extending and strengthening his original criticism of the Augustinian picture. He showed that the *Bedeutungskörper*-model of language was, as it were, *twice* removed from reality. For there is typically no such thing as a set

45

of rules for the use of an expression which cannot be misinterpreted, and which cannot be extended without resulting in redundancy or inconsistency; this ideal of completeness is empty. Nor is there any such thing as a rule that determines, independently of our practice of applying rules, whether an expression is used correctly or not; this ideal of objectivity is incoherent. The conception of language as a calculus invites philosophers to subscribe to both of these bogus ideals. Unless this mythology is exploded, the original demythologizing of the Augustinian picture may be more harmful than beneficial. Without supplementation by the remarks on rule-following in the *Investigations*, it certainly would not yield a clarification of the concepts of understanding, meaning and explanation.

3   Once Wittgenstein directed his attention to the ingredients of the calculus model of language, there was a noticeable evolution in his thought. Perhaps the most crucial question is what it is for the explanation of a word to 'enter into' its use. This is a special case of the question what it is to follow a rule (as opposed to behaving in conformity with a rule). Wittgenstein canvassed a variety of unsatisfactory answers (e.g. BB, 12f.; PG, 89ff.). The reflections on rule-following in the *Investigations* are a great advance on their published predecessors. They are the culmination of the attempts of more than a decade to demythologize the calculus model characteristic of his initial rejection of logical atomism. This spotlights these remarks as the centre-piece of a lengthy campaign to clarify the fundamental defects of the Augustinian picture of language.

A third confirmation of the proposed global interpretation of §§ 147–242 is that these remarks, if construed as perfectly general context-free observations about rules and rule-following, would be open to serious objections. Indeed, by Wittgenstein's own lights, they would have to be condemned as very poor. This unfavourable verdict can be forestalled only to the extent that they can be assigned another strategic purpose. Construing them as part of a criticism of the Augustinian picture transforms into a strength what would otherwise appear to be a weakness, namely exclusive concern with a particular way of following a special kind of rule. Therefore there are two further reasons here supporting the claim that these remarks have this definite strategic purpose.

1   Wittgenstein made a point of stressing the diverse kinds of

rules even within grammar. Explanations take many forms: ostensive definitions with or without permanent samples, charts or
diagrams, explanations by complete enumeration (e.g. of 'primary
colour') or by examples with or without explicit similarity-riders
(e.g. of 'number' or 'game'), definition by *Merkmale* (e.g. of
'triangle') or by necessary and sufficient conditions involving generality (e.g. of 'prime numbers' or 'ancestor'), truth-tables, con-
textual paraphrase (e.g. of many prepositional phrases and
connectives), etc. More generally, rules take many forms, e.g.
rules of games: there are duty-imposing rules, rules conferring
powers or rights, rules granting permissions, rules modifying the
application of other rules, ideal rules (e.g. 'a goalie should always
be alert'), so-called 'constitutive' rules (e.g. 'a goal is scored when
the ball is fairly kicked between the posts'), general and particular
rules, conditional and unconditional rules, etc. Wittgenstein was
well aware of this diversity.[19] Surely he would have thought it
relevant to any adequate *general* treatment of the question of
what a rule is, yet §§ 143–242 do not even begin to make an
attempt to encompass this vast range of phenomena. The justification for this procedure is that philosophers in the grip of the
calculus model have in view only a single kind of rule, exemplified
by the definition of a mathematical function (e.g. 'For all n, let
$F(n)$ be $n^2 + 2$'). They do not recognize the legitimacy of any
explanations apart from definitions in terms of necessary and
sufficient conditions of application. In tackling this illusion, it is
a viable strategy to ignore all the other kinds of rules and to
concentrate on this preferred type in order to demonstrate that
philosophers make a fundamental error in holding these to be
ideal, i.e. 'complete' and immune from misapplication. Only rules
of this kind are plausible candidates for the rules hidden in the
medium of the understanding. For, if philosophers acknowledged
that other kinds of meaning-rule could be admitted to this select
company, they would not have to search for any rules beneath
everyday explanations of word-meaning.

2 Similarly, there is a wide variety of ways in which explanations of meaning 'enter into' the uses of the words. A *Merkmal*-
definition may be employed to construct an incontrovertible justification for applying a concept-word to an object; an explanation
by example may be appealed to as defeasible justification; and
many ostensive definitions (e.g. of 'red') cannot be used for the

purpose of such justification at all (§§ 380–1). More generally, there are many different kinds of consideration that bear on whether acting in a particular way (or forbearing to act) counts as following a given rule. Indeed, even cursory reflection on the diverse kinds of rules reveals that the very idea of *following* a rule becomes problematic in many contexts of activity. Can anybody follow a 'constitutive' rule (e.g. the rule that a goal is scored whenever the ball is fairly kicked between the posts)? Or a 'secondary' rule (e.g. the rule laying down the jurisdiction of a small-claims court)? Can anybody obey or disobey a rule granting a permission (e.g. the rule permitting castling in chess)? Wittgenstein himself stressed the variety of circumstances that justify us in describing a speaker as following a meaning-rule, and he explored the more general issue about the criteria for following a rule (e.g. BB, 85ff., 98ff.). Surely he would have thought a survey of these diverse phenomena to be an essential part of a competent *general* account of what it is to follow a rule. Yet §§ 143–242 are silent on most of these matters. The justification for his preoccupation with a single kind of rule-following is the same as before. The philosophical misconception that he attacked takes calculation (e.g. the computation of the value of a function for a given argument) as the paradigm to which all cases of following a meaning-rule are to be assimilated. This rests on the illusion that calculation is the ideal case of rule-following, i.e. a procedure uniquely immune from error and yielding singularly conclusive and objective verdicts. In tackling this illusion, it is perfectly appropriate for Wittgenstein to focus the microscope of criticism on this single form of rule-following. If calculation is demoted to the ranks, then the kind of rule associated with calculations will lose its aura of uniqueness and hence too its power to fascinate philosophers.

The length of this description of the stage-setting for *Investigations* §§ 143–242 is commensurate with the importance of the exercise. It is a matter commonly neglected. Yet its neglect can make nonsense of any attempt at a a detailed exegesis, interpretation and evaluation of Wittgenstein's remarks. Locating these remarks in a campaign of battle against the Augustinian picture may not answer every question about them, but it will provide pertinent questions for many of the standard answers about their significance. Moreover, by connecting them with a mythology of rules that is currently widespread and influential, it will make their interpretation of vital relevance to modern philosophy of language.

3 *INVESTIGATIONS* §§ 143–242: A PRELIMINARY SYNOPSIS

Evaluation of the philosophical theory that understanding consists in operating a calculus according to definite rules might profitably begin from a clarification of what it is to operate a calculus, i.e. what it is to derive particular verdicts within a system of rules. A naïve approach to this question would start from a list of paradigms of this kind of rule-following. Candidates for such a list would surely include calculating the successive terms of the series 1, 4, 9, 25 . . . from the algebraic formula '$a_n = n^2$', deriving the Russian spelling of 'Eisenhower' from the principles for transliterating from the Roman into the Cyrillic alphabet or working out how to pronounce the word 'counterintuitive' from its spelling. Untutored reflection on such cases is apt to focus on two features. The first is that in calculating a result one follows a rule; one has the feeling of being guided or directed by this rule, just as one may be guided in a dance by one's partner. Being guided seems to belong to the essence of rule-following (cf. §§ 170–8). The second feature is that in calculating (correctly) one merely recognizes or discovers a result that is already laid up in the system of rules. The calculus already contains all particular results, and hence it is the impersonal arbiter of whether one has succeeded in following the rule. Rigidity and inexorability seem also to belong to the essence of rule-following. These two features might be called the 'subjective' and the 'objective' aspects of rule-following. They generate a mutual tension. The experience of being guided is no guarantee of following a rule, i.e. of applying it correctly. Conversely, conformity of a calculation with the output of a calculus is no guarantee of following the rules of the calculus, for the correspondence may be mere coincidence. Neither of these conflicting features can be jettisoned from our concept of rule-following. Neither something that failed to guide behaviour nor something that failed to provide an external standard of correctness would count as a rule. The normativity of rules gives rise to a predicament about characterizing rule-following. 'This isn't how it is!' we say; but then add 'Yet this is how it has to be!' (cf. § 112).

§§ 143–242 are intended to dissolve this puzzlement by exposing the misconceptions giving rise to it. The primary focus of §§ 143–84 is the philosophical illusions enveloping the subjective aspects of rule-following. §§ 185–252 are a complementary investigation concentrating on the objective aspects of rule-following. Together these remarks are meant as antidotes to the poison given off by an absurd idealization of operating a calculus of rules. They have effected a cure only if we lose all inclination to dismiss a series of signposts along a footpath as a less complete or perfect expression of a rule than an algebraic formula generating the terms of a series.

§§ 143–84 are a tight-knit dialectical exploration of misconceptions about calculating, deriving and being guided. Its core (§§ 156–78) is a long analysis of reading, conceived simply as mastering the 'rule of the alphabet' for transforming written words into spoken ones. The purpose of this 'digression' is to provide a focus for the diagnosis of philosophical illusions about the subjective aspects of rule-following. Three sources of error are stressed.

1 Although we naturally explain by examples such expressions as 'calculating', 'deriving', 'being guided' or 'following a rule', we are not content to accept these explanations as complete. We are loath to acknowledge that each of these expressions applies to a family of cases (cf. §§ 164, 234–6; BB, 123ff.) and that our explanations by example completely express our concepts (§ 71). Instead, in each case we subscribe to the dogma that there must be something which all the phenomena have in common. We strip away the particularities of each case of 'deriving' in search of the underlying essence of deriving (§ 164). Finding no obvious common properties, we are prone to consider that 'deriving' names a psychological process, though this process is not something familiar, but something difficult to apprehend and still awaiting a clear description (PG, 74f.). Hence the path to further clarification of the term 'derive' is to scrutinize very carefully what really happens when we carry out derivations, for only by such examination can the requisite unifying mental process be brought to light.

2 We note that calculating may be carried out in the head; we speak of the experience or feeling of being guided; and we remark

that following a rule, as distinct from acting in conformity with one, is an intentional act. These observations lend support to the idea that calculating, deriving, being guided, etc., are essentially mental activities, processes or states. They also interlock with the inner/outer picture of the contrast between mind and behaviour. We are prone to consider what is 'inner' as inaccessible and hidden from all but its owner, whose access to it, through introspection, is direct and infallible. This picture supports the contention that only I can know whether I am making a particular calculation or following a given rule; others, it seems, can merely make conjectures based on observation of my behaviour.

3   We appreciate that calculating a term in a series does not consist merely in writing down a number *after* contemplating an algebraic formula; to calculate, a person must produce a particular number *because of* the formula generating the number series. This launches a search for some special connecting experience or mental mechanism that will serve to distinguish coincidental conformity with a calculation-rule from genuine calculation. Something must make this difference, so we postulate an intermediate explanatory link. We seek to substantiate its existence by reputable scientific procedures. We inspect limiting cases in extreme conditions, e.g. examining what happens in reading a text in Cyrillic script, where the process of reading will be greatly slowed down.[20]

These three distinct sources of misconception in philosophy interlock to yield a gross misunderstanding of what it is to calculate and, more generally, of what it is to follow or be guided by a rule. We thereby make a mystery of the subjective aspects of the normativity of rules. In the search for the essence of calculation and of guidance, we misguidedly study our own experiences in following rules. We vainly hope to find some experience of a causal nexus, some feeling of guidance or of a motivating force, or some peculiar intimations given off by rules. Disappointed, we conclude that the experience of normativity is something altogether ineffable, elusive and mysterious. Instead of wallowing in this mystery-mongering, we should call into question the whole chain of reasoning leading into this cul de sac. In particular, we should re-examine the very first step of conceiving of deriving, calculating, being guided and following rules as being 'mental processes'. Though apparently innocuous (§ 308), this initial move is pregnant with confusion (§ 154). It would be prophylactic to remind ourselves that mental processes or acts are mere *accompaniments* of rule-following (cf. § 152). The *criteria* for somebody's following a rule, or for his calculating or deriving something, are not mental performances, but overt acts, including his citing rules as justifications for what he has done.

§§ 185–242 are a somewhat less systematic exploration of misconceptions about what it is for a certain consequence to be determined by or to follow from a rule. Here Wittgenstein concentrated on the case of continuing a series of numbers. Illusions about the 'objective' aspects of rule-following cluster most densely around instances of calculation. Mathematical calculations are therefore the most suitable objects to examine in pursuit of sound understanding of these aspects of rule-following. Wittgenstein meant to pinpoint certain sources of error. He particularly stressed four.

1 We note the possibility of mistakes in calculations. We say that somebody has made a mistake when he has not made the correct move at some stage of his calculating. This seems to presuppose that the system of calculation-rules supplies an independent standard of correctness, against which we can measure the performances of particular persons or even mankind at large. Somehow, it seems, a calculus already contains all of its (correct) applications. It takes care of itself; what we have to do is to see how it does so. More generally, we note the possibility of misapplying rules. This leads us to contrast the 'rule of law' with the 'rule of man' and to hold up the first as an ideal of impartiality. We are then seduced by this metaphor into cancelling out mankind altogether. The rule of law seems grounded in the principle that rules, if properly drafted, determine their own applications quite independently of how we apply them, as if verdicts in particular cases were already foreshadowed in the rules. In the resulting mythology, rules became absolutely rigid bodies, and systems of rules became peculiarly adamantine machines, not subject to wear and tear, friction, free-play and distortion of the parts. By constructing a calculus, we set a machine in motion which inexorably grinds out all of its correct applications, without any further interventions by us (cf. §§ 189–94).

2 This picture of a calculus as an adamantine machine carries with it a temptation to redraw the boundary between the logical and the psychological. Initially we are inclined to claim that many

judgments about correctness or incorrectness of rule-applications are quite objective. We would say, e.g., that someone who arrives at the answer 25 when asked to calculate the value of $n^2 + 2n + 1$ for the argument 3 has made a mistake; saying this is simply stating a fact. But all of this easily comes to look questionable. I can make judgments about correctness of rule-applications only according to my understanding of the rule and my perception of the circumstances in which it is to be applied. I must make use of my 'interpretation' of the rule. But my calculations are fallible. Hence my standards of correctness are merely *my* standards. What holds in my case holds for everybody. Our standards of correctness of calculation are merely *our* standards, not *the* standards which are embodied in the system of rules. We are tempted to conclude, therefore, that whether something conforms to a rule is a logical question, in contrast to the psychological question of how we determine whether it so conforms (cf. § 377). Real objectivity becomes an unattainable ideal. Correctness becomes a transcendent concept.

3   The notion that a rule determines its application exploits an analogy between rules and (mathematical) functions (cf. §§ 189–90). Rules are here conceived to be general, so that application is a matter of instantiation, parallel to calculating the value of a polynomial by substituting a number in place of a variable. Rules are also thought to be comparable to functions in being single-valued; for a single argument, a function must yield a unique entity as its value. Taken together, these two features of rules seem to yield an external check on the correctness of sets of rule-applications. Consistency appears to be a necessary condition for over-all correctness of applications, and it seems to be a matter independent of any grasp of the rule the correctness of whose applications is to be determined. For surely if something conforms to a given rule, so too must anything else which is exactly the same. But identity is an issue logically independent of conformity with rules. Hence a minimal condition of correctness of applications is that a rule must be applied in the same way to instances that are the same. Inconsistencies in applications afford a short-cut to determine incorrectness of rule-applications.

4   A calculus, or even a game, is a system of rules. We are apt to cash this platitude in terms of a particular paradigm of a system, viz. deductive unification as exemplified by Euclidean geometry.

The propositional calculus formulated as a system of natural deduction provides a model for a system of rules. Starting from a set of intuitively sound rules of inference, we work upwards to discover a set of primitive rules from which all of them can be deduced and we work downwards to generate new derived rules of inference. What informs this conception of systems of rules is the idea that any consequence of a set of rules must itself be a rule already contained in that set. In the propositional calculus, e.g., acceptance of the primitive rules is thought to necessitate acceptance as a (derived) *rule* of any sequent obtained through repeated applications of the primitive rules. The converse is not held to be valid. Deductive unification by constructing axioms is a form of inductive inference, and therefore yields results which are neither unique nor conclusively supported. But in the interests of maximizing the systematic character of a set of rules, it is legitimate to formulate rules as *hypotheses*. In two different ways a system of rules may be supposed to contain hidden rules.

These four sources of misconception in philosophy interlock to yield a distorted conception of the objective aspect of rule-following. Our thought is dominated by mechanical pictures. We conceive of a system of rules as a huge machine in motion, which turns out applications and derived rules; all of this is as independent of our will as the motion of the stars. Or we think of a calculation-rule as a railway track laid to infinity; so correctness of application consists of our staying on the rails. These pictures have a baleful influence. They dress up certain truths of grammar as metaphysical principles. We are in danger of confusing ourselves if we contend that anybody who correctly follows the rule 'add 2' *must* get the answer '1002' for the argument '1000'; the point is that getting this answer in this particular case is a *criterion* for a person's following this rule. The same mechanical pictures tempt us to ignore the fact that whether something counts as a rule depends solely on how we collectively *use* it. The normative uses of a rule as a guide to behaviour, and as a standard for judging correctness of rule-applications, are not something extrinsic. They do not 'fit' the concept of a rule, but rather 'belong' to it (cf. § 136). The idea of a rule functioning as a transcendent standard of correctness is incoherent. Surrendering this idea does not, however, entail abandoning the claim that there are objective standards for judging the correctness of applications of rules.

Criteria for following rules discharge this role. Superimposed on instinct, training and drill suffice to inculcate practices of rule-application. The performance of any individual constitutes correct application of a rule only if it satisfies the criteria of correctness enshrined in the general practice of following rules of the relevant kind. Conformity or non-conformity with a practice is an objective matter. Indeed, it is not a whit less objective than identity, since the concepts of identity and agreement 'belong' to the concept of a rule (§ 225; cf. §§ 185, 208; RFM VII, §§ 39f.).

The primary aim of §§ 185–242 is negative, to explode a mythology that clouds philosophers' vision of the phenomena of normativity. The picture of systems of rules as machines grinding out derived rules and applications is to be discarded. As a prophylactic, we might liken rules to signposts (§ 85). A signpost may serve to guide a walker along a footpath, but not by dragging him along an invisible set of rails. Its power to guide is parasitic on the existence of a practice. For erecting a signpost would be pointless unless there were in the community at large a general disposition to respond to its presence in a particular way. Given the background of the practice of following signs marking paths, a signpost has, as it were, a trajectory (cf. § 87). It thus 'determines' which way to go. Divorced from this practice, it would be a mere object on the trail-side. We are under no compulsion to employ signposts as we do. But, of course, if we were not to employ an object in this way, it would not correctly be characterized as a 'signpost' at all. Following a signpost is a paradigm of guidance without mechanism.

Recognizing their predominantly negative aim is crucial to correct understanding of §§ 185–242. It should serve as a warning against misconstruing destructive arguments directed against philosophical preconceptions as constructive arguments supporting fresh 'positive' philosophical theses. This mistake is tempting. Can we not describe Wittgenstein's purpose as showing that there is no objectivity, no 'fact of the matter', about conformity with rules? Or that all necessity is merely psychological? Or that identity is relative? Or that decisions alone cement rules together into systems and link them with their applications? Or that rule-following boils down to regularity in behaviour and dispositions? Each of these interpretations is profoundly misleading. Each of these 'positive' theses is the fountainhead of fresh misconceptions.

Indeed, each embodies the very misconception that Wittgenstein meant to extirpate. The idea, e.g., that he argues against there being any fact of the matter about conformity with a rule presupposes the intelligibility of explicating the notion of objectivity in terms of the mechanical picture of rules as adamantine machines grinding out their applications; for otherwise what is it that is claimed not to exist? The targets of Wittgenstein's criticism are not mistakes properly countered by assertions, but a form of mythology whose grip on our thinking must be loosened.

Though predominantly negative in aim, §§ 185–242 are by no means purely negative. These remarks do not leave a lacuna to be filled by some novel and more viable theory of rule-following. Wittgenstein meant his clarification of the grammar of 'rules' and 'rule-following' to be definitive. He aimed at a complete clarification of these phenomena, i.e. at a clarification that made our puzzlements disappear completely (§ 133). The key to clarity is a set of reminders of familiar aspects of our practice of explaining the expressions 'rule' and 'to follow a rule'. Two matters are of vital importance. First, there are distinct criteria for the existence of rules, for a person's trying or intending to follow a given rule and for his following this rule correctly. We appeal to the first kind of criterion to determine what are the rules of chess, what are the statutes of a college or what are the current tax laws in respect of royalties. We employ the second kind to settle whether an individual is playing chess or trying to meet his tax liabilities, or whether a college is engaged in electing a master according to the provisions of its statutes. The third kind of criteria are applied in determining whether a person has castled correctly in chess or has met his tax liabilities, or whether a college has properly elected a new master. It is obvious that these sets of criteria are distinct, for a person may well not try to conform to an established rule, and he may intend to follow a rule without doing so correctly. Moreover, satisfying criteria is not a matter of conferring mere inductive support on an hypothesis. That someone meets the criteria for castling correctly in chess makes it certain, *ceteris paribus*, that he has followed this rule of chess correctly. The second crucial feature of the grammar of rules and rule-following is a network of internal connections. In particular, to try to follow a rule is to try to follow this rule correctly; to explain a rule regulating behaviour is to explain what to do to follow this rule; and to do what a rule requires (e.g. for a private to salute an officer in uniform) is to follow this rule (viz. the rule that a private should salute an officer in uniform). Like orders and their executions, or like expectations and their fulfilments, rules and their applications make contact in language (cf. § 197; PR, 65ff.; PG, 157; PLP, 116ff.).

The cash value of these platitudes is the spotlighting of certain misconceptions that serve as the foundations for building philosophical theories of rules and rule-following. Two misconceptions are very prominent. The first amounts to a denial that there are criteria. It is thought, e.g., that whether a person follows a rule correctly has the status of a hypothesis more or less strongly confirmed by his past and present behaviour; his observed actions are held to stand to a rule in the same relation that a set of experimental data stand to a scientific explanation. The second misconception is tantamount to the denial of an internal connection. It is thought, e.g., that the pattern of actual or potential behaviour of the members of a relevant community of rule-followers is a *tertium quid* that mediates between a rule-formulation and its applications; as if to determine whether a person is following a particular rule correctly (e.g. following a signposted footpath to Grantchester) we have to settle whether he reacts to a given rule-formulation (e.g. a signpost inscribed 'Grantchester') in the way that most others would in the same circumstances. Though regularities in behaviour are of paramount importance, they have an altogether different status in the grammar of rules. They are presupposed in the identification of symbols as the formulations of rules (e.g. in the identification of a bit of painted wood as a signpost). They also account for the utility of concepts whose applications are governed by sets of logically independent criteria. Without this regularity, our actual multifaceted concept of following a rule would fall apart (cf. BB, 61f.), for its application in accord with the diverse accepted criteria would lead to discordant judgments about whether individuals were following particular rules.

Wittgenstein thought that all of these observations are uncontroversial descriptions of familiar aspects of our practice of explaining and using the expressions 'a rule' and 'to follow a rule'. Together they were meant to give an *Übersicht* of what it is to follow a rule. To the extent that this attempt succeeds, it is an achievement as positive as the construction of any theory of rule-following. By eliminating the illusion that anything stands in need of theoretical explanation, it pre-empts the place occupied by any possible theory of rule-following.

4   ON SEEING NEW ASPECTS OF *INVESTIGATIONS*
§§ 185–242

All of this stage-setting should be a prolegomenon to a detailed exegesis of §§ 185–242, and to a careful examination of the puzzles generated by them. That enterprise goes far beyond the scope of a single paper. It would ramify into an investigation of Wittgenstein's extensive writings on rule-following, only some of which are published. It would also ramify into debates on many of the topics central to philosophical logic or the philosophy of language. This programme remains to be executed. Even if it were completed, trying to summarize its main features would probably be futile. §§ 185–242 are Wittgenstein's own attempt to give a synopsis of a vast skein of argument. Any duplicate attempt would produce a text less elegant and forceful than the original, and it would no doubt reiterate points from the original that strike many contemporary philosophers as *crazy*. A widespread reaction to the material epitomized in §§ 185–242 is that there we have stumbled across a hitherto unknown kind of madness. As a consequence, philosophers often lack the patience to try to understand Wittgenstein's arguments. Certainly these arguments have received no decisive refutation.

In desperate bid to remedy this situation, I shall abandon sobriety – or at least academic caution – and present something radically different from detailed exegesis. It is evident that §§ 185–242 cover a host of issues at the core of any serious philosophical analysis of language, meaning and understanding. Wittgenstein was eager to eliminate obstacles to our seeing these matters aright. Yet what distorts our vision is as much defects of the *will* as it is defects of the intellect. We are rightly impressed by the notion that in many respects language-use is a rule-governed activity. The normativity of language is of crucial importance. Ignoring it leads to a very crude form of behaviourism. 'Following according to the rule is at the BOTTOM of our language-game' (RFM VI, § 28). On the other hand, the results of emphasizing the normativity of language may be just as grotesque as crude behaviourism. We have a powerful desire to display rules as entities altogether unique. We sublime the concept of a rule. Thereby we generate a mystery about what it is to be guided by a rule, and we concoct a myth about what it is for an act to conform to a rule (cf. § 221). As a cure for these misconceptions 'we must ensure that in philosophy (i.e. in clarifying grammatical questions) we really speak of *rules* – only thus can we keep our feet on solid ground and avoid building castles-in-the-air' (BT, 243). To accomplish this, however, we need to neutralize the desire for mythopoesis and for prostrating ourselves in the face of apparent mysteries. Here arguments are powerless. But pictures might succeed if they were endowed with sufficient charisma. They might help us to see new aspects of the phenomena of normativity (cf. § 144). By doing so, they might make it possible for us really to *listen* to Wittgenstein's arguments and to weigh these up. I shall offer a pair of pictures, one of rules and one of rule-following, not in the expectation of effecting any philosophical conversions, but only in the hope of enhancing receptivity to the arguments in §§ 185–242.

Rules as instruments. Philosophers are prone to think of rules as abstract entities. Most commonly they are conceived of as either parallel or subordinate to propositions, i.e. as the meanings of sentences of certain kinds (e.g. of sentences containing such 'prescriptive' expressions as 'must', 'may', 'shalt not'). As an antidote, Wittgenstein recommended viewing rules as *symbols* or *instruments* with particular uses or ranges of use. This is an application of a more general policy. For he urged us to regard sentences as instruments and the sense of a sentence as its employment (§ 421). Descriptions, commands, expressions of intention, etc., are sentences used in particular ways (cf. §§ 21–5; BB, 102f.), not Platonic entities nor even sentences characterized by certain intrinsic properties. Similarly, samples are merely objects used in a distinctive way, not extraordinary entities endowed with 'normative properties'.[21] Rule-formulations may take the form of sentences, or of concrete symbols such as samples, traffic lights and authoritative examples (e.g. a demonstration of how to behave in church);[22] or they may combine both kinds of symbol, as on signposts or colour-charts. But in all these cases rules are to be viewed as instruments or symbols with particular uses. This has therapeutic value for combating illusions that arise from considering rules as abstract objects.

1 Any sentence used to formulate a particular rule can also be used for other purposes; typically it can be used to report that a rule is in force,[23] and often it can be used as a description. Compare pictures: a picture of a boxer in a particular stance can be used to express a number of different rules, and also to describe an historical event (cf. p. 11n.). Wittgenstein suggested a more radical generalization: any experiential sentence (*Erfahrungssatz*) can be used to express a rule (RFM, vii, § 74). Whether or not this is correct, the use of a sentence as a rule is not something determined by the sentence itself, any more than the use of an object as a sample is somehow determined by the nature of the object.

2 Therefore its status as a rule-formulation is not an intrinsic property of a symbol. *A fortiori*, this does not follow from the *form* or *structure* of a sentence. It depends on external facts about how the symbol is used. There is no short-cut in identifying rules. In particular, scrutiny of form cannot be substituted for inspection of use without grave risk of error. Any given use of a symbol may be transitory, intermittent or localized. These matters are perhaps clearest if we focus on the use of objects as samples.

3 If rules are symbols with particular uses, then rule-following might be viewed as a relation of actions to *symbols*. Wittgenstein hinted that this idea should be taken seriously. (Compare Z, § 290: ' "He did *what* I told him." – Why should one not say here: There is an identity between the action and the *words*?!') Where a concrete symbol (sample, colour-chart, diagram) occurs in the formulation of a rule, application of the rule may involve comparison of objects with these symbols. This is a clear instance of the truth of grammar that an order and its fulfilment, a rule and its correct applications, make contact *in language*.

4 The only ground for characterizing a symbol as a rule is that *it* is used in the ways distinctive of rules (RFM III, § 65). This is true of rule-formulations whether they are in the form of sentences or of concrete symbols (samples, authoritative examples, etc.). Therefore there is no such thing as a hidden, or hitherto unacknowledged, yet operative rule. We cannot discover *rules* of grammar, games, law, etc. The fact that one sentence entails another, even if combined with the hypothesis that the first sentence is standardly used to formulate a rule, does not entail that the second

sentence is a *rule*, i.e. that it is actually used in the ways characteristic of rules. It is merely a possible rule, and that was obvious
prior to the demonstration of entailment. This point is perhaps
even clearer where rules are formulated by means of concrete
symbols. The fact that the edge of my desk coincides in length
with a metre-stick, together with the fact that the metre-stick is
used as a sample (e.g. in explaining the expression 'one metre
long'), does not entail that edge of my desk is a *sample* of the
length one metre (though it is, of course, a possible sample). The
use of one symbol is connected with the use of others only in so
far as we *make* connections by using them alike.

No doubt this picture of rules as instruments seems very crude.
Any competent philosopher will at once object to the identification of rules with symbols (their expressions). But rather than
making excuses for these alleged defects and attempting to introduce saving qualifications, I am inclined to justify appealing to
this picture. First, the point of presenting this picture is not to
encapsulate the whole truth and nothing but the truth about rules,
nor even to give a perfect picture of Wittgenstein's reflections.
Rather, it is meant to remove blind prejudices and thus to open
our eyes to new possibilities worthy of detailed exploration (cf.
§ 52). Such a picture has a function comparable to that of a
scientific paradigm, e.g. Bohr's model of the atom. It may well
have a value just *because* it is very simple and hence very crude.
Second, in its apparent commitment to a form of nominalism, this
picture chimes with a conspicuous element of Wittgenstein's
thought. He derided excessive nicety about mention and use (e.g.
§ 143), and he was attracted by the idea of incorporating expressions of rules into an account of what is to *follow* a rule (e.g. BB,
12f., 28; RFM VII, § 26). His general recipe for escaping from
misconceptions about rules is to avoid telling 'fairy-tales about
symbolic processes' (PG, 256, my italics). Hence the picture of
rules as instruments, however crude and objectionable, captures
an important element of his thinking.

Rule-following as making measurements. Philosophers are inclined to think of rule-following as something passive. We are
guided by something external; we are driven along a pre-existing
track; we are compelled by the rule as by an alien will. The focus
of attention is shifted away from what we do to what we experience. Rules, as independent entities, are surrounded by fields of

force that impinge on our lives and shape them from without. Wittgenstein often employed a picture of rule-following that is deeply antithetical to this widespread one. He recommended viewing measuring as the model for following a rule. This is a natural counterpart of the picture of rules as instruments. For in so far as a rule is an instrument, applying a rule must be making a particular use or application of an instrument, and measuring obviously involves the use of such instruments as yardsticks or kilogram weights. Wittgenstein showed a predilection for extending this model and applying it to the special case of following rules of grammar. He compared a rule of grammar with a decision establishing a unit of measurement, e.g. with the choice of the standard metre for defining the unit of metric linear measure. Following a rule of grammar, i.e. using an expression in accord with its explanation, is parallel to putting a system of measurement to work to make measurements of objects. Setting up and applying systems of measurement are models for the explanation and use of expressions in speech (PLP, 13f.). Both the more general and the more particular pictures have therapeutic value.

1   Although in measuring something a person follows a procedure, his measuring is an activity devoid of any aura of passivity. Nor is there any grip here for the notion of compulsion. Of course, if he is to measure something correctly, he must follow an appropriate procedure. But this merely reformulates the truism that he can be correctly described as making a measurement only if he does something the performance of which counts as making a measurement.

2   It is patently absurd to claim that a yardstick contains the acts of particular persons in using it to take linear measurements of objects. Nor would it make sense to suppose that a yardstick contained or determined the practice of using it to make measurements. These claims contain obvious category mistakes. Hence the picture of rule-following as measurement helps to make latent nonsense into patent nonsense.

3   Whether employing instruments counts as making measurements depends on how these instruments are used, i.e. on the circumstances surrounding their employment on particular occasions. It seems obvious here that a verdict never turns on the occurrence or non-occurrence of some epistemically private mental act, but only on observable public features of the use of in-

struments. There are indeed *criteria* for whether someone is measuring (trying to measure) an object, also *criteria* for whether he has measured it correctly (succeeded in measuring it). Like all criteria, these ones are public and defeasible. *Ceteris paribus*, that somebody has satisfied a criterion of measuring something correctly makes it *certain* that he has measured it correctly, though this inference is not incontrovertible. The defeasibility of such inferences is what generates the illusion that Wittgenstein adumbrated a form of scepticism concerning judgments about the correctness of rule-following. This is as far from his thought as the sceptical thesis about the possibility of explaining meanings of words by ostensive definitions.

4   Although describing methods of measurement is distinct from applying these methods to describe objects, 'what we call "measuring" is partly determined by a certain constancy in results of measurement' (§ 242). The concept of measurement presupposes (in some way) agreement in judgments. Regularities in behaviour underpin the unity of this concept, since otherwise the wide range of independent criteria for making correct measurements would produce a random scatter of often conflicting applications of this concept in place of the coherent pattern actually observed. This point about regularities is what Wittgenstein meant to stress by calling measuring and (more generally) rule-following *practices*.

5   Setting up a system of measurement involves singling out certain instruments and formulating rules for their use. Any attempt to stipulate how to apply these rules in making measurements is obviously an extension of the original set of rules, in that it formulates further rules for the use of the very same instruments of measurement. Consequently, directions for applying a system of measurement simply swell the rules of the system to be applied, but cannot themselves bridge the 'gap' to the applications. Measurement therefore makes clear the fact that 'there is a way of grasping a rule which is *not* an *interpretation*, but which is exhibited in what we call "obeying the rule" and "going against it" in actual cases' (§ 201). The obverse side of this coin is that in any rule-governed procedure, justifications come to an end (BB, 13ff.; Z, § 301). In following a particular rule on a given occasion, my reasons for what I do soon give out (§ 211). 'If I have exhausted the justifications I have reached bedrock, and my spade

is turned' (§ 217). Exhaustion of justifications for particular applications of rules is a transparent aspect of making measurements of objects.

6 As a model for applying rules of grammar, making measurements of objects clarifies some aspects of the 'autonomy of grammar'. In particular, it underlines that rules of grammar are arbitrary (cf. §§ 372, 497; PG, 184ff.). For the choice of a unit of measure is not grounded in some essential or metaphysical truth about the object taken as a sample of the unit, but rests simply on a decision to use an object as a 'standard of comparison' (cf. § 50). Nor are regularities, whether natural or human, necessary conditions for establishing something as a unit of measurement. The utility, not the possibility, of metric concepts presupposes such regularities (§ 142). Concept formation is shaped by the natural history of mankind, but not beholden to it (cf. p. 230, RFM VI, § 49).

Once again this picture will seem very crude. Using metre-sticks to measure carpets is only a particular application of a special system of rules. Only a grotesque reification of rules would make it even a plausible candidate for a general model of what it is to follow a rule. The answer, as before, is that this picture sketching has a purpose not vitiated by crudeness in the brushwork. The aim is to manufacture an inoculation effective against a prevalent mythology characteristic of philosophical reflection on rule-following. We move in the gravitational field of other crude pictures, especially when we view following a calculation-rule as being driven along tracks leading to infinity (§ 218). Wittgenstein combatted this source of misconceptions with a battery of images and slogans: 'There is nothing behind the rules' (PG, 244), 'There is no logical machinery' (LFM, 194ff.), and 'Rules do not act at a distance' (BB, 14; cf. PG, 81). These ideas seem ludicrous and inconsequential to some, evocative and forceful to others. My purpose is to make sense of the thought that informs this position, and to make its attractiveness intelligible. To think of following a rule in terms of using instruments to make measurements is the key to unpacking the complex argumentation of §§ 185–242, as well as a nucleus of condensation for independent philosophical investigations. If it were to become entrenched and unassailable, this picture might in due course become a strait-jacket for our thinking, but this danger now seems remote.

5 THE ISSUE OF RELEVANCE

The clarification of the arguments of *Investigations* §§ 143–242 might be supposed to be a properly 'academic' exercise, without any interest save for antiquarians. We are disposed to think that the entire framework of Wittgenstein's thought about language is outmoded. It belongs to the stone ages of the philosophy of language – an era bereft of the benefits of modern psycholinguistics and of transformational grammar. The burning issues of the present day are not liable to be illuminated by Wittgenstein's remarks on rules or rule-following.

In one respect, this harsh verdict is clearly justified. We would look in vain for Wittgenstein's contribution to detailed debates in the philosophy of language. Only *per accidens* did he contribute anything to a theory of adverbial modification or to a semantic analysis of intensional contexts. On the other hand, this does not merit our contempt. His silence on these issues is not a matter of neglect and ignorance, but one of principle. He was attracted by the idea of exhibiting language as a calculus. He was sensitive to a current of thought that is now prominent. But, instead of trying to execute this philosophical programme, he challenged and repudiated it. This makes his remarks on meaning relevant to the whole framework of controversy in the philosophy of language. *A fortiori*, §§ 143–242, being the core of the *Investigations*, are of the utmost importance.

Far from having left him far behind, we have only recently arrived at the point from which Wittgenstein set off in the early 1930s.[24] In his own critical reflections on logical atomism, his initial attempt to free himself from the Augustinian picture of language led him to a demythologized account of word-meaning. The meaning of a name is not the object named, but rather the totality of rules governing its use, or the role of the word in the calculus. Understanding a sentence still consists in operating a calculus of meaning-rules, one for each logical constituent of the sentence. The advantage of this conception over its predecessors is abstention from unnecessary metaphysics. Such obscure entities as Frege's senses, or the 'objects' of the *Tractatus*, are replaced by sets of conventions for using the expressions of a language. Mythology is not merely reduced, but seemingly eliminated once for all. Philosophy can concentrate on describing a language completely by supplying a complete meaning-rule for the use of each individual word.

This general picture of language as a calculus, which was a transient phase of Wittgenstein's thought, is now dominant among the host of contemporary philosophers who quest after 'theories of meaning for natural languages'. There are many and important differences even among the leaders of this movement. Yet these are superimposed on a general agreement about certain fundamental principles. Apparent controversies notwithstanding, there is much that is common to the work of Quine, Davidson, Dummett, Chomsky and generative semanticists. The meaning of a word can in principle be given by an all-embracing rule for its correct application; its meaning is, or is 'represented by', such a semantic rule. The meaning of a sentence is a resultant of the meaning of its constituents and its structure; the meaning is, or perhaps merely can be, calculated in this way. Understanding a sentence consists in deriving its meaning from the meanings of its constituents and its structure; it is, or can be 'represented by', a set of transformations in a calculus of meaning-rules.[25] Speakers of a language need not, and typically do not, have the ability to state the semantic rules governing the words that they use. Hence a semantic theory need pay no special attention to speakers' explanations of words in their language; their explanations may fail to 'specify the meanings' of the explained expressions, and a semantic rule 'giving the meaning' of a word might be none the worse for having no intelligible role in the practice of teaching or explaining this word. A philosophical understanding of an expression may be as far removed from the conscious transactions of a competent speaker as the theory of quantum mechanics is from what a savage knows about fire.

It is immediately noteworthy how strongly Wittgenstein fought against the tides of such scientific philosophy. He advanced general arguments against its methodology. It seeks explanations of phenomena; it tries to penetrate beneath what is apparent to disclose the hidden mechanism of language; and it cheerfully explains away much of what we suppose ourselves to understand. It treats certain philosophical puzzles about language as genuine problems and proposes novel solutions for them, instead of dissolving them by showing how they originate in misunderstandings. Wittgenstein also opposed many of the leading ideas of the mod-

ern scientific philosophy of language. This movement must hold
that semantic rules can act at a distance. It does seek to lay bare
the logical machinery that underlies our everyday rules of
language. It is trying to refine or complete in unheard-of ways the
system of rules for the use of our words (§ 133). To the extent
that it considers understanding at all, it must presuppose that
understanding a sentence is a complex, articulated mental (or
neural!) process (cf. § 154), and that it consists in operating a
calculus of semantic rules (cf. § 81). Similarly, it must treat explanations diverging from the canonical form of semantic rules as
mere hocus-pocus (cf. PG, 273). In the short run at least, con-
frontation with Wittgenstein's thinking is the most testing examination which the current philosophy of language is likely to
undergo. The *Investigations* may not contain the answers to all of
our questions about language, but it elaborates many of the questions that should be addressed to the questions and answers now
fashionable in constructing theories of meaning for natural
languages.

The mainspring of Wittgenstein's criticism is his insistence on
scrupulous respect for the conceptual connections among explanation, meaning and understanding.[26] Understanding is the correlate
of explanation. The content of understanding (i.e. the meaning of
an expression) cannot transcend the practice of explaining an
expression. The meaning of a word, phrase or sentence is what is
explained in explaining it. Ordinary explanations of meaning are
to be taken at face value; they have many different forms, and
they function in many different ways. Explanations are *rules* for
the correct use of the expressions explained. Understanding an
expression is to know how to use it. Hence understanding presupposes knowing how to explain an expression in at least some of
the ways acknowledged to be correct in the actual practice of
explanation.

At one or more points, the project of exhibiting language as a
calculus of semantic rules breaks this network of internal connections. It openly scorns any close attention to actual explanations
of meaning, contending that only a properly drafted semantic rule
can 'give the meaning' of a word or sentence. It also distorts the
concept of a rule by identifying as 'semantic *rules*' sentences that
have no normative functions at all in our everyday use of language.
To remedy this defect by elevating 'semantic rules' to the status

of *hypotheses* in a complex scientific theory of language is to convert a covert inconsistency into a blatant contradiction. Wittgenstein's objections to treating language as a calculus do not concern matters of detail. They completely undermine the claim that meaning is the subject-matter under study. There are no such things as hidden *rules* in our practice of explaining and using expressions. To the extent that 'specifications of meaning' in a semantic theory diverge from ordinary explanations, they are not *explanations* of meaning at all, and hence have nothing whatever to do with *understanding*. There is typically no such thing as an explanation of meaning that is immune to misinterpretation, and hence never liable to non-trivial extension. The very idea of such a *complete* semantic rule for each expression of language is incoherent. In so far as philosophy aims to clarify our *understanding* of expressions that we employ, it should skate on the surface of our variegated practices of giving *explanations*. Any attempt to penetrate deeper by constructing a theory or system of semantic rules would be as futile as seeking to explain the observed behaviour of objects in the looking-glass world by reference to their molecular structure. Quite literally, the investigation of *meaning* can consist only in reminders of *explanations* that we already acknowledge and use to guide our linguistic behaviour.

In retrospect, Wittgenstein rejected his initial attempt to demythologize logical atomism. It had merely substituted a mythology about rules for the metaphysics of the *Tractatus*. The Fates have ordained that this mythology should become the wisdom of the present age. Perhaps the most striking evidence of its power is our inability to see the wider point of a certain philosophical joke. In one lecture, having noted that we have been drilled in the technique of counting in Arabic numerals, Wittgenstein asked Turing how many numerals he had learned to write down. The answer was guarded: 'Well, if I were not here, I should say $\aleph_0$'. Far from objecting, Wittgenstein expressed his agreement, thereby rejecting by implication such stock finitist responses as 'The number of numerals that I will *ever* write down'. But he then continued: 'Now should we say: "How wonderful – to learn $\aleph_0$ numerals, and in so short a time! How clever we are!"'?' (LFM, 31). This is clearly intended to be a joke, and many of us perceive it to be a joke, even if we would vary in how we explained the absurdity. A parallel case does not evoke the same response.

Consider the phenomenon called the 'creativity of language'.[27] In learning to speak English we have all mastered a technique of using and understanding sentences. If asked how many sentences we have learned to understand, we are advised by linguists and philosophers alike to reply '$\aleph_0$'. What if Wittgenstein were to interject 'Now should we say: "How wonderful – to learn to understand $\aleph_0$ sentences, and in so short a time! How clever we are!"'?' Would we perceive this to be a *joke*? More probably we would reply that Wittgenstein had here put his finger on something deep. We must humble ourselves before the mystery of the creativity of language. If blessed with scientific curiosity, we should embark on a programme of research to explain our seemingly god-like powers. Anybody who reacted to Wittgenstein's comment with laughter rather than solemnity and awe would be open to the charge that he was shallow, a philosophical philistine or an intellectual Luddite. Differences here cut very deep. They concern a contrast of climates of thought, almost of forms of intellectual life. No wonder Wittgenstein felt so profoundly alienated from the mainstream of contemporary western civilization (PR, 7). He thought that philosophical clarification necessitated the ridiculing of much of what advanced intellectuals most reverenced.

The task of clarifying *Investigations* §§143–242 is monumental, difficult and important. It extends from deciphering Wittgenstein's numerous manuscripts to the foundations of the philosophy of language. A single insight at the beginning is worth ever so many somewhere along the line. For in gazing into the limpid waters of the *Investigations* we are liable to ape Narcissus by falling in love with what we see. This paper is a stone thrown to shatter the surface reflection in the hope that we may see what is really there.

NOTES

1 This paper draws extensively on research carried out in collaboration with Dr Peter Hacker. The analysis of *Investigations* §§ 1–184 is derived from our joint commentary (G. P. Baker and P. M. S. Hacker, *Wittgenstein: Understanding and Meaning*, Blackwell, Oxford, 1980). The rest of the paper, more speculative and perhaps rash, is my sole responsibility, although it is greatly influenced by his generous and penetrating criticism of a preliminary draft.
2 Saul Kripke, unpublished lecture presented in Ontario (1976) and

Cambridge (1978). Crispin Wright, *Wittgenstein on the Foundations of Mathematics*, Duckworth, London, 1980, esp. Chapters 2 and 12.

3 Cf. Baker and Hacker, *op. cit.*, pp. 110–32, 140–57 and 395–431.

4 *Ibid.*, pp. 367–85.

5 *Ibid.*, pp. 33–59, 110–32, 664–86.

6 *Ibid.*, pp. 492–530, 546–59.

7 Cf. G. P. Baker and P. M. S. Hacker, critical notice of Wittgenstein's *Philosophical Grammar*, *Mind*, 85 (1976), pp. 270–2. Also G. P. Baker, 'Verehrung und Verkehrung: Waismann and Wittgenstein', in C. G. Luckhardt (ed.), *Wittgenstein: Sources and Perspectives*, Cornell, Ithaca, 1979, pp. 266–80.

8 A noteworthy instance is the preamble to § 79. Cf. Baker and Hacker, *op. cit.*, pp. 426.

9 *Ibid.* pp. 33–47 gives a detailed anatomization of the Augustinian picture.

10 *Ibid.*, pp. 47–52.

11 *Ibid.*, pp. 168–205.

12 *Ibid.*, pp. 320–43.

13 *Ibid.*, pp. 69–85.

14 Cf. F. Waismann, 'Verifiability', in A. G. N. Flew (ed.), *Logic and Language*, First Series, Blackwell, Oxford, 1960, pp. 117–29; also his *Principles of Linguistic Philosophy*, Macmillan, London, 1965, pp. 69–81 and *Logik, Sprache, Philosophie*, Reclam, Stuttgart, 1976, pp. 612–43.

15 Baker and Hacker, *op. cit.*, pp. 367–85.

16 *Ibid.*, pp. 531–45.

17 *Ibid.*, pp. 89–98.

18 It is a tempting strategy to short-circuit any criticism of Frege's metaphysical 'realm of sense'. For, it is alleged, 'Frege thought of language as a game played with fixed rules' (M. Dummett, *Truth and Other Enigmas*, Duckworth, London, 1978, p. 135). Consequently, he held that 'the sense of a word consists in a *rule* which, taken together with the rules constitutive of the senses of the other words, determines the condition for the truth of a sentence in which the word occurs' (M. Dummett, *Frege: Philosophy of Language*, Duckworth, London, 1973, p. 194, my italics.)

19 Cf. especially PLP, Chapter VII.

20 Wittgenstein, *Manuscript* (von Wright catalogue no. 152), p. 5, quoted at Baker and Hacker, *op. cit.*, p. 644.

21 Baker and Hacker, *op. cit.*, pp. 184–201.

22 Cf. H. L. A. Hart, *The Concept of Law*, Oxford University Press, pp. 120ff.

23 Cf. G. H. von Wright, *Norm and Action*, Routledge & Kegan Paul, London, 1963, pp. 104ff.

24 Logical positivists, too, spent many years exploiting a specific paradigm of meaning that Wittgenstein had briefly advocated and then abandoned.

25 For detailed criticism of these accounts of sentence-meaning and of understanding sentences see Baker and Hacker, *op. cit.*, pp. 258–83.
26 *Ibid.*, pp. 69–85, 664–86.
27 Cf. N. Chomsky, *Aspects of the Theory of Syntax*, MIT Press, Cambridge, Mass., 1965, pp. 6ff and N. Chomsky, *Reflections on Language*, Fontana/Collins, Glasgow, 1976, pp. 138f.

II

REPLY: RULE-FOLLOWING: THE NATURE OF WITTGENSTEIN'S ARGUMENTS[1]

Christopher Peacocke

I find myself in considerable disagreement with Dr Baker's provocative paper. The two main areas of disagreement are the interpretation of Wittgenstein and the question of whether, if Wittgenstein's arguments about rule-following are correct, they exclude the possibility of systematic semantic theories. But although in what follows there is much disagreement with Dr Baker, there is an underlying point of agreement, viz. that Wittgenstein's arguments about following a rule should not be treated with 'contempt', or regarded as 'outmoded'. If what Wittgenstein says about following a rule is correct, our pre-philosophical ideas not only about meaning and psychological states are misconceived, but also our ideas about objectivity; and I would agree with Dr Baker's statement that Wittgenstein's claims have never received a decisive refutation.

1   THE INTERPRETATION OF WITTGENSTEIN

The rival interpretation which I would offer in place of Dr Baker's is, in outline, this. The conclusion of Wittgenstein's arguments about following a rule is, in his own words, that ' "obeying a rule" is a practice' (§ 202). By 'practice' here he means the practice of a community; as he puts it, 'a rule is an institution' (RFM VI, § 31). And again, 'The application of the concept "following a rule"

72

Christopher Peacocke

presupposes a custom. Hence it would be nonsense to say: just once in the history of the world someone followed a rule' (RFM VI, § 21). This claim is also present in such remarks as: 'The word "agreement" and the word "rule" are *related* to one another, they are cousins. If I teach anyone the use of the one word, he learns the use of the other with it' (§ 224). Wittgenstein's point is not the banale claim that in a community with a conventional rule, persons attempt to make their individual rule accord with the conventional rule; his claim is a more radical one, that what it is for a person to be following a rule, <u>even individually</u>, cannot ultimately be explained without reference to some community.

In arguing for this claim, Wittgenstein considers various kinds of facts about individuals in virtue of which it might be said that rule-following is an individual matter; facts about what goes on in someone's consciousness, about his brain states, about his use of examples, tables or formulae. He finds all of these wanting. In the end, Wittgenstein holds, the only thing that must be true of someone who is trying to follow a rule, so long as we consider just the individual and not facts about some community, is that he is <u>disposed to think</u> that certain cases fall under the rule and others do not. But this is something which is also true of a person who falsely believes that he is conforming to a rule. His general argument is that only by appealing to the fact that the genuine rule-follower agrees in his reactions to examples with the members of some community can we say what distinguishes him from someone who falsely thinks he is following a rule. Wittgenstein develops this point in application to arithmetical and logical vocabulary, and to talk about sensations.

This is an extremely crude description of a set of complex and powerful arguments. But a statement even at that level of generality is rather different from the interpretation suggested by Dr Baker. Dr Baker writes (p. 42): 'The maximum of seamlessness in the web of Wittgenstein's argument is obtained by treating §§ 143–242 as a criticism of the notion that anyone who utters a sentence and *means* or *understands* it is operating a calculus according to definite rules (§ 81)'. Wittgenstein is nowhere denying that the ability to follow a rule is something employed in understanding and speaking a language; he is rather saying that we must not have a false view of what it is to follow a rule. The rules may or may not be definite: in the arguments about following a rule,

73

definiteness is not the crucial issue. What then is going on in § 81, the passage Dr Baker cites to support his interpretation? For here Wittgenstein certainly does say that it is false that anyone who 'utters a sentence and *means* or *understands* it is operating a calculus according to definite rules'. The answer to this question seems to be that in the section of the *Investigations* from which this quotation is taken, Wittgenstein is discussing definiteness, and not rule-following in general. In the section immediately preceding the one containing this quotation, Wittgenstein discusses an example of what seems to be a chair which regularly disappears and reappears: Wittgenstein says that it is wrong to think that we do not really 'attach any meaning to [the word 'chair'] because we are not equipped with rules for every possible application of it' (§ 80). And three sections after the one from which Dr Baker quotes, Wittgenstein summarizes his own discussion of the immediately preceding sections in the words 'I said that the application of a word is not everywhere bounded by rules' (§ 84). A further indication that definiteness is not the crux is the fact that the examples of rules which Wittgenstein does discuss, when developing the rule-following arguments, are not indefinite : for instance the rule 'add 2' or the table for transcribing printed into cursive script.

Of course, on the community interpretation of Wittgenstein I offer, it is true that indefiniteness and rule-following are not completely *unrelated*: if Wittgenstein can show that there can be meaning and understanding of expressions the extension of which is unified only by a family resemblance, and in particular a resemblance explicable only in terms of the agreement of the members of some community, then that may help to throw doubt on the idea that in rule-following there must be properties the presence of which can guide someone in the application of a rule quite independently of the properties of anyone else in any community. But this is just a plausibility consideration: the arguments Wittgenstein offers are meant to show that there cannot be individual rule-following independently of the properties of some community, even where there is no indefiniteness in the rules.[2]

If indefiniteness is not the point, does Dr Baker then deny that rule-following is involved in meaning and understanding at all? No: his claim seems rather to be that rule-following in general is to be explained by giving examples, that following a rule is a family resemblance concept and that following a rule should be compared with using a measuring instrument. It is hard to know, then, how Dr Baker would explain those passages in which Wittgenstein says that a rule is an institution; for *prima facie* there would be no contradiction in holding that following a rule is a family resemblance concept, but one which can be applied at the individual level without taking account of the properties of any community.

Dr Baker does indeed say, in developing the analogy between following a rule and measuring, that there are criteria for whether someone is following a rule, and these criteria are public. But on Dr Baker's reading this fact comes out of the blue: I suggest that in Wittgenstein's thought it is the conclusion of an argument. Here is an initial, crude statement of that argument.

Wittgenstein thought that if only the rule-follower and not anyone else could know whether he is following a rule, we would not in such a case be able to say what is the difference between there really being a rule the agent is following and his being under the false impression that there is. This, Wittgenstein continues, is an unacceptable conclusion if following a rule is to place any restrictions of what the rule-follower does. Hence it is not possible that the subject alone can know whether he is following a rule : the conclusion is that there must be public criteria for whether someone is following a rule. I am not endorsing this argument, and its formulation contains an ambiguity which we will consider below: but it does seem to express the thought which Wittgenstein summarizes at § 202:

> And hence also 'obeying a rule' is a practice.
> And to *think* one is obeying a rule is not to obey a rule.
> Hence it is not possible to obey a rule 'privately': otherwise thinking one was obeying a rule would be the same thing as obeying it.

The argument I have just stated, of which the publicity of criteria for rule-following is the conclusion, does not of course take the community view as a premise. Rather it has as one of its starting points a condition of adequacy, of which it can be said that it is one of the virtues of the community view that it meets this condition. The dialectical situation reached by § 202 is this. In earlier sections, the community view has been made plausible by negative considerations against various individualistic accounts of rule-following. The later discussion of the impossibility of a private language is not only a discussion of what may seem to be an especially problematic case for the community view. It also contains arguments which, if sound, independently favour the community view: for to say that the criteria for rule-following must be public, while not strictly equivalent to the community view, is something implied by that view. Here we have an example of Wittgenstein's own description of his writing as a criss-cross investigation, with 'the same or almost the same points . . . being approached afresh from different directions' (Preface, p. v).

Pivotal in Wittgenstein's discussion of rule-following and the impossibility of a private language are the correlative ideas that a genuine rule must impose restrictions on the actions of a rule-follower, and that there must then be a distinction between really following a rule and merely being under the impression that one is following a rule. Since these ideas receive no attention from Dr Baker, and seem to me to have been misunderstood by others, I will consider them further.

The second sentence of § 202 of the *Investigations*, 'And to *think* one is obeying a rule is not to obey a rule', is ambiguous. One claim which might be intended in saying of someone that he is mistaken in thinking he is following a rule is this:

he believes ∃R (R is a rule which he is following)
and in fact ~∃R (R is a rule which he is following).

Here the first occurrence of the quantifier '∃R' has narrower scope than 'believes'. I will call such a mistake 'a mistake about existence'. A person who uses an expression when disposed to think it correctly applies, even though the expression means nothing on his lips and he expresses no belief in sincerely uttering would-be sentences containing it, is someone who is making such a mistake about existence. Statements of mistakes about existence need not be relativized to particular occasions on which a person thought he was acting in accordance with some rule. One can say outright that someone is mistaken in thinking that there is a rule he is following in his use of some expression in his vocabulary.

The other way in which someone can be mistaken in thinking that he is following a rule *is* relativized to some particular occasion of action. This kind of mistake occurs when:

∃R (R is a rule he intends to follow, and he believes that in performing action *a* he was following R, when in fact he was not).

Here the quantifier '∃R' has wider scope than 'believes' and 'intends'; so when such mistakes occur, there is a rule which is the agent's intended rule. I will call these mistakes 'mistakes in application'.

Was Wittgenstein talking in § 202 about mistakes about existence or mistakes in application? I will argue, first, that a theory of mistakes about existence is more fundamental than a theory of mistakes in application; and, second, that in propounding the community view, Wittgenstein was offering a theory of mistakes about existence.

An account of the distinction between cases in which someone's action accords with his intended rule and cases in which his actions do not accord with his intended rule does not, by itself, say what it *is* for a given rule to be someone's intended rule. Yet the notion of a rule being someone's intended rule is fundamental even to the explanation of mistakes in application. Suppose we represent the rule to perform an action of kind F in circumstances G by (F,G). As soon as we have explained what it is for (F,G) to be someone's intended rule, we can go on to say: someone is making a mistake in application on a particular occasion iff there is some rule (F,G) which is his intended rule and on this occasion circumstances are G and he does not perform an F action. Clearly, a philosophically adequate converse explanation of mistakes about existence, in terms of the notions used in the distinction between mistakes in application and correct application, would not be possible : for in that distinction, what it is for (F,G) to be someone's intended rule is taken for granted.

Of course there is room for a theory of how we can come to know there has been a mistake in application of one rule, as opposed to a correct application of a slightly different rule. But we would expect such an account to be determined by what having (F,G) as one's intended rule consists in, together with general principles about evidence, explanation and human action. We can also say that if an account of what it is to have (F,G) as one's intended rule determines an unsatisfactory account of mistakes in application, then that is an objection to the account of intended rules. But this point is not only consistent with the priority of the notion of (F,G) being a person's intended rule; it also rests on the fact that the concept of a mistake in application is defined in terms of the notion of some (F,G) being the agent's intended rule.

There are several arguments for saying that we misrepresent Wittgenstein's intentions if we ignore the notion of a mistake about existence. In offering these arguments, I do not imply that the notion of a mistake in application has no role in Wittgenstein's thought; on the contrary, it explicitly enters some passages of the *Investigations* (e.g. § 288), and is employed in one of the arguments to be attributed to him below. My point is just that it should not be represented as concerned *only* with mistakes in application.

A simple argument that he was concerned with mistakes about existence is simply that when he states the community view, his formulation contains no mention of mistakes in application. The passages quoted at the start of this paper seem to be offered as unrestricted claims about what it is for someone genuinely to be following a rule. One who interprets Wittgenstein as concerned only with mistakes in application will, secondly, have difficulties over §§ 138–242 of the *Investigations*, which contain an extended argument that if you conceive of rule-following individualistically, you will be unable to avoid the consequence that any course of action whatever can be regarded as in accordance with the agent's rule. Nowhere in these sections does Wittgenstein discuss mistakes in application. We should infer that he thought that these (negative) arguments for the community view could proceed even if we do not consider mistakes in application. How could this be so if one of his major objections to an individualistic theory of rule-following was that it offered no account of mistakes in application? The absence of discussion of mistakes in application is especially striking in passages in which Wittgenstein is explicitly drawing the conclusion that individualistic accounts of rule-following allow any behaviour to be counted as in accord with a particular rule. For one would expect, if one was interpreting Wittgenstein as concerned only with mistakes in application, the argument to be that one needs to bring in the community if one is to distinguish a series of actions as a following of rule (F,G), rather than as a following of a different rule (F,G′) with mistakes in application. Such a line of thought cannot be expressed without talking about

78

mistakes in application: the fact that there is no mention of them is hard to reconcile with the interpretation.

An important third argument that Wittgenstein was concerned with mistakes about existence concerns the connection in Wittgenstein's thought between the rule-following arguments and the private language argument. In particular, let us compare two different arguments which might be suggested as representing Wittgenstein's reasons for holding that the grammar of 'pain' is not to be construed on the model of object and designation (§ 293). The first argument – let us label it 'A' – is the interpretation offered by one who thinks Wittgenstein was concerned only with mistakes in application. It runs:

Argument A:
1 If we construe the grammar of 'pain' on the model of object and designation, then mistakes in the application of 'pain' must be possible.
2 It is not possible for someone who understands 'pain' to say sincerely 'I am in pain' and not be in pain.[3]

_____

3 The grammar of 'pain' is not to be construed as the model of object and designation.

The second argument, labelled 'E', is the interpretation offered by one who thinks that the possibility of mistakes about existence plays a role in Wittgenstein's argument. Argument E runs:

Argument E:
4 There must always be a distinction between the case in which someone is making a mistake about existence and the case in which he is not.
5 If there were a state such that only the subject could know whether he is in that state, there would be no distinction between the case in which the subject is making a mistake about existence and the case in which he is not.
6 For any state such that others can know that the subject is in that state, the subject can be in error about whether he is in that state.
7 It is not possible for someone who understands 'pain' to say sincerely 'I am in pain' and not be in pain.

_____

   8 The grammar of 'pain' is not to be construed on the
      model of object and designation.[4]

Arguments A and E have their conclusion and their last premise
in common. (We can call this common conclusion 'the non-designative claim'.) As interpretations of Wittgenstein's thought, they
differ in that interpretation E regards this last part as a component
of a larger argument.

There are many arguments in favour of interpretation E. One
overriding consideration in its favour is simply that premise (4)
explicitly connects Wittgenstein's thoughts about rule-following
with the non-designative claim: as we saw, Wittgenstein explicitly
drew conclusions about privacy from his views on rule-following.
Considerations such as this one about rules in general are inter-
woven with the discussion of privacy:

> Don't always think that you read off what you say from the
> facts; that you portray these in words according to rules. For
> even so you would have to apply the rule in the particular
> case without guidance (§ 212).

The argument for attributing premise (5) to Wittgenstein is
primarily that it makes sense of those famous passages in which
Wittgenstein says that there is nothing for the correctness of the
use of an expression in a private language to consist in. When he
writes, 'One would like to say : whatever is going to seem right
to me is right. And that only means that here we can't talk about
"right" ' (§ 258) he is saying that in the case of a private language,
there is no account of there really being a rule someone is following other than various applications of a rule striking the subject
as correct. Such an account must be inadequate, because an
impression of correctness could be present even if the subject
were making a mistake about existence. This is a constitutive
argument about what is required for a particular distinction to
hold, the distinction between someone making or not making a
mistake about existence. It is not a verificationist argument. A
user of an alleged private language can have only an illusion of
understanding, since there is nothing for that distinction to consist
in : this is why Wittgenstein writes, 'And sounds which no one
else understands but which I *"appear to understand"* might be
called a "private language" ' (§ 269).[5]

Premise (5) is of course entirely consonant with the community view. There are later passages, after Wittgenstein has developed the private language argument, in which he commits himself to (5):

> I could not apply any rules to a *private* transition from what is seen to words. Here the rules really would hang in the air; for the institution of their use is lacking (§ 380).

> 'Before I judge that two images which I have are the same, I must recognise them as the same.' And when that has happened, how am I to know that the word 'same' describes what I recognise? Only if I can express my recognition in some other way, and if it is possible for someone else to teach me that 'same' is the correct word here (§ 378).

The hypothesis of a private language was a hypothesis of a language which 'another person cannot understand' (§ 243): so if 'same' is a word of that language, it is not possible for someone else to teach me that it is the correct word here.[6]

I do not know of a passage in which Wittgenstein explicitly commits himself to premise (6); but it is needed if the argument for the non-designative claim is to go through, and it is a consequence of several of his statements taken collectively. He says (§ 288), 'if I assume the abrogation of the normal language-game with the expression of a sensation, I need a criterion of identity for the sensation; and then the possibility of error also exists.' This gives us the conditional that if there is a criterion of identity, there is the possibility of error. But Wittgenstein also held the view that there is a genuine criterion of identity iff others can know that 'the same' applies in particular cases. § 378, quoted above, gives the 'only if' part of this biconditional; and he nowhere suggests that any more than agreement in judgments on sameness is required for the presence of a genuine criterion of identity. Indeed he emphasizes that agreement 'is part of the framework on which the working of our language is based (for example, in giving descriptions)' (§ 240). All this, together with his statements of the community view, suggest that he held the sufficiency component of the conditional : agreement in judgments involving 'the same' is sufficient for the existence of a genuine criterion of identity. Putting this together with the conditional from § 288 we can arrive at the conclusion that, if others can know that I am in a certain state, I can be in error about whether I am in that state.

Again, I endorse (6) here only as a statement of what Wittgenstein held, and not as a truth. It seems to be the weakest premise of argument E. To assert (6) is to rule out the correctness of a combination of views according to which others can understand and know the statement that I am in pain, while also I cannot be in error about my being in pain. Such a combination of views does not involve admitting the possibility of a language only one person can understand, and by the same token the community view by itself cannot exclude the combination.[7] But it is also important to note that rejecting (6) is consistent with accepting (4) (and (5) too), and the arguments for them. Someone who does reject (6) while accepting (4) and (5) then finds himself with constraints on any satisfactory replacement for (6). Thus someone who is unable to believe the non-designative claim can still find permanent value in Wittgenstein's thought on (1) and (2).

One thinker who seems to me to miss the relevance of the distinction between mistakes in application and mistakes about existence is Judith Jarvis Thomson. In her stimulating paper 'Private Languages'[8] she takes Norman Malcolm (in his *Philosophical Review* notice of the *Investigations*) to be interpreting Wittgenstein as concerned solely with mistakes in application; she goes on to criticize the argument which appeals only to a requirement of the possibility of mistakes in application. Malcolm's own text is often ambiguous as between a concern with mistakes in application and mistakes about existence, and he never clearly draws the distinction: nevertheless certain passages (especially at the end of his section entitled 'Private language') seem clearly to be discussing mistakes about existence. As we might expect from what I have said so far, Thomson's attempt to link the concern that a rule not be vacuous with a requirement that mistakes in application be possible is open to objection. She states a link as follows: 'if from the fact that I think *x*-ing is following rule R it follows that it is following rule R, I am then free to do anything or nothing. That "rule" doesn't point in any direction' (p. 190). She then replies to this that adoption of rule R *does* impose a restriction on me : I must not do something which I think is violating rule R. But this does not show the rule not to be vacuous. Suppose there were a nonsense word, which I quite wrongly think has significance; I am disposed to use the word on some occasion and not others, but there is nothing relevant beyond my disposition to apply or to withold the term which unifies these occasions. Here there is no genuine rule which I am following – I merely believe there is a rule which I am following – but of course it remains the case that I must not do something which strikes me as violating the rule.[9]

Suppose we accept that argument E and not argument A represents Wittgenstein's thought. Then, while it remains the case that in holding (7) Wittgenstein was making a claim about the possibility of mistakes in application, this claim is not strictly part of the private language argument. We can already conclude from (4) and (5) that we cannot make sense of the idea that someone is following a rule which concerns a state which only he can know he is in; on the interpretation E, the impossibility of mistakes in application of 'pain' is not used in reaching that conclusion. (This is as it should be, since in Wittgenstein's thought the private language argument aims at refuting an alleged possibility; it is not a thesis *per se* about the concept of pain, a concept we actually possess, but rather a thesis about any allegedly private state. Any conclusions we can draw about pain from the argument will be drawn from some more general conclusion which does not explicitly mention pain.) On interpretation E, the premise about mistakes in application is used only in establishing the non-designative thesis, and is not strictly used in the private language argument itself.

But is it correct to ascribe the non-designative claim to Wittgenstein? What are we to say about the many passages in which Wittgenstein writes without qualification of certain words as naming sensations?[10] It is helpful here to consider Wittgenstein's acceptance of

<blockquote>'pain' names a kind of sensation   (10)</blockquote>

in the light of an analogy, and indeed a connection, with the redundancy theory of truth. Wittgenstein in the *Investigations* appears to have adopted the redundancy theory of truth. He writes (§ 136)

<blockquote>'p' is true = p
'p' is false = not-p</blockquote>

(This is not just an endorsement of the correctness of a homophonic theory of truth for a notion of truth which has some independent elucidation; Wittgenstein uses these equivalences in order to reject the suggestion that the concepts of truth and falsity can be employed in an account of what it is for something to be a proposition.) Now (10) above follows immediately from the uncontroversial object language sentence 'Pain is a kind of sensation' and the disquotational

$$\text{'pain' names pain} \qquad (11)$$

I suggest that Wittgenstein often used 'refer' and 'name' in accordance with a redundancy theory of reference, similar to and connected with the redundancy theory of truth. Wittgenstein held (or must have held) that there is no inconsistency in saying that an utterance of 'He is in pain' is true, while also rejecting, as he did, the view that 'pain' is a predicate true of certain events or objects in the world (§§ 293, 304); what reconciles these two in his thought is the redundancy theory of truth. Similarly for reference: ' "pain" refers to pain' is regarded as a triviality, providing no substantive constraint on what is required for understanding 'pain' (beyond the fact that it has the syntactic role of a predicate). It is, of course, a more complicated matter to state a redundancy theory of reference than to state a redundancy theory of truth: there is no simple analogue for reference of the familiar equivalences Wittgenstein gives for the case of truth. But one would expect the redundancy theorist of truth and reference to take the following line. We should count as true precisely those sentences containing 'refers' which we need to if we are both to count as true all instances of ' "p" is true iff p' and also to accept such principles linking truth and reference as 'Any sentence of the form ⌜Fa⌝ is true iff the object denoted by a has the property referred to by F'.[11] Certainly there is no passage known to me in which Wittgenstein explicitly states that his use of 'refers' is sometimes governed by such principles. But there is a section in *Zettel*, § 487, which makes it clear that what he wants to agree with, in the statement of one who insists that I have a real feeling of joy when I can correctly say 'I feel joyful', is that I really am then joyful. But in the same section he almost immediately makes clear, too, that he thinks that what he has just said in no way rules out the non-designative claim, in what must be some other sense of 'designate':

'But I do have a real *feeling* of joy!' Yes, when you are glad you really are glad. And of course joy is not joyful behaviour, nor yet a feeling around the corners of the mouth and the eyes.

'But "joy" surely designates an inward thing.'

No. 'Joy' designates nothing at all. Neither any inward nor any outward thing.

The nature of what for Wittgenstein is sufficient for saying that an expression is a name of a sensation is shown in such passages as this, which is found at the end of the section on the manometer:

And what is our reason for calling 'S' the name of a sensation here? Perhaps the kind of way this sign is employed in this language-game. – And why a 'particular sensation', that is, the same one every time? Well, aren't we supposing that we write 'S' every time? (§ 270.)

Wittgenstein himself indicated that he did not think that 'name' is used uniformly when we say that some words name physical objects and others name sensations:

What does it mean 'to use a word as a designation, a name, of a sensation'? Isn't there something to investigate here?

Imagine you were starting from a language-game with physical objects – and then it was said, from now on sensations are going to be named too. Wouldn't that be as if first there were talk of transferring possessions and then suddenly of transferring joy in possession or pride in possession? Don't we have to learn something new here? Something new, which we call 'transferring' too (Z, § 434).

What, then, is this claim that 'pain' does not designate anything, a claim which is meant to be consistent with ' "pain" refers to pain' as we construed it? It is the claim that: there is no kind of thing, object or event such that (a) an account of what it is to understand 'pain' ineliminably requires intentional behaviour sensitive to the presence of instances of that kind and (b) 'pain' refers to things of that kind. On Wittgenstein's view, there need be no harm in saying that understanding 'pain' involves the possibility of intentional behaviour sensitive to whether someone is in pain: but this reference to pain is not ineliminable. It is eliminated in a statement of the criteria for someone's being in pain, and grasp of these can for a human being suffice for understanding of 'pain'.[12] (Clause (b) is present because Wittgenstein need not be committed to denying that, for instance, grasp of the identity conditions of *persons* is required for understanding 'pain'.)

This suggestion about how Wittgenstein thought to reconcile the non-designative claim with his talk of 'pain' naming a sensation places me in disagreement with Kenny's attempt to resolve this difficulty. Kenny writes:

> To sum up: if by 'name' one means 'word whose meaning is learnt by bare ostensive definition', then 'pain' is not the name of a sensation: but if by 'name' one means what is ordinarily meant by that word, then of course 'pain' is the name of a sensation.[13]

I am not, of course, disputing that Wittgenstein held that the meanings of names of sensations are not learned by bare ostensive definition. The point is rather that Kenny's resolution fails to accommodate the fact that, in both § 293 and the passage recently quoted from *Zettel*, it is our *familiar* words 'pain' and 'joy' which are said to be non-designative, and not just the expressions which the private linguist attempts to introduce. An interpretation of Wittgenstein should do justice to this fact.

This reflection leads to a more general issue. Commentators on Wittgenstein sometimes discuss the question of whether there is a consistent alternative to Wittgenstein's own position, an alternative which admits the truth of the main theoretical points made in the private language argument while still construing discourse containing the word 'pain' as having subjective experience as its subject matter. If the interpretation I have given so far is correct, then two points follow about such speculations. First, it is important to make clear that in such speculations one is concerned with designation, as discussed in the last paragraph but one above, rather than with reference as construed by the redundancy theory; otherwise one may not be considering a theory distinct from Wittgenstein's own.[14] Second, such speculations are often motivated by a desire to reject the Wittgensteinian thesis that 'I know I am in pain' is in some way nonsense (§ 246). This desire, in its turn, sometimes results from a desire to reject the view that an utterance of 'I am in pain' is an avowal, or even to be compared with moaning. It is hard not to sympathize with these desires; but on my interpretation, *none* of these theses about 'I am in pain' is a premise in the argument for the non-designative claim; so Wittgenstein would not have thought rejection of these theses sufficient by itself to reinstate a designative vew. One must also give a reasoned rejection of at least one of the premises of the argument for the non-designative conclusion. If one attempts to develop a designative view without attacking the premises of argument E, one's view will still be open to the Wittgensteinian dilemma 'Can the speaker alone know whether he is in the state actually designated by "pain", or can others know it too?' Whichever way one answers, Wittgenstein will still be able to apply one part of argument E against the view. One cannot, then, avoid attacking some premise of argument E if one wishes to combine a designative theory with the view that it is not possible sincerely to utter 'I am in pain', understand it, make no error in action and not be in pain.[15]

A quite different objection to my attribution to Wittgenstein of a specific argument for the non-designative claim would be that the first sixty-four sections of the *Investigations* show that he held a non-designative view of *all* expressions. I disagree. At *Investigations* §§ 2–3 he says explicitly that the Augustinian description of language is correct for some but not all parts of language. Wittgenstein's concern is rather to argue for such claims as these: a specification of what a word names determines its role in the language only against a certain presupposed background of kind of use (§§ 6, 10, 13, 26); the meaning of a proper name should not be identified with its bearer (§ 40); ostensive definition suffices to explain the meaning of a word only when its kind of role in the language is known (§§ 28–30). These claims are jointly consistent with the view that some words designate objects or kinds of object; and Wittgenstein himself says, in passing, 'In a sense, however, this man is surely what corresponds to his name' (§ 55). Wittgenstein's claims are rather claims about what it is to understand an expression.

Let us now return to Dr Baker's paper. Dr Baker suggests that the versions of the rule-following arguments put forward by Kripke and by Wright may be 'latter day developments' that are 'perhaps altogether alien' to Wittgenstein's own thought. If the interpretation of Wittgenstein which I have given is correct, these suggestions are false. Suppose one holds that there are no facts about an individual in virtue of which it can be true that he means one thing rather than another by an expression, or indeed something rather than nothing: then one striking way of presenting this claim is to say that so long as we are confined to facts about an individual, and truths about his community are not considered, then there is no satisfactory way of answering the sceptic who puts forward a claim that in the past I meant some function other than addition by the plus sign. The questions about the objectivity of rule-following discussed by Wright are similarly queries not about the objectivity of the claim that someone is following a rule in performing such and such actions, but are rather questions about the objectivity of such claims *if* their truth is to supervene on facts about the individual by himself.

Dr Baker, without saying which other interpretations he has in mind, raises the question of whether Wittgenstein's arguments might be 'construed as perfectly general context-free observations about rules and rule-following' and remarks that if they are so construed then, 'by Wittgenstein's own lights, they would have to be condemned as very poor' (p. 46). He says this is so because Wittgenstein does not discuss the wide variety of kinds of rule and different sorts of rule-following. This criticism seems to me to be addressed to the wrong party to the dispute. It is for the person who claims that Wittgenstein is arguing that rule-following is a family-resemblance concept to be embarrassed by the fact that Wittgenstein does not cite the many different kinds of rule or sorts of following. On the community interpretation there would be no need to do so. In arguing for the community view one needs to make it plausible that if one looks solely to facts about the individual, then one cannot make sense of the distinction between meaning one thing rather than another by an expression, and correspondingly of one's meaning something rather than just thinking one means something by it. The *kinds* of features that might allegedly be constitutive of individual rule-following – such features as the state of consciousness of the individual rule-follower, or what dispositions he has, or some causal story – these kinds are clearly common to the various different sorts of rule and rule-following which Dr Baker mentions. If Wittgenstein's arguments are mistaken, it is not from consideration of too limited a variety of rules.

Another consequence if it is correct to attribute the community view to Wittgenstein concerns his anti-revisionism. What is the nature of the link between the community view and Wittgenstein's anti-revisionism? Suppose an individual can mean something by himself, and that the distinction between really following a rule and it just being the case that one thinks there is a rule one is following can be drawn without bringing in some community. Then one can make sense of the suggestion that someone's practice is not in accord with what he means by his expressions. The practice may do no harm, may not be in conflict with what he meant, but one could still draw a distinction between what the meaning required (in the circumstances) and what is optional. Now it may be asked: 'If meaning and rule-following generally are determined by the practices of the community, that makes no difference: once we allow the idea of the meaning of some expressions, we can ask whether the practice is in accordance with them or not. The community view is of no special relevance here.' But this would be to ignore Wittgenstein's views about the *way* in which whether someone is following a rule or not is determined by practices of the community. According to Wittgenstein, it is, roughly speaking, the way that others go on in new cases in applying a word, and my conformity with their practice, which determines whether I am following a rule, whether I mean something by an expression or not; and if this is the account, then it is not clear how someone could still mean the same as the other members of the community by some expression and yet try to revise the judgments which, according to Wittgenstein, help to determine its meaning. One might expect anti-revisionism from one who wrote at the end of his general discussion of rule-following that, 'If language is to be a means of communication there must be agreement not only in definitions but also (queer as this may sound) in judgements' (§ 242). I am not endorsing any of the steps in this argument either, but I do suggest that a connection between anti-revisionism and Wittgenstein's views on rule-following and meaning is part of his thought; and this outline makes the community view an essential part of the link.

Dr Baker writes that his reading makes Wittgenstein's thought in the *Investigations* grow naturally out of his middle-period views. But the evidence he gives for this view equally supports the community interpretation. This is transparently the case for the appearance of the notion of a language game in the later philosophy. His second piece of argument is that on his interpretation the *Investigations* pushes further the middle-period criticism of the *Tractatus* views; Dr Baker says that the view of the *Philosophical Remarks* that the meaning of an expression is the totality of rules for its use is replaced by the more radical view that there is typically no such thing as an unextendable set of rules for the use of an expression, and there are no rules which, independently of us, determine the use of an expression as correct or incorrect. The community interpretation will agree with this very last point, but will note that in it 'independently of us' must not be taken merely *in sensu diviso*: the true construal must have it meaning 'independently of the community's reactions'. This is still a radical extension of the middle-period views. Dr Baker's final piece of evidence is that on his construal it is intelligible how explanations could come to play a normative role in the application of expressions. But this is just as vividly the case on the community interpretation: on the community interpretation, following a rule, and hence meaning and understanding, are possible only because of the brute fact that given similar training with the explanations of the expressions, the members of a community in fact go on to new cases in the same way. This is a brute fact not necessarily in the sense that there may not be some scientific explanation of this uniformity, but in the sense that there is no propositional attitude explanation in terms of an individual agent's reasons for going on from the initial explanations of the expression in the way he does.

2   DOES WITTGENSTEIN'S VIEW PROVIDE AN OBJECTION TO SYSTEMATIC THEORIES OF MEANING?

Dr Baker holds that Wittgenstein's views about following a rule, meaning and understanding show that the conception of the theory of meaning in 'Quine, Davidson, Dummett, Chomsky and generative semanticists' is radically erroneous (p. 66). The differences between the writers on this list seem at least as important as their similarities, and the charge that they divorce the theory of meaning from what it is to understand a sentence or an expression sticks better against some than others. For definiteness I will discuss Dr Baker's complaints in relation to the idea that a theory of meaning should take the form of a recursive specification of truth conditions.[16]

It has been taken as a condition of adequacy, by those working within a broadly Davidsonian conception of a theory of meaning, that anyone who knows of a truth theory for a particular object language that it is interpretational is in a position to understand the object language in question. I will not discuss the question of whether the theory is one that must be implicitly known to speakers of the language, partly because this will come up in the next session of this conference, but also because even on the minimal condition of adequacy we can give reasons for not adopting Dr Baker's recommendations.

Dr Baker's point is that what is treated as a specification of the meaning of an expression in a theory of truth is not what is given in explanation of the expression to one who is being trained to understand it; and, Dr Baker writes, 'The content of understanding (i.e. the meaning of an expression) cannot transcend the practice of explaining an expression. The meaning of a word, phrase or sentence is what is explained in explaining it.' (p. 67).

Consider 'plus', for simplicity as a three-place predicate of numbers. Here the explanation of meaning will consist of what Dr Baker calls 'authoritative examples': the trainee will be told that 1, 1 and 2 and again 3, 4 and 7 and so forth all stand in this relation. Can we then say that

> 'plus' concatenated with terms a, b and c is true iff the
> denotations of a, b and c stand in the same relation as the
> triples 1, 1, 2 and 3, 4, 7 and so forth (for as long a list as is
> in fact used in explanations of meaning)?

To think that such a rule, together with knowledge that it is interpretational, would yield understanding of the object language in question would be not to conform to but to violate a Wittgensteinian thought, one which Dr Baker himself emphasizes. On Wittgenstein's views there is no such thing as *the* relation in which any finite set of triples stand; and someone who knew only that there is *some* relation under which these examples fall, and which is such that a predication of 'plus' of certain numbers is true iff they stand in that relation, is certainly not in a position to understand the language. This illustrates a general point that does not emerge in Dr Baker's paper: the point is that meaning is not determined just by the examples given in explanation of the word in question, but by those examples *together with* the disposition of members of the community to go on in certain ways and not others. If we omit reference to these ways, it will not be surprising if we do not capture the meaning of the expression.

What then of this different clause?

> 'plus' concatenated with terms a, b and c is true iff the denotations of a, b and c stand in the relation which members of such and such community find it natural to continue from the set of samples 1, 1, 2 and 3, 4, 7, etc.

But again, someone who knows just this is not in a position to understand our language: the person needs also to know *which* relation it is that the community finds it natural to continue from this set of examples. Clearly we are not going to solve this problem until we write 'plus', or some synonym of it, on the right-hand side of the truth-theoretic clause. When we do, we could also drop the examples if we wished; examples would, however, still be there in the background, in that manifestation of knowledge of such a semantic clause would involve having the right reactions to such simple examples.

So far I have just defended writing the clauses in a truth theory in a certain way; but these observations are internal to a programme, and Dr Baker is questioning the point of the whole programme. He says that 'there can in principle be nothing to discover about meaning rules'. Now I do not see how this follows from either his or my interpretation of Wittgenstein. He does not give an argument explicitly, but I suspect he is influenced by the following line of thought: 'If there could be discoveries about meaning, there could be explanatory theories about meaning, and prediction of semantic facts, predictions and explanations which need not be obvious to one who just knows the language. But such a state of affairs would be incompatible with Wittgenstein's idea that "grammatical rules do not act at a distance".'

This argument is fallacious. Suppose, just for the sake of argument, we hold the view of necessity which Stroud attributes to Wittgenstein[17]: on this account, a similar community view is given of what it is to follow a meaning-rule for a logical expression as we earlier regarded Wittgenstein giving for other expressions. It does *not* follow from such a view that there are no unobvious logical truths; a series of individually compelling steps, steps that you in fact find compelling even though there is no truth in the idea that you are forced to take them by what you previously meant, can carry you from the obvious to the unobvious. A corresponding point holds in the semantical case too: there may for instance be unobvious consequences of the interaction of our various ways of going on. Let us take an extremely simple and familiar example. Someone may predict, on the basis of the functioning of participles and modals in a language, that a language will contain a sentence 'Flying planes can be dangerous', and that it will have a particular ambiguity: and he will say what the ambiguity is. Though someone who understands the language will already know that, he need not have the theory that if a language has such-and-such sentences, it is likely to have such-and-such others with so-and-so semantic properties; or to lack such-and-such others. We need, then, to consider the question of whether Dr Baker considers such theorizing illegitimate. Perhaps in these last paragraphs I have been doing too much reading between the lines, and Dr Baker has in mind some entirely different argument from Wittgenstein's thought about rule-following to show that the idea of systematic semantics rests on a mistake. If so, not only should we examine the argument he does accept, but we should also consider whether generalizations and extensions of the legitimate simple example I just cited would not be sufficient to give the systematic semantic theorist all he ever needed.

NOTES

1 This text includes some discussion of the private language argument which was not read in the original reply. The fact that Wittgenstein himself regarded his conclusions about private languages and his views on rule-following as intimately related provides a constraint both on one's interpretation of his views on rules and on one's interpretation of his views on sensations. I have also in the main confined myself to interpretation rather than assessment.
2 Nothing in the community view as I have stated it excludes the possibility of a permanently isolated desert-islander rule-follower. The community view can count such a person as a genuine rule-follower if he reacts to new examples in the same way as would members of

our own community, or of some other conceivable community. The community need not be that (if any) of the rule-follower himself.

3 In the case of both arguments I am ignoring the possibility of slips of the tongue as not central to the issue.

4 It may be helpful if I set out this argument formally. With the same numbering of the premises it has the form

$$(4)\ ArF(r)$$
$$(5)\ (D\ \&\ K)\&{\sim}F(c)$$
$$(6)\ (D\ \&\ {\sim}K)\&E$$
$$(7)\ \underline{{\sim}E}$$
$$(8)\ {\sim}D$$

Here 'F(ξ)' abbreviates 'ξ is a rule such that there is a distinction between a person's really following ξ and falsely believing there is a rule he is following'; 'c' names the alleged rule ' "pain" is to be used to designate pain'; 'D' abbreviates the statement that 'pain' designates a state; 'K' abbreviates the statement that the state designated by 'pain' is one which only the subject can know himself to be in; and 'E' abbreviates the statement that the subject can be in error about whether he is in pain. (5) as formalized here is strictly an instance of (5) in the text.

5 Cp. also § 270: 'the hypothesis that I make a mistake [in identifying the sensation] is mere show'.

6 § 270 seems to imply that I could introduce a sign to be used when my blood-pressure rises and which I use non-inferentially. This is a possibility on the present interpretation because others can also know, though not non-inferentially, that my blood-pressure is rising.

7 It would not be open to Wittgenstein to argue that the community view must exclude this combination on the ground that I can always be mistaken about how members of some community will go on in new cases. Wittgenstein is surely right in insisting that the content of an object-language sentence does not have the agreement of people as its subject-matter: see for instance RFM VI, § 49.

8 *American Philosophical Quarterly*, 1 (1964), pp. 20–31, reprinted (with changes) in O. R. Jones (ed.), *The Private Language Argument*, Macmillan, London 1971. Page references are to this last volume.

9 Having made this criticism, I ought to emphasize the following points of agreement between Thomson and myself: we agree (i) on the correctness of a non-verificationist interpretation of Wittgenstein, (ii) that mistakes in the application of 'pain' were supposed by Wittgenstein not to be possible and that this belief plays some role in his thought, (iii) that Wittgenstein sought to reconcile this belief in incorrigibility with his thoughts about rule-following by holding that 'pain' is not, as Thomson expresses it, a 'kind-name'.

10 See for instance: § 244 and § 270. Norman Malcolm, in his well-known notice of the *Investigations* in the *Philosophical Review*, raised this

point against Strawson's notice of the same work in *Mind*. If the points in the text below are correct, Malcolm's criticism is naive.

11 Cp. H. Putnam, *Meaning and the Moral Science*, Routledge & Kegan Paul, London, 1978, p. 31.

12 The phrase 'for a human being' is present here to signal the possibility of an interpretation of Wittgenstein's notion of a criterion thus: the criteria for 'pain' are those circumstances such that, if a human is taught that 'pain' applies in those circumstances, he goes on to apply the expression correctly in new cases. On this interpretation, the criteria for an expression do not determine even its extension: that is determined by the criteria together with the way humans go on in new cases. This view, unlike some other interpretations of 'criterion' in Wittgenstein, is consistent with the view that there is no way at all of stating the meaning of 'pain' without using the notion of pain, regardless of the degree of complexity or kind of accounts permitted.

13 A. J. P. Kenny, *Wittgenstein*, Penguin, London, 1973, p. 183.

14 This distinction is not drawn in the otherwise valuable penultimate chapter of P. M. S. Hacker's *Insight and Illusion*, Oxford University Press, 1972.

15 This criticism applies for example to pp. 280–2 of Hacker, *op. cit.*

16 In fact, the particular observations I make will still hold if the meaning theory for a language is formulated using a 'means that' operator, so that nothing more need be required of the theory itself than its truth.

17 'Wittgenstein and logical necessity', *Philosophical Review*, 74 (1965), pp. 504–18.

PART TWO

FOLLOWING A RULE: OBJECTIVITY AND MEANING

III

RULE-FOLLOWING, OBJECTIVITY AND THE THEORY OF MEANING

Crispin Wright

When we think of a question in some area of enquiry as an *objective* issue, what we have in mind, I take it, is – very crudely – that a two-fold distinction is required to do justice to the situation; there is our, perhaps settled, opinion on the one hand, and, on the other, the (hopefully concordant) true facts of the matter. For the believer in objectivity, human opinion in no sense constitutes truth; truth is in no sense supervenient upon human opinion.

Realism about verification-transcendent statements – the view, that is, that we are capable of intellectual grasp of the character of a range of facts, or at least possible facts, to which we can have no cognitive access – obviously believes in the objectivity of such statements. With decidable statements, however, – whatever may prove to be the correct general characterization of that class – the belief in objectivity cannot have to do with possible verification-transcendence. Rather, what is in play is something like this notion: confronted with any decidable, objective issue, there is *already* an answer which – if we investigate the matter fully and correctly – we will arrive at. The objectivity of decidable statements consists, in this way, in their possession of determinate, investigation-independent truth-values – in their, as I shall call it, *investigation-independence*.

I believe, rightly or wrongly, that the Wittgenstein of the *Investigations* and *Remarks on the Foundations of Mathematics* is, rightly or wrongly, sceptical about investigation-independence, and that the grounds for that scepticism are embedded in his discussions of rule-following. In the first part of what follows, I

99

want to try to convey, all too hastily I fear, something of the character of that scepticism. And in the second part, though again I shall have space only to pose certain questions and adumbrate certain theses, I shall attempt to sketch some of the challenges which I think Wittgenstein's later thought poses to recent approaches in the philosophy of language.

I

Investigation-independence requires a certain stability in our understanding of our concepts. To think, for example, of the shape of some particular unobserved object as determinate, irrespective of whether or not we ever inspect it, is to accept that there are facts about how we will, or would, assess its shape if we do, or did, so *correctly*, in accordance with the meaning of the expressions in our vocabulary of shapes; the putative investigation-independent fact about the object's shape is a fact about how we would describe it if on the relevant occasion we continued to use germane expressions in what we regard as the correct way, the way in which we have always tried to use those expressions when aiming at the truth. The idea of investigation-independence thus leads us to look upon grasp of the meaning of an expression as grasp of a general pattern of use, conformity to which requires certain determinate uses in so far unconsidered cases. The pattern is thus to be thought of as extending *of itself* to cases which we have yet to confront.

It has to be acknowledged, however, that the 'pattern' is, strictly, inaccessible to absolutely definitive explanation. For, as Wittgenstein never wearied of reminding himself, no explanation of the use of an expression is proof against misunderstanding; verbal explanations require correct understanding of the vocabulary in which they are couched, and samples are open to an inexhaustible variety of interpretations. So we move towards the idea that understanding an expression is a kind of 'cottoning on'; that is, a leap, an inspired guess at the pattern of application which an instructor is trying to get across. It becomes almost irresistible to think of someone who is learning a first language as if he were forming general *hypotheses*. 'Cottoning on' would be forming the right hypothesis; and failing to do so would be forming the wrong, or no, hypothesis. And the leap involved would just be that with the best will in the world we – the instructors – cannot do better than leave an indefinite variety of hypotheses open for selection.

Well, what is wrong with that picture of the business? On occasion, no doubt, we do self-consciously form hypotheses in order to interpret what somebody means; people are, for example, sometimes embarrassed to confess that they do not know the meaning of a particular expression. What is wrong with thinking that, when we are learning a new expression, it is always *as if* we formed a hypothesis? It rather depends how circumspect we are in our application of the resulting picture. For it makes sense to think of someone as having a hypothesis only if *he* knows what it is, that is, what its correctness will require. So the question is whether it is legitimate to think of a first-language trainee as knowing what he himself has come to mean by an expression, what hypothesis about its correct use he has formed. If the 'as if' is to be taken literally, we have to be able to credit the trainee with knowledge about what we – the instructors – will allow in a particular new case if his hypothesis is correct, if his conjectural understanding of the relevant expression coincides with ours. So the picture encourages, if it does not make absolutely inevitable, our drift into the idea that each of us has some sort of privileged access to the character of his own understanding of an expression. Each of us, that is to say, knows of a particular idiolectic pattern of use which he intends his use of an expression to subserve, and for which there is a strong presumption, when sufficient evidence has accumulated, that it is shared communally.

The hypothetico-deductive picture thus encourages us to accept as a matter of course the rider of certain knowledge of the character of one's own understanding of an expression. And this idea is fundamental to our whole conception of concepts, or meanings, as stable, on which the idea of investigation-independence feeds. But the rider is not a matter of course. It involves an over-dignification. In cases where there really *is* a hypothesis, as in the case of the embarrassed man who is trying to guess the meaning of some expression, this hypothesis can be formulated and its correct application will be open to communal assessment. But when it is merely a matter of an 'as if', the trainee will not have the vocabulary to tell us what it is he thinks we mean. To be sure, the idea of a hypothesis is then psychologically artificial – but it was

101

already conceded to be a mere picture anyway. The more fundamental objection is that nothing can be done to defend the description that the trainee *recognizes* how, if his conjectural
understanding is right, we will treat a particular new case, against
the more austere account that he simply expects *this* application
to be acceptable to us.

The trouble is to prise apart the fact of what his 'as if' hypothesis
requires from his expectations about the new case – or, what
comes to the same thing, his response to it. For *we* cannot tell
whether he implements his hypothesis correctly, that is, whether
his expectations here really are consonant with the interpretation
he has put on our treatment of, say, the samples which we gave
him; and *he* cannot provide any basis for a distinction between
their really being so and its merely seeming to him that they are.
It would make all the difference if he could tell us what his
hypothesis was; then there could be a communal assessment of
the situation. But this is just what he cannot do in the fundamental
case when the whole idea of a hypothesis about a pattern is meant
merely as an 'as if' idea.

The proper conclusion is not merely that the hypothetico-deductive picture is potentially misleading, but that there cannot be
such a thing as first-person privileged recognition of the dictates
of one's understanding of an expression, irrespective of whether
or not that understanding is shared. For the only circumstance in
which it makes sense to think of someone as correctly applying a
non-standard understanding of, for example, 'square' is where
there is a community of assent about how, given that *that* is what
he means, he ought to characterize this object.

Now, how exactly do these reflections bear on the idea of
investigation-independence? What they bear on is the implicit
idea that if we do not allow the description of certain so far
uninvestigated objects in certain particular predeterminate ways,
we shall have broken faith with the patterns of use which we have
given to the relevant vocabulary. The question is whether it is
legitimate to think of our mastery of a language as involving
anything properly seen as a capacity to recognize what preserva-
tion of such patterns requires. For suppose that you find yourself
incorrigibly out of line concerning the description of some new
case. We have just seen that you can't, single-handedly as it were,
give sense to the idea that you are at least being faithful to your

own pattern; that is, that you recognize how you must describe this new case if you are to remain faithful to your own understanding of the relevant expressions. How, then, would your disposition to apply the expression to a new case become, properly speaking, recognition of the continuation of a pattern if it so happened that you were *not* out of line, if it so happened that there was communal agreement with you?

If there can intelligibly be such a thing as a ratification-independent fact about whether an expression is used on a particular occasion in the same way as it has been used on previous occasions, then the fact ought to be something which we can recognize – or at least be justified in claiming to obtain. Otherwise the correct employment of language would become on every occasion radically transcendent of human consciousness. But I cannot legitimately credit myself with the capacity to recognize that *I* am here applying an expression in the same way as *I* have used it before, so long as this capacity is to be indifferent to whether I can persuade others of as much or whether that is the way in which the community in general uses the expression. How, in that case, is it possible for me to recognize that I am using the expression in the same way that *we* used it before? How, where it seems that I cannot significantly claim to have grasped an idiolectic pattern, can I claim to have grasped a *communal* one? How does others' agreement with me turn my descriptive disposition into a matter of recognition of conformity with a pattern, recognition of an antecedent fact about how the communal pattern extends to the new case?

To put the point another way: none of us, if he finds himself on his own about a new candidate for φ-ness, and with no apparent way of bringing the rest of us around, can sensibly claim to recognize that the community has here broken faith with its antecedent pattern of application for φ; the proper conclusion for him is rather that he has just discovered that he does not know what φ means. So there can be no such thing as a legitimate claim to unilateral recognition that here a community's pattern of application of a particular expression is contravened. So long as the 'recognition' is unilateral, it cannot legitimately be claimed to be recognition, nor can that state of affairs of which it is supposed to be recognition be legitimately claimed to obtain; (though if the community can be brought around, it will later be legitimate to claim that the unilateral verdict *was* correct). But how, in that case, can there ever be such a thing as a legitimate claim to unilateral recognition of how any particular expression should be applied in particular circumstances, if it is to be applied in the same manner as previously? How can the mere *absence* of the information that the community at large does not agree legitimize the claim to recognition of the fact whose status is supposed in no sense to await our ratification?

Virtually everyone, myself included, will be tempted to reply here that a solicitable community of assent just does make the relevant difference, just does supply the objectivity requisite to transform one's unilateral response into a matter of recognition or mistake. Thus in the absence of the information that the community at large does not agree with one's verdict, standard inductive grounds will remain intact for the supposition that there will be sufficient agreement; and one's claim to have recognized how the 'pattern' extends to the particular new case will be justified accordingly. But ask, what *type* of bearing would the discovery that one was in line with the rest of the community concerning this case have on the question of the correctness of the original unilateral verdict? How does finding out that other people agree with one make it legitimate to claim apprehension of a fact whose status does not require that we acknowledge it at all? Is it that it is somehow less *likely* that lots of people are in error? To suppose that such was the correct account would be to confront the unanswerable challenge to explain how the probabilities could be established.

Assuredly, there is truth in the idea that it is a community of assent which supplies the essential background against which alone it makes sense to think of individuals' responses as correct or incorrect. The question is whether it can be explained why there should be any truth in this idea unless the correctness or incorrectness of individuals' responses is precisely *not* a matter of conformity or non-conformity with investigation-independent facts; for if the contrary account were correct, the role of communal assent in determining the correctness of individuals' responses would require the capacity of the *community as a whole* to recognize what conformity to antecedent patterns of use required of us. And now essentially the same problem arises again that beset the attempt to make unilateral sense of correct employment of an idiolect. What is it for a *community* to recognize that it here continues a pattern of application of an expression on which it previously embarked? What does it add to describe the situation in two-fold terms, of the fact of conformity to the pattern *and* the community's recognition of the fact, rather than simply saying that there is communal agreement about the case? It is unclear how we can answer. We are inclined to give new linguistic responses on which there is communal consensus the dignity of 'objective correctness'; but we have, so to speak, only our own word for it. If 'correctness' means ratification-independent conformity with an antecedent pattern, the uncomfortable fact is that there is apparent absolutely nothing which we can do to make the contrast active between the consensus description and the correct description. Of course it may happen that a community changes its mind; and when it does so, it does not revise the judgment that the former view at one time enjoyed consensus. But that is a fact about our cultural procedures; to call attention to it is to call attention to the circumstance that we make use of the notion that we can all be wrong, but it is not to call attention to anything which gives sense to the idea that the wrongness consists in departure from a ratification-independent pattern.

This, I believe, is the fundamental point of the 'Limits of empiricism' remarks (RFM III, § 71; IV, § 29; VII, §§ 17, 21; cf. OC §§ 110, 204). None of us unilaterally can make sense of the idea of correct employment of language save by reference to the authority of securable communal assent on the matter; and for the community itself there is no authority, so no standard to meet. It is another matter why we find the idea so attractive that the communal language constitutes a network of determinate patterns, and that our communal judgment is somehow in general a faithful reflection of the world. Probably it is because we do not pause to consider how much sense we can really give these ideas; and their opposites seem intolerable.

To put the point in the starkest possible way: how can we penetrate *behind* our consensus verdict about a particular question in order to achieve a comparison of our verdict with the putative investigation-independent fact? Once we accept the double-element conception of the situation, verdict and investigation-independent fact confronting one another, we feel constrained to say that all we can know for sure is how things *seem* to us to deserve description; certainly, we may come to revise our assessment – but then, again, the revised assessment would be merely what *seems* right. The dilemma we then confront as a community is thus essentially that of the would-be private linguist: faced with the impossibility of establishing any technique of comparison between our judgment and the putative objective fact, we must construe the fact either as something we cannot know at all, or – the classic choice for the private linguist about sensations – as something which we cannot but know. Wittgenstein's response is to urge that both courses are equally disreputable; and that we should therefore abandon the conception which leads to the dilemma. If we do so, we shall reject the idea that, in the senses requisite for investigation-independence, a community goes right or wrong in accepting a particular verdict on a particular decidable question; rather, it just goes.

II

Some philosophers, of whom Davidson has been perhaps the most committed representative, have recommended work towards the construction of formal theories of meaning for natural languages as a fruitful way of approaching traditional problems in the philosophy of language. Others have agreed at least to the extent of accepting that extensive philosophical gains can be expected to accrue from consideration of the question: what exact form should such a theory ideally take?[1] What does Wittgenstein's later philosophy of language have to say to proponents of these views?

The question is of course very wide-ranging, and raises a host of exegetical problems about Wittgenstein's writings and an army of questions concerning the claims which might legitimately be made on behalf of the sort of formal theory typically proposed. My aim here is not to answer questions but to ask them: questions which, I think, will fairly rapidly occur to anyone familiar with Wittgenstein's later writings who devotes some thought to the sort of programme being advocated by the philosophers of language referred to.

The relevant sort of formal theory of meaning for a natural language will consist in an axiomatic system whose deployment will enable us, in principle at least, to resolve any well-formed declarative sentence in the language into its essential semantically contributive constituents, and to determine its meaning on the basis of the structure thereby revealed and the assigned semantic values of those constituents. The theory may, as Davidson proposed, incorporate an axiomatic theory of truth; or it may utilize as its central semantic concept something other than truth. In what follows we shall be concerned with the constraints which Davidson imposes on any axiomatic theory of truth which is to be suitable for the purposes of a theory of meaning; but these constraints would be no less intuitively cogent if the central theory was to be, say, a theory of assertability. And the points to be made are applicable equally, if at all, to all theories of meaning fitting the above general characterization.

The crucial issue is of course: to what questions is such a theory necessarily able to give answers? Clearly, there are plenty of well-established questions in the philosophy of language which a theory of this kind need not be capable of addressing at all. To begin with, a theory meeting the characterization just given would not be required to say anything about commanding, asking whether, or wishing; it would need supplementation with, in the Frege/Dummett terminology,[2] a theory of *force* – a theory which makes explicit what difference it makes whether a sentence to which the original theory assigns a particular truth-condition, say, is understood as a command, or question, or wish, or assertion, or any other kind of linguistic act which we deem to constitute a further kind of force with which an utterance can be made; and goes on to describe the grammatical indicators, if any, which the studied language uses to mark these various kinds of force.

It is clear, second, that a whole range of limitations are consequent upon the fact that, in the case where the language in which the theory is stated is the same as, or an extension of, its object-language, the theory need not, in order to comply with the characterization given, say any more about the meaning of any particular semantically atomic expression than can be conveyed by incorporation of an appropriate 'homophonic' axiom; that is, an axiom in which that very expression is *used*, in whatever way the theory considers appropriate, to state its own meaning. For suppose that such an axiom is all the theory has to offer by way of elucidation of the semantic role of a particular predicate, ø. Then the construction of the theory will neither deliver nor presuppose any account of the *vagueness* of ø, if it is vague; the *theoreticity*, or *observationality*, of ø, if it is theoretical, or observational; the *reducibility* of ø in terms of other predicates, if it is so reducible. In these ways, and in general, the theory will fail to speak to the question: in what does an understanding of ø consist – what are the criteria for mastery of the use of ø? And it will keep silence, third, on perhaps the most fundamental question of all: what *is* a language – what distinguishes language-use from any other rule-governed, goal-directed activity, and what makes mouthings and inscriptions into uses of language?

Where, therefore, will light be cast? One answer would be that a theory of the kind characterized can still be a theory of speakers' understanding of the object-language. For we ought to distinguish between giving an account of what an understanding of any particular expression consists in – what, that is, distinguishes anyone who possesses that understanding from someone who lacks it – and giving an account of what is known by anyone who understands that expression. It is in general one thing to state a particular item of knowledge, another further to explain what having that knowledge essentially is. So, *prima facie*, a theory of the 'modest'[3] kind may still be presented as an account of understanding; it is just that it will purport to characterize only what is understood by anyone who knows the meaning of a particular expression, and will not attempt to explain what having this understanding amounts to. It appears to be open, then, to the proponents of such a theory to present it as a theory of understanding, a theory of speakers' knowledge. Now, that Davidson originally so intended his particular brand is strikingly suggested by his insistence that an adequate such theory must supply the means to derive for each declarative sentence in the language a meaning-delivering theorem in (i) a *structure-reflecting way* on the basis of (ii) a *finite axiomatization*.[4] The intention of this pair of constraints would appear to be to ensure the capacity of the theory to explain the familiarly stressed fact that mastery of a typical natural language will involve the ability, on the basis of finite training, to understand indefinitely many sentences which its speakers have never heard before. The goal is, apparently, a model of this epistemic capacity; it is desired to understand how it is *possible* for us to recognize the meaning of any given new significant sentence in our language. The answer is to be: by deploying the information encapsulated in the axioms germane to the parts of the sentence in the manner determined by the structure of the sentence, that is, the manner reflected by the mode of derivation within the theory of the relevant meaning-delivering theorem.

Naturally, it would be unwise to insist that *only* this underlying conception of the significance of such a theory could vindicate the organization which Davidson proposed it should have. It could very well make a difference, to begin with, whether, for example, the theory was being constructed as the end of a programme of radical translation, in one language for another, or whether the goal was rather to use a particular language to state its own semantics. It might be that in the former case it would only be by observing Davidson's constraints that we could actually construct a theory yielding a meaning-delivering theorem for each of the object-language's declarative sentences. But in the latter case, unless the conception described is presupposed, it is, to say the least, a very nice question why, assuming that we have available an effective criterion for determining whether an arbitrary sequence of symbols is a significant declarative sentence in the language in question, we should not simply arrogate the general form of T-theorem, or whatever form the meaning-delivering theorems take, as an infinitary *axiom schema*, thereby saving a great deal of work. If the goal is not to provide a model of how the meaning of an arbitrary declarative sentence in the language can be recognized but merely to state what its meaning is, then – putting on one side presently irrelevant complications about the appropriate form for such a statement to take – it is hard to see what objection there could be to such a course.

How, though, ought we to receive the suggestion that a theory which both correctly characterized the meaning of all significant expressions in the object-language, and satisfied Davidson's two constraints, would *explain* the capacity of speakers of the object-language to recognize the sense of new sentences? It is part of mastery of a language neither to know a theory of this kind explicitly, nor to be able to formulate one, nor even to be able to recognize a satisfactory formulation if one is presented. (For aught we know, there may *be* no such satisfactory theory for English.) But it seems that if such a theory really is to explain the performance of speakers of the object-language, then there has to be a sense in which knowledge of its content can be attributed to them.

Accordingly, there has been a tendency to invoke some sort of notion of *implicit* knowledge to supply the needed contact of the theory with the studied speakers' actual performance.[5]

This notion can certainly seem natural enough. Suppose, for example, that we were to teach certain dumb illiterates to play chess; that is, not merely to mimic chess play, but to play correctly, and strive to win. Then it would seem unexceptionable to describe such people as possessing *knowledge*, albeit inarticulately, of exactly that information which someone who understands an explicit formulation of the rules of chess knows articulately. Taken in one way, there is, indeed, nothing objectionable about such a description. For giving such a description need commit one to no more than that the people in question habitually comport themselves in such a way when playing chess as to satisfy any criteria which we might reasonably wish to impose on someone's having understood an explicit statement of the rules of the game. But in that case, to attribute implicit knowledge of such a 'theory' of the game to them is to do no more than obliquely to describe their behaviour; it is to say that they behave in just the way in which someone would behave who successfully tried to suit his behaviour to such an explicit statement.[6]

It is doubtful, however, whether it can be this notion of implicit knowledge which is relevant to the concerns of a theorist of meaning who conceives his goal to be an explanation of how a master of the object-language is able to recognize the senses of novel sentences, and accepts Davidson's two constraints as necessary if that goal is to be achieved. For to have, in the described sense, implicit knowledge of the content of a theory of meaning amounts to no more than being disposed to employ the object-language in the manner which would be followed by anyone who, being sufficiently agile intellectually and knowing sufficiently much about the world, successfully tried to suit his practice with the object-language to an explicit statement of the theory. So construed, talk of speakers' implicit *knowledge* of the theory is, indeed, misleading; there is no real suggestion of an internalized 'programme'. All that such talk need involve is that speakers' practice fits a certain compendious description. But now the question resurges: what reason would the theorist have to accept Davidson's two constraints, that the theory be finitely axiomatizable and that the mode of derivation of each meaning-delivering theorem reflect the structure of the relevant sentence, if his objective were only the achievement of such a description? For the fact is that it is only the lowest-level output of the theory – the T-theorems, or their counterparts in a non-truth-theoretic theory – which purport to describe isolable aspects of speakers' practice. So if, as when the theory is stated in a language for that very language or a fragment of it, it is possible to peel off, as it were, the descriptive part of the theory, for example by taking the general form of T-theorems as an infinitary axiom schema, there is apparent, once the objective is restricted merely to describing speakers' practice, no reason for having the full-blown theory. To suit one's behaviour to what is stated by the theory is just to suit one's behaviour to what is stated by its practice-describing part. So if the theorist's aim was merely to formulate a theory knowledge of which would suffice for competence in the object-language, there would not necessarily be any point in observing Davidson's constraints; no advance reason why it would not serve his purpose to axiomatize more simply, even if infinitistically, the descriptive part of a theory which met those constraints.

A theory of that truncated form would, of course, seem *hugely* trivial and unexplanatory. It would contribute not a jot to the purpose of devising a framework by reference to which traditional philosophical questions about language-mastery could be formulated and answered. But if the aim were no more than deliverance of an account of the meaning of each declarative sentence in the object-language, and if we were content that each instance of the relevant axiom schema was of an appropriate form for such an account to take, then what more could we want?

One reason why Davidson's idea has occasioned interest, it seems to me, is because it aspires to cast philosophical light on the concept of meaning without overt recourse to any intensional notions; an attractive promise to any philosopher who sees these problems in the way that Quine has taught us to see them. But a more fundamental reason for the 'Davidsonic boom', at Oxford at any rate, was that a framework seems to be suggested in which it would be possible to *explain* the potentially infinitary character of mastery of the sort of natural language which we all speak. What I am suggesting is that unless this prospect is to be illusion, it has to make sense to attribute to speakers of the studied language implicit knowledge of the whole of an appropriate theory of meaning for that language, and to mean by this attribution something richer than a mere imputation to speakers of a disposition to suit their practice to the theory's requirements. For implicit knowledge, in the latter, weaker sense, of the content of a Davidsonian theory would be just the same thing as implicit knowledge of its T-theorems; and it is manifestly no *explanation* of a man's ability to understand novel sentences in his language that he has *that* knowledge – to attribute that knowledge to him is no more than to attribute to him the very ability that interests us. A more substantial notion of implicit knowledge of its content is therefore going to be required if a theory of meaning is to explain how speakers of its studied language are able to recognize the meanings of new sentences. The question is whether there is any respectable such 'more substantial' notion.

Wittgenstein's later thought contains a number of *prima facie* challenges to the idea that has emerged: the idea that the potentially infinitary character of mastery of a typical natural language can be explained by appeal to its speakers' implicit knowledge, appropriately richly interpreted, of the contents of a suitable-theory of meaning.

First, and most obviously, the thesis seems to involve thinking of mastery of the language as consisting in (unconscious) equipment with the information which the axioms of the theory codify, information which systematically settles the content of so far unconstructed and unconsidered sentences. Such a conception is far from patently coherent with the repudiation of the objectivity of sameness of use involved in the scepticism about investigation-independence sketched above. The first challenge is to demonstrate *either* that it is right to repudiate that scepticism *or* that there is no real tension – that the explanatory claim made by the thesis does not require that we conceive of the meanings of novel sentences as investigation-independent, nor presuppose that people's agreement in their use of language has a foundation of the sort which the rule-following considerations would argue to be mythical.

There immediately arises, second, the challenge to show that the thesis is not, at bottom, simply an inflated version of the old muddle about 'universals' and predicate understanding. It is at best harmless to talk of understanding a predicate as 'grasp of a universal'; and it is harmless only if we do not think that we have thereby achieved some sort of *explanation* of people's capacity to agree about the application of the predicate. All that such terminology actually achieves is a measure of embroidery upon the phenomenon of agreement; for there is no criterion of what it is for us to have 'grasped' the same universal save a disposition to agree in application of the predicate. But if the fiction of universals is no explanation of people's disposition to agree in their basic predicative classifications, it is far from clear that the assumption of shared implicit knowledge of the content of a theory of meaning can provide any genuine explanation of the capacity of speakers to agree in their use of new sentences.

The third challenge is anti-realist in the sense of Dummett. No one is in a position to verify that a particular theory of meaning states precisely what some speaker implicitly knows. For the theorist, the theory has, like any theory, the status of a compound general hypothesis; and it ought by now to be clear just how hard it would be to defend the view that a speaker of the studied language was somehow better placed than an observer of his practice to recognize the correctness of a particular theory of meaning for his language. But it is unclear how we can achieve the kind of explanation of the open-ended character of a speaker's competence which is under consideration here unless it is legitimate to suppose that there is at large some 'fact of the matter', that is, that the speaker's use of his language is essentially the deployment of some *particular* body of information which some specific theory states. Each axiom of *that* theory will actually be true of the speaker in question. And the challenge is to defend this particular invocation of a verification-transcendent notion of truth; or to show that it is not needed.

Each of these challenges deserves a separate, detailed treatment, which I cannot attempt here. Certainly, no scepticism is yet justified that these challenges can be met, either by an appropriate refinement of the requisite notion of implicit knowledge or by some more direct defence of it. What I do claim is that, until it is shown that the play which the thesis makes with a rich notion of implicit knowledge can be defended against these three challenges at least, there is no reason to think that it is within the power of the sort of theory which we are considering to serve up anything which could rightly be considered an *explanation* of the open-ended character of the competence of its object-language speakers.

As noted, it is one thing to interpret a theory of meaning as codifying information which speakers in some sense possess and deploy, another to see it merely as an attempt systematically to describe their linguistic practices. I think it is fair to say that it is the latter type of interpretation which has held sway among most of those philosophers of language who have interested themselves in formal theories of meaning, Davidsonian or otherwise. The problem, as we have seen, is then to motivate the constraints which these philosophers typically wish to impose upon interesting such theories. But supposing that this problem could be solved, there may still seem to be a very fundamental tension between thinking of language as amenable even to description by the sort of theory envisaged and the rule-following considerations. For surely, it might be supposed, it is necessary, if such a theoretical description is to be possible, that what will constitute an admissible use of each new sentence whose construction the language in question permits is something settled in advance, predetermined by the language's semantic essence. The theory is not going to confine itself to recording actual, historic uses; its role will be to formulate *generalizations* furnishing predictions about what will be counted as correct use, or appropriate response to the use, of new sentences, and of old sentences used on new occasions. So it seems to be presupposed that the language in question *has* a certain general character, capturable by an appropriate generalization-venturing theory. Whereas the moral of the rule-following considerations was – wasn't it? – that we have to regard correct use, or correct response to the use, of any particular sentence on a new occasion as objectively indeterminate; it is what competent speakers do – where competence is precisely *not* a matter of a disposition to conformity with certain investigation-independent facts – which determines the correct use of expressions, rather than the other way about. Now, how can there be such a thing as a general, correct, systematic description of a practice which at any particular stage may go in *any* direction without betrayal of its character? There is simply nothing *there* systematically to be described.

If this doubt was correct, it would not, of course, be merely a certain post-Wittgensteinian conception of the proper objectives and methods of the philosophy of language which was in jeopardy. Wittgenstein's own presented methodology of assiduous attention to facts about the 'grammar' of our expressions would be equally guilty of attempting to penetrate through to general traits in our linguistic practices. In fact, though, the difficulty is surely quite spurious; for there is no reason to suppose that all the purposes which we might have in attempting to generalize about aspects of our own or others' linguistic practices could be served only if it is legitimate to think of those practices as having an objective general character, as having investigation-independent aspects. *If* the goal of a particular theory of meaning was simply to contribute towards supplying a framework in one language for describing what counted as correct linguistic practice in the same, or another, language, no need for any assumption is really apparent which the rule-following considerations would call into question – or better, if there was a need for such assumptions, then the difficulty would be one not merely for the theory of meaning but for predictive theorizing of all kinds. In order for a particular prediction about what would be accepted as correct use of an object-language sentence in particular circumstances to have practical content from the *theorists'* point of view, it is required neither that they conceive of the relevant hypotheses in the theory as codifying certain investigation-independent general features of object-language practice, nor that they conceive of it as predeterminate what behaviour by object-language speakers they – the theorists – will count as meeting the relevant prediction if they judge correctly. All that *is* required is that they can secure a consensus among themselves about whether, in any particular situation, the initial conditions of the prediction are fulfilled, and about whether, if they are, the performance of object-language speakers meets the prediction's requirements. More generally, in order for any hypothesis to have a determinate meaning it is required neither that we can render philosophically respectable the conception that it depicts some objective general trait in the studied range of phenomena, nor that it be objectively predeterminate what will have to happen if it is to be falsified in any particular situation; our securable consensus about its standing in any particular situation is enough.

The principal effect in this vicinity of the rule-following considerations is to caution a believer against allowing his interpretation of a theory of meaning to aspire to a bogus objectivity. But they do not, or so it seems to me, impugn the legitimacy of at least the most basic purpose with which such a theory might be devised: that of securing a description of the use of (part of) the object-language of such a kind that to be apprised of that description would be to know how to participate in the use of (that part of) the language.

The position at which we arrive is therefore as follows. Whatever goals theories of meaning are to aspire to, there are no legitimate constraints on the form such theories should take, save those neglect of which would frustrate the achievement of those goals. So if the goal is to be the purely descriptive one adumbrated, there will be no point in paying attention to semantic *structure* unless a complete description of the use of (the relevant part of) the object-language cannot be given if we do not do so. We observed earlier that, where the metalanguage contains the object-language there seems to be no very clear reason why it should be necessary for the theory to discern structure in order for it to fulfil that limited descriptive purpose. And, of course, almost all the philosophical interest thought to attach to formal theories of meaning depends upon preoccupation with semantic structure. So we confront a fundamental question: if, for Wittgensteinian reasons or others, an appeal to rich implicit knowledge is thought illegitimate, can any adequate motive be elucidated for the belief that an interesting theory of meaning must be structure-discerning? It is to this question that Gareth Evans is now, I believe, going to present one strategy for giving an affirmative answer.

NOTES

1 See, for example, Foster, 'Meaning and truth-theory', in Evans and McDowell (eds), *Truth and Meaning: Essays in Semantics*, Oxford University Press, 1976, p. 4; McDowell, 'Truth conditions, bivalence and verificationism', in Evans and McDowell (eds), *op. cit.*, p. 42; and Dummett, 'What is a theory of meaning?' in Guttenplan (ed.), *Mind and Language*, Oxford University Press, 1975, p. 97.
2 See Dummett, *Frege: Philosophy of Language*, Duckworth, London, 1973, pp. 302–3.
3 'What is a theory of meaning', *op. cit.*, p. 102.
4 See, for example, Davidson, 'In defense of convention T', in LeBlanc

(ed.), *Truth, Syntax and Modality*, North-Holland, Amsterdam, 1973, p. 81.

5 See, for example, Dummett, 'What is a theory of meaning? (II)' in Evans and McDowell (eds), *op. cit.*, pp. 69–72.
6 Cf. Foster, *op. cit.*, pp. 1–4.

IV

REPLY: SEMANTIC THEORY AND TACIT KNOWLEDGE[1]

Gareth Evans

I

In his provocative paper, Prof. Wright threw down several challenges to philosophers like myself who have been attracted by, and supposed themselves to be participating in, the enterprise of constructing a systematic theory of meaning for a natural language. I shall have time this evening to take up only one of his challenges, which I hope is the most important.

Prof. Wright notes that those who are interested in constructing a theory of meaning for a natural language insist that it should be what he calls 'structure-reflecting'; as he says, all the interest of the theories or sub-theories which have been constructed lies in their capacity to exhibit the meanings of complex expressions as a function of the meanings of their parts. Prof. Wright then takes this 'structure-reflecting' requirement in one hand and examines various accounts of the nature of a theory of meaning which might justify its imposition. He considers three such accounts.

The first is this: the task of a theory of meaning is simply to enable one to state what each of the sentences of a language means. He argues, I think correctly, that if this is the task of a theory of meaning, the structure-reflecting requirement cannot be justified; indeed, and here again I agree with him, in the special case in which the language under study is included in the language in which the theory is being stated, a single axiom schema:

118

$$\text{True } (\bar{\varphi}) \equiv \varphi$$

will serve the purpose.

(Like Prof. Wright, I will concentrate upon theories of meaning which yield statements of sentences' truth-conditions, since, as he says, his scepticism about theories of meaning arises equally for theories whose central motion is not that of truth but, say, warranted assertibility, or falsifiability. In order to focus upon the question of structure, we can assume that no question is being raised about the empirical content of the *theorems* of the theory of meaning; the question is about the significance of their being derived from a finite set of principles (axioms) in a structure-revealing way.)

Prof. Wright argues that if the structure-reflecting requirement is to be justified, a theory of meaning must in some way or other be regarded as a theory of the competence of speakers of the language, but in what way? We can say that the theory states something which speakers of the language tacitly know, but what does this mean? Two interpretations provide the second and third account which Prof. Wright considers. One he finds relatively weak, and acceptable, but unable to justify the requirement; the other he finds inadequately explained and open to serious objection.

According to the weak sense of 'tacit knowledge', 'to attribute implicit knowledge of such a "theory" . . . is to do no more than obliquely to describe their behaviour; it is to say that they behave in just the way which someone would behave who successfully tried to suit his behaviour to . . . an explicit statement [of the theory]' (p. 110). Let us call two theories of meaning which attribute the same meanings to sentences of a language – which agree in their theorems – *extensionally equivalent* (by analogy with the notion of extensional equivalence applied to grammars). According to Prof. Wright, to suit one's behaviour to a theory of meaning is to suit one's behaviour to its theorems. Consequently, if the behaviour of native speakers is the same as one who suits his behaviour to the explicitly formulated theory T, it is the same as one who suits his behaviour to an explicit statement of any extensionally equivalent theory T. Hence, native speakers tacitly know all extensionally equivalent theories, whether those theories discern different structures in native sentences or, in the case of a theory formulated with a single axiom schema, do not discern structure in their sentences at all. So, while this weak notion of tacit knowledge is perfectly clear, it does not provide one with the basis for preferring one extensionally equivalent theory to another.

We come then to the third account which Prof. Wright considered. It would be quite unfair to complain that Prof. Wright did not make this third option terribly clear, for it is one of his points that it is not very clear. But in the absence of an explicit statement, we must rest content with hints. The notion of tacit knowledge is richer, and allows for the idea of 'unconscious deployment of information'. It is also capable of figuring in an *explanation* of a speaker's capacity to understand new sentences. Though this indicates the kind of direction in which Prof. Wright thinks one who seeks to justify the structure-reflecting requirement must be pushed, he expressed doubt about whether a genuine explanation could be provided by the use of the notion of tacit knowledge; to invoke tacit knowledge of a theory of meaning to explain a speaker's capacity to understand new sentences is vacuous, in the way in which explanations invoking the notion of a universal are vacuous. Secondly, he suggests that any such rich notion of tacit knowledge of a theory of meaning is only dubiously consistent with Wittgenstein's rule-following considerations:

the thesis seems to involve thinking of mastery of the
language as consisting in (unconscious) equipment with the
information which systematically settles the content of so far
unconstructed and unconsidered sentences. Such a conception
is far from patently coherent with the repudiation of the
objectivity of sameness of use involved in the scepticism about
investigation-independence sketched above (p. 112).

Though it is not my intention to focus on this aspect of his paper, I am unsure how Wittgenstein's considerations, at least as interpreted by Prof. Wright, can threaten this, as yet unborn, third option. Prof. Wright says that Wittgenstein's rule-following considerations

do not . . . impugn the legitimacy of at least the most basic
purpose with which such a theory might be devised: that of
securing a description of the use of . . . the object language of
such a kind that to be apprised of that description would be

to know how to participate in the use of . . . the language
(pp. 115–16).

Someone who knows a finite theory for an infinite language is in
some sense in possession of information which *settles in advance*
(allows him to predict) the meanings of as yet unconstructed
sentences. It is unclear to me why those who wish to argue that
speakers of an infinite language tacitly know a finite theory of
meaning need suppose the theory to determine the meanings of
unconstructed sentences in any stronger, or more objectionable,
sense than the one Prof. Wright implicitly accepts in the passage
I have just quoted.

However good or bad the reasons for Prof. Wright's pessimism
might be, he certainly threw down a challenge, and I want to take
it up. I want to try to explain how the structure-reflecting requirement might be justified. But I must immediately mention two
limitations on my attempt. I do not pretend that it is the only
possible way of replying to Prof. Wright's challenge, nor do I
think that it would command universal assent among theorists of
meaning. For example, I am fairly sure that Prof. Davidson would
dissent from it, since, contrary to what Prof. Wright suggests, he
has conspicuously avoided reference to the psychological states of
language users in his explanation of the nature of a theory of
meaning. Second, I propose to do merely what I say: to defend
the enterprise on which the structure-reflecting requirement is a
constraint. I do not propose to defend the claim that philosophical
insights and benefits accrue from taking the enterprise seriously.

Those who have followed recent debates in grammatical theory
will be aware that Prof. Wright's challenge to the theorist of
meaning is very similar to Quine's challenge to the grammarian:

> Implicit guidance is a moot enough idea to demand some
> explicit methodology. If it is to make sense to say that a
> native was implicitly guided by one system of rules rather
> than another, extensionally equivalent one, this sense must
> link up somehow with the native's dispositions to behave in
> observable ways in observable circumstances.[2]

However, in a way Prof. Wright's challenge is more radical, because it is not possible to formulate even a merely extensionally
adequate grammar by the use of a single axiom schema. But this

idea, that all a semantic theorist needs to say about English in English can be encapsulated in a single axiom schema, must surely lead us to begin upon our task of meeting Prof. Wright's challenge with a conviction that it can be met. Can it seriously be suggested that there is nothing to be said about the semantics of specific constructions – of adverbs, tense, modality, intensional contexts, pronouns, quantifiers, proper names, definite descriptions and the like? A good deal has already been said on these subjects by Frege, Russell, Davidson, Geach, Dummett and many others, and though I can detect deficiencies in this work, they do not lead me to think that there are simply no questions of the kind these theorists are attempting to answer. Prof. Wright has criticized semantic theorists for ignoring the ideas of 'the most original philosophical thinker of the twentieth century', but it is surely equally deplorable if students of those ideas act as intellectual Luddites, dismissing the entirety of a sophisticated and developing intellectual tradition without a detailed consideration of its findings, and an alternative account of the enterprise to which the obviously compelling distinctions and observations it contains do properly belong. I do not say that Prof. Wright would himself join, or even encourage, the fanatics wrecking the machines, and I am prepared to concede that his challenge has not been squarely faced, but I should have liked to see a little more evidence that the questions he posed were 'expecting the answer "Yes" ', rather than 'expecting the answer "No" '.

II

Let us begin by considering a little elementary and finite language which contains ten names, $a, b, c, \ldots$ and ten monadic predicates $F, G, H, \ldots$; in all, the language has 100 possible sentences. I consider this case partly for simplicity, but also in order to stress that the structure-reflecting requirement has nothing whatever to do with *finiteness*. The fact that a language has an infinite number of possible sentences is a sufficient but not necessary condition of its having semantically significant structure, as our little language will illustrate. (It is unfortunate that Chomsky's writings have led people to equate the *creativity* of language use with the *unboundedness* natural languages display. Linguistic creativity is manifested in the capacity to understand new sentences, and the speaker of a finite language such as the one I have described can manifest it.) I want to consider two possible theories of meaning for this language. T_1 has 100 axioms; one for each sentence of the language. Examples would be;

> *Fa* is true iff John is bald
> *Fb* is true iff Harry is bald
>
> . . .
>
> *Ga* is true iff John is happy
> *Gb* is true iff Harry is happy

T_1 treats each of the sentences as unstructured. T_2, on the other hand, has twenty-one axioms – one for each 'word' of the language, and a general, compositional one. Ten of the axioms are of the form:

> *a* denotes John
> *b* denotes Harry

and ten are of the form

> An object satisfies *F* iff it is bald
> An object satisfies *G* iff it is happy.

The compositional axiom is:

> A sentence coupling a name with a predicate is true iff the object denoted by the name satisfies the predicate.

One can derive from these twenty-one axioms a statement of the truth-conditions of each of the 100 sentences of the language – the very statements which T_1 takes as axioms. T_2 treats a sentence like *Fa* as structured; it discerns two distinct elements in it; the name *a* and the predicate *F*. Thus, T_1 and T_2 are extensionally equivalent in our sense, and our question is: what can be meant by saying that the practice of speakers of the language shows that one of these is to be preferred to the other, or equivalently, that they tacitly know one of these theories rather than the other?

It is tempting to answer this question by saying that T_1 is a theory tacitly known by someone who has had to receive training with, or exposure to the practice with, each one of the 100 sentences taken individually – someone who had not realized, or who could make no use of the fact, that the same expressions occur in different sentences – whereas T_2 is tacitly known by someone who has the capacity to understand *new* sentences of this simple subject-predicate form (e.g. *Kc*), provided that he has been exposed to the practice with a sufficiency of sentences containing the name *c* and the predicate *K*. However, though this contains the essence of the answer, it will not do as it stands, since it may reasonably be objected that T_1 also comprises a statement of what *Kc* means, so that someone who tacitly knew T_1 would be able to understand it.

I suggest that we construe the claim that someone tacitly knows a theory of meaning as ascribing to that person a set of dispositions – one corresponding to each of the expressions for which the theory provides a distinct axiom. In the case of T_1, it is easy to see what these dispositions are: one tacitly knows T_1 iff one has 100 distinct dispositions, each one being a disposition to judge utterances of the relevant sentence type as having such-and-such truth-conditions. It is more difficult to specify the dispositions which tacit knowledge of T_2 requires of a speaker, because they are interconnected. The only judgments which we are prepared to ascribe to speakers are judgments about the truth-conditions of whole sentences – this, of course, is why we must speak of the knowledge of the axioms being tacit. However, if the subject tacitly knows T_2, we shall regard any such judgment as the exercise of two distinct dispositions. Consequently, the dispositions which tacit knowledge of T_2 requires can never be manifested singly. The dispositions must be inter-defined, but though this makes the task of specifying the dispositions more difficult, it does not make it impossible.

For example, we might say that a speaker U tacitly knows that the denotation of *a* is John iff he has a disposition such that:

$(\Pi\Phi) (\Pi\Psi)$ if

   (i)   U tacitly knows that an object satisfies Φ iff it is Ψ
   (ii) U hears an utterance having the form $\widehat{\Phi}a$,
then U will judge the utterance is true iff John is Ψ

Connectedly, we say that a speaker U tacitly knows that an object satisfies *F* iff it is bald iff he has a disposition such that:

$(\Pi x) (\Pi\alpha)$ if

   (i)   U tacitly knows that the denotation of α is x,

(ii) U hears an utterance having the form $\widehat{F\alpha}$,
then U will judge that the utterance is true iff x is bald.

In these formulations, 'Π' is a universal substitutional quantifier, with variables having the following substitution classes: Φ, names of predicate expressions of the (object) language; α, names of names of the (object) language; Ψ, predicate expressions of our language (the metalanguage); and 'x', proper names of our language.

Now, it is essential that the notion of a disposition used in these formulations be understood in a full-blooded sense. These statements of tacit knowledge must not be regarded as simple statements of regularity, for if they were, anyone who correctly judged the meanings of complete sentences would have a tacit knowledge of T_2. When we ascribe to something the disposition to V in circumstances C, we are claiming that there is a state S which, when taken together with C, provides a causal explanation of all the episodes of the subject's V-ing (in C). So we make the claim that there is a common explanation to all those episodes of V-ing. Understood in this way, the ascription of tacit knowledge of T_2 does not merely report upon the regularity in the way in which the subject reacts to sentences containing a given expression (for this regularity can be observed in the linguistic behaviour of someone for whom the sentence is unstructured). It involves the claim that there is a single state of the subject which figures in a causal explanation of why he reacts in this regular way to all the sentences containing the expression. Tacit knowledge of T_2 requires that there should be twenty such states of the subject – one corresponding to each expression of the language which the theory treats separately – such that the causal explanation of why the subject reacts in the way that he does to any sentence of the language involves two of these states, and any one of these states is involved in the explanation of the way he reacts to ten sentences containing a common element.

The difference between the ascription of tacit knowledge of T_1 and T_2 can be brought out diagrammatically, with the diagrams representing two extremely abstract and schematic psychological models of a subject's capacity to understand sentences. Tacit knowledge of T_1 and T_2 are incompletely represented in figures 4.1 and 4.2 respectively. Forget about the dotted lines for a mo-

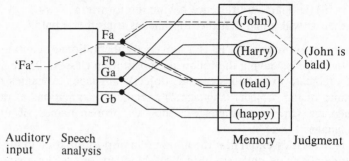

Figure 4.1

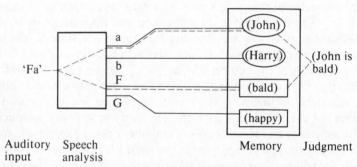

Figure 4.2

ment. You will observe that in the first model, there are two *independent* links between the speech-analysing device and the subject's store of knowledge of John (and in a full representation there would be ten such independent links), whereas in the second model, there is just one link between the speech-analysing device and the subject's store of knowledge of John. The dotted lines are intended to indicate what happens when the subject hears the sentence *Fa*. If you imagine dotted lines drawn to trace the consequences of the subject's hearing the sentence *Ga*, you will observe that in the former case they will not, and in the latter case they will, share a pathway with the dotted line already on the diagram. This is a representation of the fact that in the former case there is not, and in the latter case there is, a common factor which must be invoked in the explanation of the speaker's reaction to the two sentences.

126

It appears to me that there is a clear empirical difference between these two models of competence, and hence between tacit knowledge of T_1 and T_2 interpreted in the way I have suggested.

The decisive way to decide which model is correct is by providing a causal, presumably neurophysiologically based, explanation of comprehension. With such an explanation in hand, we can simply see whether or not there is an appeal to a common state or structure in the explanation of the subject's comprehension of each of the sentences containing the proper name *a*. However, even in the absence of such an explanation, we can have very good empirical reasons for preferring one model of competence to the other.

In the first place, we can examine the way in which the dispositions to react to sentences (the capacity to understand them) are acquired. We might find that the acquisition of the language progressed in quite definite ways, and involved a subject's acquiring the capacity to understand sentences he had never heard before. For example, suppose a subject had progressed in his mastery of the language to the point where he understood all of the sentences which could be constructed from the vocabulary *a*, *b*, *c*, *d*, *e*, and *F*, *G*, *H*, *I*, *J*. Suppose further that he is exposed to the sentences *Ff* and *Gf* in surroundings which, or with instructions which, made it clear what they mean. Whether this exposure leads to his acquiring the capacity to understand new sentences, and which new sentences he was able to understand, would cast very considerable light upon the structure of his competence with the language, both antecedent and subsequent to the introduction of new vocabulary.

If he acquired the capacity to understand the sentences *Hf*, *If*, *Jf*, never having heard them before (and no others), this would strongly confirm the second model of his competence, for this is exactly what it predicts. On the second model, the understanding of these sentences is consequential upon the subject's possession of dispositions specific to the expressions *H*, *I*, *J*, and *f*. Further, if the second model is correct, the subject's understanding of the fragment of the language without the new name *f* showed that he possessed the first three relevant dispositions, while the exposure to just two sentences containing the name *f* can suffice for the establishment of the fourth, provided the circumstances are such that it is clear what those sentences mean. So, according to the second model, all the ingredients of understanding of some sentences are present before any of them have been heard, and they are specifically the sentences *Hf*, *If*, *Jf*.

The first model generates no predictions as to the understanding of unheard sentences. According to it, the understanding of each sentence is a separate capacity, and there is absolutely no reason why the inculcation of competence in the two sentences *Ff* and *Gf* should induce competence with any others. If it does so, this can only be accommodated on the first model by additional postulates, but why light dawns upon the particular sentences *Hf*, *If*, *Jf*, rather than *Li* or *Mj*, must be left totally unexplained.

Thus, we can see more clearly what bearing the capacity to understand new sentences has upon the choice between T_1 and T_2. The fact that someone has the capacity to understand the unheard sentence *Hf* does not refute the ascription to him of tacit knowledge of T_1 *outright* – it just makes the ascription extremely implausible.

Evidence of a parallel kind can be derived from the way in which competence is lost. Suppose a subject is such that, if he loses his competence with any sentence of the form $\widehat{\Phi a}$ (while retaining his competence with some sentences of the form $\Phi\beta$), he simultaneously loses his competence with *every* sentence of that form. This would also favour the second model of the subject's competence, since this is, once again, what that model predicts. On the first model, however, it is *inexplicable* why the loss of the capacity to understand one sentence should drag the comprehension of other sentences with it. (Evidence of this kind would be equally valuable whether the loss of competence was simply due to the subject's forgetting the meanings of words, or to brain damage.)

There is evidence of a third kind which might be used to decide between the models, since they carry with them different accounts of sentence perception. The second model requires that the subject perceive the sentence *Fa*, for example, *as* structured, that is to say, as containing the expression *a*. There is a clear difference between perceiving a sentence which does in fact contain the expression *a*, and perceiving a sentence *as* containing the expression *a*. Consequently, we can regard as relevant to the decision between the two models the various psychological tests which have been devised for identifying perceived acoustic structure, for example, the click test originally devised by Ladefoged and Broadbent.[3]

Thus, it seems to me that Prof. Wright's challenge can be met. It is possible to link tacit knowledge of one theory (rather than one of its extensionally equivalent rivals) to 'the native's dispositions to behave in observable ways in observable situations'. But to do this, one must look further than just to the dispositions to respond to, or to use, whole sentences. It is possible that the scepticism which Prof. Wright expresses is due in a small way to the mistaken thought that facts of native usage which bear upon the content possessed by whole sentences are all the facts to which a theory of meaning can or need be sensitive.

Bearing in mind the interpretation of 'tacit knowledge' which I have proposed, let us briefly consider infinite languages. What would be involved in the tacit knowledge of the theory for such a language which is formulated with the use of a single axiom schema?

An axiom schema is not a theory; it is a compendious specification by their syntactic form of the sentences which do constitute the theory. In the case of an infinite language, there are an infinite number of such sentences. Someone would possess tacit knowledge of such a theory only if he possessed an infinite number of *distinct* linguistic dispositions: one corresponding to each of the sentences of the language. This we know no one can possess. I have concentrated upon the more challenging case of a finite language because it is important to stress the point that there can be compelling evidence that someone *does* not possess a battery of distinct dispositions other than the fact that no one *can* possess them, so that we may want to do for a speaker of a finite language what we are forced to do for a speaker of an infinite language.

Infinity in language results from recursiveness; syntactic and semantic rules which operate upon their own output. A standard clause for the recursive element 'and' runs like this:

A sentence of the form S $^\frown$ 'and' $^\frown$ S' is true iff S is true and S' is true

Generalizing the procedure used earlier, we can say that a speaker U tacitly knows this principle iff he has a disposition such that:

$(\Pi S)\ (\Pi P)\ (\Pi S')\ (\Pi P')$ if:

(i)   U is disposed to judge that S is true iff P
(ii) U is disposed to judge that S' is true iff P'
(iii) U hears an utterance having the form $S\frown$ 'and' $\frown S'$,
then U will judge that the utterance is true iff P and P'

(The substitution classes for the variables S and S', and P and P', are names of sentences of the object language, and sentences of the metalanguage, respectively.) More difficult is the clause for an existential quantifier. It might run:

A sentence of the form '$(\exists x)$'$\frown\Phi$ is true iff there is something y such that, letting β be its name, the sentence Φ^β/x is true.

This is a simplified 'Fregean' clause for an objectual quantifier.[4] 'Φ^β/x' abbreviates 'the result of substituting β for all occurrences of x in Φ'. Then we can say that U tacitly knows this principle iff he has a disposition such that:

$(\Pi\Phi)$ $(\Pi\Psi)$, if:
(i) $(\Pi\beta)$ (Πx) (If U tacitly knows the denotation of β is x, then U is disposed to judge that the sentence Φ^β/x is true iff x is Ψ)
(ii) U hears an utterance of the form '$(\exists x)$'$\frown\Phi$ then U is disposed to judge that the utterance is true iff something is Ψ.

(In this instance, the substitution class for Φ are structural-descriptive names of object-language propositional functions in the variable x.)

III

Prof. Wright and I are agreed that tacit knowledge of the semantic rules of a language is a 'logical construction' out of the use of whole sentences. I have suggested that the idea that we may tacitly know one rather than another of two extensionally equivalent theories which differ in the amount of structure they discern in sentences leads one to the thought of a correspondence between the separable principles of a theory and a series of internal states of the subject, dispositionally characterized. Nevertheless, I would agree with Prof. Wright that to regard these states as states of knowledge or belief, that is to say, states of the same kind as are identified by the ordinary use of those words, is wrong and capable of leading to confusions of the kind he gestures at. To establish this point would require another paper. However, I shall say a brief word about it now, since I believe it is to this point, rather than the very idea of a psychological underpinning to the theory of meaning, that Prof. Wright's criticisms are legitimately directed.

There is no doubt in what the similarity between the states of tacit knowledge and the ordinary states of knowledge and belief is taken to consist. At the level of output, one who possesses the tacit knowledge that p is disposed to do and think some of the things which one who had the ordinary belief that p would be inclined to do and think (given the same desires). At the level of input, one who possesses the state of tacit knowledge that p will very probably have acquired that state as the result of exposure to usage which supports or confirms (though far from conclusively) the proposition that p, and hence in circumstances which might well induce in a rational person the ordinary belief that p. But these analogies are very far from establishing tacit knowledge as a species of belief. After all, similar analogies at the level of input and output exist between the state of a rat who avoids a certain food which has upset it in the past ('bait-shyness') on the one hand, and the belief that a man might have that a certain food is poisonous, on the other.

It is true that many philosophers would be prepared to regard the dispositional state of the rat as a belief. But such a view requires blindness to the fundamental differences which exist between the state of the rat and the belief of the man – differences which suggest that fundamentally different mechanisms are at work. We might begin with this disanalogy: The rat manifests the 'belief' in only one way – by not eating – whereas there is no limit to the ways in which the ordinary belief that something is poisonous might be manifested. The subject might manifest it by, e.g., preventing someone else from eating the food, or by giving it to a hated enemy, or by committing suicide with it. These variations stem from the different projects with which the belief may interact, but similar variations arise from combining the belief with other beliefs. It might, for example, lead to a subject's consuming a small amount of the food every day, when combined with the belief that the consumption of small doses of a poison renders one immune to its effects. (The existence of other beliefs induces a similar variability in the ways in which the belief that something is poisonous might be established.) It is of the essence of a belief state that it be at the service of many distinct projects, and that its influence on any project be mediated by other beliefs. The rat simply has a disposition to avoid a certain food; the state underlying this disposition is not part of a system which would generate widely varying behaviour in a wide variety of situations according to the different projects and further 'beliefs' it may possess.

So, one who possesses a belief will typically be sensitive to a wide variety of ways in which it can be established (what it can be inferred from), and a wide variety of different ways in which it can be used (what can be inferred from it) – if we think of plans for intentional action as being generated from beliefs by the same kind of rational inferential process as yields further beliefs from beliefs. To have a belief requires one to appreciate its location in a network of beliefs; this is why Wittgenstein says, 'When we first begin to *believe* anything, what we believe is not a single proposition, it is a whole system of propositions. (Light dawns gradually over the whole.)' (OC, §141.) To think of beliefs in this way forces us to think of them as structured states; the subject's appreciation of the inferential potential of one belief (e.g. the belief that *a is F*) at least partly depending upon the same general capacity as his appreciation of the inferential potential of others (e.g. the belief that *b is F*). After all, the principle of an *inference*, of *reasoning*, can never be specific to the set of propositions involved.[5] Possession of this general capacity is often spoken of as mastery of a concept, and the point I am making is frequently made by saying that belief involves the possession of concepts (e.g. the concept of *poison*). Behind the idea of a system of beliefs lies that of a system of concepts, the structure in which determines the inferential properties which thoughts involving an exercise of the various component concepts of the system are treated as possessing. At the ground floor of the structure will be observational concepts whose possession requires the subject to be able to discriminate (in suitable favourable circumstances) instances of the concept. Inferential links connect these concepts with more theoretical concepts 'higher' in the structure, and they in their turn will be connected with concepts yet more remote from observation.

Concepts are exercised in the first instance in thoughts; beliefs may be regarded as dispositions to entertain thoughts in the 'believing mode' – i.e. to make judgments; if we think of belief in this way, we shall not be prepared to attribute to a subject the belief that *a is F* (for some particular object *a*, and property *F*) unless we can suppose the subject to be capable of entertaining the supposition (having the thought) that *b is F*, for every object *b* of which he has a conception. For example, we will not be inclined to explain a subject's actions by attributing to him the belief that *he* is F (e.g. he is in pain) unless we suppose him capable of entertaining the supposition with respect to individuals distinct from himself that they are F (e.g. that the person is in pain).[6] Now, it is true that the 'believing mode' of thought cannot be characterized without reference to its influence upon the subject's actions; the traditional accounts of belief which I am largely following went wrong in trying to identify the difference between judgment and mere thought in terms of some introspectible feature of accompaniment of the thought. A judgment is (*ceteris paribus*) a thought one acts upon (if a suitable plan for action is derived from it). But we are now far away from the rat's disposition to avoid certain food. For one thing, there is an enormous gap between belief (a disposition to judge that p when the question whether p is raised) and action. Even though a subject believes a substance is poisonous he may not slip it to an enemy he wants to kill and knows no other way to kill either because he 'didn't think of it' or because, having thought of it, he 'forgot' what to do when the time came.

Tacit knowledge of the syntactic and semantic rules of the language are not states of the same kind as the states we identify in our ordinary use of the terms 'belief' and 'knowledge'. Possession of tacit knowledge is exclusively manifested in speaking and understanding a language; the information is not even potentially at the service of any other project of the agent, nor can it interact with any other beliefs of the agent (whether genuine beliefs or other tacit 'beliefs') to yield further beliefs. Such concepts as we use in specifying it are not concepts we need to suppose the subject to possess, for the state is inferentially insulated from the rest of the subject's thoughts and beliefs. There is thus no question of regarding the information being brought by the subject to bear upon speech and interpretation in rational processes of thought, or of making sense of the subject's continued possession of the information despite incorrect performance, due to his 'not thinking' of the rule at the appropriate time, etc. Remarks which Prof. Wright makes ('unconscious deployment of information', etc.) suggest that he considers the proponent of his third option as holding that tacit knowledge is a real species of belief, but with all the relevant inferential processes made by the subject somehow taking place outside his ken. This is certainly a mysterious and confused position.

I disagree with Prof. Wright only in denying that the proponent of a structure-reflecting theory of meaning need have anything to do with it.

IV

I come finally to the question of whether there is any sense in which the theorist of meaning provides an explanation of a speaker's capacity to understand new sentences. Now it is implicit in what has gone before that the notion of tacit knowledge of a structure-reflecting theory of meaning, explained as I have explained it, cannot be used to explain the capacity to understand new sentences. I have given a purely dispositional characterization of tacit knowledge, and though this does not just amount to a re-description of the speaker's capacities to understand sentences (including the new ones) what it provides, in addition to a description of those capacities, is not itself something that could be involved in an explanation of them. The surplus concerned the form which an explanation of the capacities would take, and to say that a group of phenomena have a common explanation is obviously not yet to say what the explanation is. So I agree with what Prof. Wright writes on p. 113:

> there is no reason to think that it is within the power of the
> sort of theory which we are considering to serve up anything
> which could rightly be considered an *explanation* of the
> infinitary character of competence with its object-language.

But while I agree with this, I disagree with his claim that a proponent of structure-reflecting theories of meaning must somehow be comitted to the view that they are providing an explanation of speakers' capacity to understand new sentences.

Nevertheless, I believe that there is a way of explaining a speaker's capacity to understand new sentences to which provision of a structure-reflecting theory of meaning is indispensable. For we can provide a genuine explanation of a speaker's capacity to understand a certain novel utterance by citing his exposure, in the past, to the elements of that sentence occurring in sentences whose meaning was, or was made, manifest. I envisage an explanatory chain like this:

Exposure to corpus of sentences containing parts of the given sentence being used in determinate ways => Complex set of dispositions = tacit knowledge of clauses in theory of meaning => Understanding of a given new sentence

This chain can be genuinely explanatory even though the last link of the chain by itself is not. The attribution to a subject of tacit knowledge of T_1 is neither more nor less explanatory of the capacity to understand the given new sentence than the attribution of T_2, but tacit knowledge of T_2 belongs in an explanation of the capacity to understand a new sentence because we understand how those dispositions might have been acquired as a result of exposure to the corpus of utterances which the subject has heard. Now, we can cite a subject's exposure to a corpus of utterances in explanation of his capacity to understand a new one only if we believe that the use of expressions in the new sentence is *in conformity with* their use in the previously heard corpus. Only in this case will we be able to show what set of dispositions the subject might have acquired which meets the two conditions: (1) exercising them yields the observed (and correct) interpretation of the new sentence; (2) it would have been exercised in, and hence could have been acquired by exposure to, the previous use. Consequently, when a capacity to understand novel sentences is observed, the theorist of meaning has an indispensable role to play in its explanation, since he must exhibit the regularity between the old and the new.

I have more or less deliberately spoken in terms which might well offend some of those present, for I believe that some of those present, though not, I think Prof. Wright, believe that Wittgenstein's arguments on rule-following show that the ambition to exhibit such regularity must be based upon some kind of mistake. Perhaps this is so, and if it is so, I hope that we shall hear tonight why it is so. Since I do not have time to discuss the arguments of such philosophers, let me end by addressing two connected questions to them.

1　Is it their opinion that all capacities to understand novel sentences (to *know*, I stress, what they mean) are equally inexplicable, or do they believe that scope is provided for one kind of explanation of how it is that a speaker knows what a new sentence means when and only when it can be shown to contain elements which also occur in sentences with whose use he is already familiar?

On the assumption that their answer to my first question is 'Yes', I come to my second:

2　Do they think that it is sufficient to provide an explanation of the kind which the occurrence of familiar expressions makes possible simply by showing that the new sentence does contain expressions which also occur in sentences with whose use he is already familiar, or do they believe, in view of the evident possibility of ambiguity, that something else must be provided? If so, how does this further part of the explanation differ from a statement of the regularity between the old use and the new?

NOTES

1 Sections I, II, IV of this paper were read at the conference in reply to the second section of Crispin Wright's 'Rule-following, objectivity and the theory of meaning'. Section III is new material.
2 W. V. Quine, 'Methodological reflections on current linguistic theory', in D. Davidson and G. Harman (eds), *Semantics of Natural Languages*, Reidel, Dordrecht, 1972, pp. 442–54.

3 P. Ladefoged and D. E. Broadbent, 'Perception of sequence in auditory events', *Quarterly Journal of Experimental Psychology* 13 (1960), pp. 162–70. See also J. A. Fodor and T. G. Bever, 'The psychological reality of linguistic segments', *Journal of Verbal Learning and Verbal Behaviour* 4 (1965), pp. 414–20.

4 For an account of the 'Fregean' approach to quantifiers, see my paper 'Pronouns, quantifiers and relative clauses (1)', *Canadian Journal of Philosophy*, 7 (1977), pp. 467–536.

5 See T. Nagel, *The Possibility of Altruism*, Clarendon, Oxford, 1970, Chapter 7.

6 See P. F. Strawson, *Individuals*, Methuen, London, 1959, Chapter 3, Section 4.

V

NON-COGNITIVISM AND RULE-FOLLOWING*

John McDowell

1   Non-cognitivists hold that ascriptions of value should not be conceived as propositions of the sort whose correctness, or acceptability, consists in their being true descriptions of the world; and, correlatively, that values are not found in the world, as genuine properties of things are. Such a position should embody a reasoned restriction on the sort of proposition that does count as a description (or at worst misdescription) of reality: not merely to justify the exclusion of value-ascriptions, but also to give content to the exclusion – to explain what it is that value judgements are being said not to be. In fact presentations of non-cognitivist positions tend to take some suitable conception of the descriptive, and of the world, simply for granted. In this paper, if only to provoke non-cognitivists to explain how I have missed their point, I want to bring out into the open the nature of a conception that might seem to serve their purpose, and to suggest that there is room for doubt about its serviceability in this context.

According to the conception I have in mind, how things really are is how things are in themselves – that is, independently of how they strike the occupants of this or that particular point of view. With a literal interpretation of the notion of a point of view, this

---

* Much of § 3 of this paper is adapted from my 'Virtue and reason', the *Monist*, 62, No. 3 (July 1979); I am grateful to the Editor and Publisher of the *Monist* for permission to use the material here. In revising the paper I read at the conference, I have been unable to resist trying to benefit from some of Simon Blackburn's thoughtful comments; but most of the changes are merely cosmetic.

idea underpins our correcting for perspective when we determine the true shapes of observed objects. But the idea lends itself naturally to various extensions.

One such extension figures in the thought, familiar in philosophy, that secondary qualities as we experience them are not genuine features of reality. If, for instance, someone with normal human colour vision accepts that the world is as his visual experience (perhaps corrected for the effects of poor light and so forth) presents it to him, then the familiar thought has it that he is falling into error. This is not merely because the appropriate sensory equipment is not universally shared. That would leave open the possibility that the sensory equipment enables us to detect something that is really there anyway, independently of how things appear to us. But the familiar thought aims to exclude this possibility with the claim that the appearances can be satisfyingly explained away. If, that is, we suppose that how things really are can be exhaustively characterized in primary-quality terms, then we can explain why our colour experience is as it is without representing it as strictly veridical: the explanation reveals the extent to which the world as colour experience presents it to us is mere appearance – the extent to which colour vision fails to be a transparent mode of access to something that is there anyway.[1]

Now an analogy between colour experience and (so to speak) value experience seems natural. We can learn to make colour classifications only because our sensory equipment happens to be such as to give us the right sort of visual experience. Somewhat similarly, we can learn to see the world in terms of some specific set of evaluative classifications, aesthetic or moral, only because our affective and attitudinative propensities are such that we can be brought to care in appropriate ways about the things we learn to see as collected together by the classifications. And this might constitute the starting-point of a parallel argument against a naive realism about the values we find ourselves impelled to attribute to things.[2]

There is an extra ingredient that threatens to enter the argument about values and spoil the parallel. In the argument about colours, we are led to appeal to the explanatory power of a description of the world in primary-quality terms, in order to exclude the suggestion that colour vision is a mode of awareness of something that

142

is there anyway. The parallel suggestion, in the case of values, would be that the members of some specific set of values are genuine features of the world, which we are enabled to detect by virtue of our special affective and attitudinative propensities. And it might be thought that this suggestion can be dismissed out of hand by an appeal to something with no analogue in the argument about secondary qualities; namely, a philosophy of mind which insists on a strict separation between cognitive capacities and their exercise, on the one hand, and what eighteenth-century writers would classify as passions or sentiments, on the other.[3] The suggestion involves thinking of exercises of our affective or conative natures either as themselves in some way percipient, or at least as expanding our sensitivity to how things are; and the eighteenth-century philosophy of mind would purport to exclude this *a priori*.

But perhaps this gets things the wrong way round. Do we actually have any reason to accept the eighteenth-century philosophy of mind, apart from a prior conviction of the truth of non-cognitivism?[4] The question is at least awkward enough to confer some attractions on the idea of a route to non-cognitivism that bypasses appeal to the eighteenth-century philosophy of mind, and proceeds on a parallel with the argument about secondary qualities, claiming that the character of our value experience can be satisfyingly explained on the basis of the assumption that the world – that is, the world as it is anyway (independently of value experience, at any rate[5]) – does not contain values. (I shall return to a version of the eighteenth-century philosophy of mind later: § 4 below.)

How is the explanatory claim made out? Typically, non-cognitivists hold that when we feel impelled to ascribe value to something, what is actually happening can be disentangled into two components. Competence with an evaluative concept involves, first, a sensitivity to an aspect of the world as it really is (as it is independently of value experience), and, second, a propensity to a certain attitude – a non-cognitive state which constitutes the special perspective from which items in the world seem to be endowed with the value in question. Given the disentangling, we could construct explanations of the character of value experience on the same general lines as the explanations of colour experience that we have in mind when we are tempted by the argument about secondary qualities: occupants of the special perspective, in making value judgements, register the presence in objects of some property they authentically have, but enrich their conception of this property with the reflection of an attitude.[6]

2   Now it seems reasonable to be sceptical about whether the disentangling manoeuvre here envisaged can always be effected: specifically, about whether, corresponding to any value concept, one can always isolate a genuine feature of the world – by the appropriate standard of genuineness: that is, a feature that is there anyway, independently of anyone's value experience being as it is – to be that to which competent users of the concept are to be regarded as responding when they use it; that which is left in the world when one peels off the reflection of the appropriate attitude.

Consider, for instance, a specific conception of some moral virtue: the conception current in a reasonably cohesive moral community. If the disentangling manoeuvre is always possible, that implies that the extension of the associated term, as it would be used by someone who belonged to the community, could be mastered independently of the special concerns which, in the community, would show themselves in admiration or emulation of actions seen as falling under the concept. That is: one could know which actions the term would be applied to, so that one would be able to predict applications and withholdings of it in new cases – not merely without oneself sharing the community's admiration (there need be no difficulty about that), but without even embarking on an attempt to make sense of their admiration. That would be an attempt to comprehend their special perspective; whereas, according to the position I am considering, the genuine feature to which the term is applied should be graspable without benefit of understanding the special perspective, since sensitivity to it is singled out as an independent ingredient in a purported explanation of why occupants of the perspective see things as they do. But is it at all plausible that this singling out can always be brought off?

Notice that the thesis I am sceptical about cannot be established by appealing to the plausible idea that evaluative classifications are supervenient on non-evaluative classifications. Supervenience requires only that one be able to find differences expressible in terms of the level supervened upon whenever one wants to make

144

different judgements in terms of the supervening level.[7] It does not follow from the satisfaction of this requirement that the set of items to which a supervening term is correctly applied need constitute a kind recognizable as such at the level supervened upon. In fact supervenience leaves open this possibility, which is just the possibility my scepticism envisages: however long a list we give of items to which a supervening term applies, described in terms of the level supervened upon, there may be no way, expressible at the level supervened upon, of grouping just such items together. Hence there need be no possibility of mastering, in a way that would enable one to go on to new cases, a term which is to function at the level supervened upon, but which is to group together exactly the items to which competent users would apply the supervening term.[8] Understanding why just those things belong together may essentially require understanding the supervening term.

I shall reserve till later (§ 5) the question whether there may be a kind of non-cognitivist who can happily concede this possibility. Meanwhile it is clear that the concession would at any rate preclude explaining the relation between value experience and the world as it is independently of value experience in the manner I described above (§ 1). And actual non-cognitivists typically assume that they must disallow the possibility I have envisaged.[9] They may admit that it is often difficult to characterize the authentic property (according to their standards of authenticity) that corresponds to an evaluative concept; but they tend to suppose that there must be such a thing, even if it cannot be easily pinned down in words. Now there is a profoundly tempting complex of ideas about the relation between thought and reality which would make this 'must' seem obvious; but one strand in Wittgenstein's thought about 'following a rule' is that the source of the temptation is the desire for a security which is actually quite illusory.

3   A succession of judgements or utterances, to be intelligible as applications of a single concept to different objects, must belong to a practice of going on doing the same thing. We tend to be tempted by a picture of what that amounts to, on the following lines. What counts as doing the same thing, within the practice in question, is fixed by its rules. The rules mark out rails along which correct activity within the practice must run. These rails are there

anyway, independently of the responses and reactions a propensity to which one acquires when one learns the practice itself; or, to put the idea less metaphorically, it is in principle discernible, from a standpoint independent of the responses that characterize a participant in the practice, that a series of correct moves in the practice is really a case of going on doing the same thing. Acquiring mastery of the practice is pictured as something like engaging mental wheels with these objectively existing rails.

The picture comes in two versions. In one, the rules can be formulated, as a codification of the practice in independently accessible terms. Mastery of the practice is conceived as knowledge, perhaps implicit, of what is expressed by these formulations; and running along the rails is a matter of having one's actions dictated by proofs of their correctness within the practice, with these formulations as major premisses. Sometimes, however, a practice of concept-application resists codification other than trivially (as in 'It is correct to call all and only red things "red" '), and in such cases we tend to resort to the other version of the picture. Here we appeal to grasp of a universal, conceiving this as a mechanism of an analogous sort: one which, like knowledge of an explicitly stateable rule, constitutes a capacity to run along a rail that is independently there.

The extending of a number series is an example of going on doing the same thing which should constitute an ideal case for the application of this picture. Each correct move in a series of responses to the order 'Add 2' is provably correct, as in what seems the clearest version of the picture. But in fact the idea that the rules of a practice mark out rails traceable independently of the reactions of participants is suspect even in this apparently ideal case; and insistence that wherever there is going on in the same way there must be rules that can be conceived as marking out such independently traceable rails involves a misconception of the sort of case in which correctness within a practice can be given the kind of demonstration we count as proof.

We can begin working up to this conclusion by coming to appreciate the emptiness, even in what should be the ideal case, of the psychological component of the picture: that is, the idea that grasp of a rule is a matter of having one's mental wheels engaged with an independently traceable rail. The picture represents understanding of, for instance, the instruction 'Add 2' – command of

146

the rule for extending the series 2, 4, 6, 8, . . . – as a psychological mechanism which, apart from mistakes, churns out the appropriate behaviour with the sort of reliability which, say, a clockwork mechanism might have. If someone is extending the series correctly, and one takes this to be because he has understood the instruction and is complying with it, then, according to the picture, one has hypothesized that the appropriate psychological mechanism, the engagement with the rails, underlies his behaviour. (This would be an inference analogous to that whereby one might postulate a physical mechanism underlying the behaviour of an inanimate object.)

But what manifests understanding of the instruction, so pictured? Suppose we ask the person what he is doing, and he says 'Look, I'm adding 2 each time'. This apparent manifestation of understanding will have been accompanied, whenever it occurs, by at most a finite fragment of the potentially infinite range of behaviour which we want to say the rule dictates. The same goes for any other apparent manifestation of understanding. Thus the evidence we have at any point for the presence of the pictured state is compatible with the supposition that, on some future occasion for its exercise, the behaviour elicited by the occasion will diverge from what we would count as correct, and not simply because of a mistake. Wittgenstein dramatizes this 'possibility' with the example of the person who continues the series, after 1000, with 1004, 1008, . . . (§ 185). Suppose a divergence of the 1004, 1008, . . . type turned up, and we could not get the person to admit that he was simply making a mistake; that would show that his behaviour hitherto was not guided by the psychological conformation we were picturing as guiding it. The pictured state, then, always transcends any grounds there may be for postulating it.

There may be a temptation to protest as follows: 'This is nothing but a familiar inductive scepticism about other minds. After all, one knows in one's own case that one's behaviour will not come adrift like that.' But this objection is mistaken in itself, and it misses the point of the argument.

First, if what it is for one's behaviour to come adrift is for it suddenly to seem that everyone else is out of step, then any sceptical conclusion the argument were to recommend would apply in one's own case just as much as in the case of others.

(Imagine the person who goes on with 1004, 1008, . . . saying in advance 'I know in my own case that my behaviour will not come adrift'.) If there is any scepticism involved, it is not especially about *other* minds.

Second, it is anyway a mistake to construe the argument as making a sceptical point: that one does not know that others' behaviour (or one's own, once we have made the first correction) will not come adrift. The aim is not to suggest that we should be in trepidation lest 'possibilities' of the 1004, 1008, . . . type be realized.[10] We are in fact confident that they will not, and the argument aims, not to undermine this confidence, but to change our conception of its ground and nature. Our picture represents the confident expectation as based on whatever grounds we have *via* the mediation of the postulated psychological mechanism. But we can no more find the putatively mediating state manifested in the grounds for our expectation (say about what someone else will do) than we can find manifested there the very future occurrences we expect. Postulation of the mediating state is an idle intervening step; it does nothing to underwrite the confidence of our expectation.

(Postulation of a mediating brain state might indeed figure in a scientifically respectable argument, vulnerable only to ordinary inductive scepticism, that some specifically envisaged train of behaviour of the 1004, 1008, . . . type will not occur; and our picture tends to trade on assimilating the postulation of the psychological mechanism to this. But the assimilation is misleading. Consider this variant of Wittgenstein's case: on reaching 1000, the person goes on as we expect, with 1002, 1004, . . . , but with a sense of dissociation from what he finds himself doing; it feels as if something like blind habit has usurped his reason in controlling his behaviour. Here the behaviour is kept in line, no doubt, by a brain state; but the person's sense of how to extend the series correctly shows a divergence from ours, of the 1004, 1008, . . . type. Of course we confidently expect this sort of thing not to happen, just as in the simpler kind of case. But a physically described mechanism cannot underwrite confidence in the future operations of someone's sense of what is called for; and once again postulation of a psychological mechanism would be an idle intervening step.[11])

What, then, is the ground and nature of our confidence? Stanley

Cavell has described the view Wittgenstein wants to recommend as follows:

> We learn and teach words in certain contexts, and then we are expected, and expect others, to be able to project them into further contexts. Nothing insures that this projection will take place (in particular, not the grasping of universals nor the grasping of books of rules), just as nothing insures that we will make, and understand, the same projections. That on the whole we do is a matter of our sharing routes of interest and feeling, senses of humour and of significance and of fulfilment, of what is outrageous, of what is similar to what else, what a rebuke, what forgiveness, of when an utterance is an assertion, when an appeal, when an explanation – all the whirl of organism Wittgenstein calls 'forms of life'. Human speech and activity, sanity and community, rest upon nothing more, but nothing less, than this. It is a vision as simple as it is difficult, and as difficult as it is (and because it is) terrifying.[12]

The terror of which Cavell writes at the end of this marvellous passage is a sort of vertigo, induced by the thought that there is nothing that keeps our practices in line except the reactions and responses we learn in learning them. The ground seems to have been removed from under our feet. In this mood, we are inclined to feel that the sort of thing Cavell describes is insufficient foundation for a conviction that some practice really is a case of going on in the same way. What Cavell offers looks, rather, like a congruence of subjectivities, not grounded as it would need to be to amount to the sort of objectivity we want if we are to be convinced that we are *really* going on in the same way.

It is natural to recoil from this vertigo into the picture of rules as rails. But the picture is only a consoling myth elicited from us by our inability to endure the vertigo. It consoles by seeming to put the ground back under our feet; but we see that it is a myth by seeing, as we did above, that the pictured psychological mechanism gives only an illusory security. (Escaping from the vertigo would require seeing that this does not matter; I shall return to this.)

The picture has two interlocking components: the idea of the psychological mechanism correlates with the idea that the tracks we follow are objectively there to be followed, in a way that transcends the reactions and responses of participants in our practices. If the first component is suspect, the second component should be suspect too. And it is.

In the numerical case, the second component is a kind of platonism. The idea is that the relation of our arithmetical thought and language to the reality it characterizes can be contemplated, not only from the midst of our mathematical practices, but also, so to speak, from sideways on – from a standpoint independent of all the human activities and reactions that locate those practices in our 'whirl of organism'; and that it would be recognizable from the sideways perspective that a given move is the correct move at a given point in the practice: that, say, 1002 really does come after 1000 in the series determined by the instruction 'Add 2'. It is clear how this platonistic picture might promise to reassure us if we suffered from the vertigo, fearing that the Wittgensteinian vision threatens to dissolve the independent truth of arithmetic into a collection of mere contingencies about the natural history of man. But the picture has no real content.

We tend, confusedly, to suppose that we occupy the external standpoint envisaged by platonism, when we say things we need to say in order to reject the reduction of mathematical truth to human natural history. For instance, we deny that what it is for the square of 13 to be 169 is for it to be possible to train human beings so that they find such and such calculations compelling. Rather, it is because the square of 13 really *is* 169 that we can be brought to find the calculations compelling. Moved by the vertigo, we are liable to think of remarks like this as expressions of platonism. But this is an illusion. To suppose that such a remark is an expression of platonism is to suppose that when we utter the words 'the square of 13 is 169', in the context 'It is because . . . that we can be brought to find the calculations compelling', we are speaking not from the midst of our merely human mathematical competence but from the envisaged independent perspective instead. (As if, by a special emphasis, one could somehow manage to speak otherwise than out of one's own mouth.) We cannot occupy the independent perspective that platonism envisages; and it is only because we confusedly think we can that we think we can make any sense of it.

If one is wedded to the picture of rules as rails, one will be inclined to think that to reject it is to suggest that, say, in mathematics, anything goes: that we are free to make it up as we go along.[13] But none of what I have said casts any doubt on the idea that the correctness of a move, in a mathematical case of going on doing the same thing, can be proved – so that it is compulsory to go on like that. The point is just that we should not misidentify the perspective from which this necessity is discernible. What is wrong is to suppose that when we describe someone as following a rule in extending a series, we characterize the output of his mathematical competence as the inexorable workings of a machine: something that could be seen to be operating from the platonist's standpoint, the standpoint independent of the activities and responses that make up our mathematical practice. The fact is that it is only because of our own involvement in our 'whirl of organism' that we can understand a form of words as conferring, on the judgement that some move is the correct one at a given point, the special compellingness possessed by the conclusion of a proof. So if dependence on the 'whirl of organism' induces vertigo, then we should feel vertigo about the mathematical cases as much as any other. No security is gained by trying to assimilate other sorts of case to the sort of case in which a hard-edged proof of correctness is available.

Consider, for instance, concepts whose application gives rise to hard cases, in this sense: there are disagreements, which resist resolution by argument, as to whether or not a concept applies.[14] If one is convinced that one is in the right on a hard case, one will find oneself saying, as one's arguments tail off without securing acceptance, 'You simply aren't seeing it', or 'But don't you see?' (cf. § 231). One will then be liable to think oneself confronted by a dilemma.

On the first horn, the inconclusiveness of the arguments results merely from a failure to get something across. This idea has two versions, which correspond to the two versions of the picture of rules as rails. According to the first version, it is possible, in principle, to spell out a universal formula that specifies, in unproblematic terms, the conditions under which the concept one intends is correctly applied. If one could only find the words, one could turn one's arguments into hard-edged proofs. (If the opponent refused to accept the major premiss, that would show that he had not mastered the concept one intended; in that case his inclination not to accept one's words would reveal no substantive disagreement.) According to the second version, the concept is not codifiable (except trivially), and one's problem is to use words as hints and pointers, in order to get one's opponent to divine the right universal. (This is really only a variant of the first version. The idea is that if one could only convey which universal was at issue, the opponent would have a sort of non-discursive counterpart to the formulable proof envisaged in the first version; and as before, if he grasped what one was trying to get across and still refused to accept one's conclusion, that would show that there was no substantive disagreement.)

If neither of these alternatives seems acceptable, then one is pushed on to the second horn of the dilemma by this thought: if there is nothing such that to get it across would either secure agreement or show that there was no substantive disagreement in the first place, then one's conviction that one is genuinely making an application of a concept (genuinely going on in some same way) is a mere illusion. The case is one which calls, not for finding the right answer to some genuine question, but rather for a freely creative decision as to what to say.

In a hard case, the issue seems to turn on that appreciation of the particular instance whose absence is deplored, in 'You simply aren't seeing it', or which is (possibly without success) appealed to, in 'But don't you see?' The dilemma reflects a refusal to accept that a genuine issue can really turn on no more than that; it reflects the view that a putative judgement that is grounded in nothing firmer than that cannot really be a case of going on as before. This is a manifestation of our vertigo: the idea is that there is not enough there to constitute the rails on which a genuine series of applications of a concept must run. But it is an illusion to suppose one is safe from vertigo on the first horn. The illusion is the misconception of the mathematical case: the idea that provable correctness characterizes exercises of reason in which it is, as it were, automatically compelling, without dependence on our partially shared 'whirl of organism'. The dilemma reflects a refusal to accept that when the dependence that induces vertigo is out in the open, in the appeal to appreciation, we can genuinely be going on in the same way; but the paradigm with which the rejected case is unfavourably compared has the same dependence, only less obviously. Once we see this, we should see that we make no headway, in face of the discouraging effects of the vertigo, by trying to assimilate all cases to the sort of case where proofs are available. We should accept that sometimes there may be nothing better to do than explicitly to appeal to a hoped-for community of human response. This is what we do when we say 'Don't you see?' (though there is a constant temptation to misconceive this as a nudge towards grasp of the universal).

Once we have felt the vertigo, then, the picture of rules as rails is only an illusory comfort. What is needed is not so much reassurance – the thought that after all there is solid ground under us – as not to have felt the vertigo in the first place. Now if we are simply and normally immersed in our practices, we do not wonder how their relation to the world would look from outside them, and feel the need for a solid foundation discernible from an external point of view. So we would be protected against the vertigo if we could stop supposing that the relation to reality of some area of our thought and language needs to be contemplated from a standpoint independent of that anchoring in our human life that makes the thoughts what they are for us.[15]

At any rate, it is a bad move to allow oneself to conceive some area of thought from the extraneous perspective at which vertigo threatens, but then suppose one can make oneself safe from vertigo with the idea that rules mark out rails discernible from that external point of view. Just such a move – seeing the anthropo-centricity or ethnocentricity of an evaluative outlook as generating a threat of vertigo, but seeking to escape the threat by finding a solid, externally recognizable foundation – would account for in-sistence (cf. § 2 above) that any respectable evaluative concept must correspond to a classification intelligible from outside the evaluative outlook within which the concept functions.[16]

The idea that consideration of the relation between thought and reality requires the notion of an external standpoint is character-istic of a philosophical realism often considered in a different, more epistemologically oriented context, and in areas where we are not inclined to question whether there are facts of the matter at all. This realism chafes at the fallibility and inconclusiveness of all our ways of finding out how things are, and purports to confer a sense on 'But is it *really* so?' in which the question does not call for a maximally careful assessment by our lights, but is asked from a perspective transcending the limitations of our cognitive powers.

Thus this realism purports to conceive our understanding of what it is for things to be thus and so as independent of our limited abilities to find out whether they are. An adherent of this sort of realism will tend to be impressed by the line of thought sketched in § 1 above, and hence to fail to find room for values in his conception of the world; whereas opposition to this kind of realism about the relation, in general, between thought and reality, makes a space for realism, in a different sense, about values.[17]

4   I want now to revert to the eighteenth-century philosophy of mind, mentioned and shelved in § 1 above, and consider one way in which it connects with the line of thought I have been discussing.

What I have in mind is an argument for non-cognitivism that goes back at least to Hume (though I shall formulate it in rather un-Humean terms).[18] It has two premises. The first is to the effect that ascriptions of moral value are action-guiding, in something like this sense: someone who accepts such an ascription may (depending on his opportunities for action) *eo ipso* have a reason for acting in a certain way, independently of anything else being true about him. The second premiss is this: to cite a cognitive propositional attitude – an attitude whose content is expressed by the sort of proposition for which acceptability consists in truth – is to give at most a partial specification of a reason for acting; to be fully explicit, one would need to add a mention of something non-cognitive, a state of the will or a volitional event. Clearly, it would follow that ascriptions of value, however acceptable, can be at most in part descriptive of the world.

The key premiss, for my purposes, is the second. Notice that if this premiss is suspect, that casts doubt not only on the non-cognitivism to which one would be committed if one accepted both premisses, but also on a different position which rejects the non-cognitivist conclusion, and, keeping the second premiss as a fulcrum, dislodges the first. This different position might merit Hare's label 'descriptivism', meant as he means it – something that is not true of the anti-non-cognitivism I would defend, which retains the first premiss.[19] (A version of descriptivism, without general insistence on the second premiss – exceptions are allowed in the case of reasons that relate to the agent's interest – but with a restricted form of it used to overturn the first premiss, is found in some of the writings of Philippa Foot.[20])

I suspect that one reason why people find the second premiss of the Humean argument obvious lies in their inexplicit adherence to a quasi-hydraulic conception of how reason explanations account for action. The will is pictured as the source of the forces that issue in the behaviour such explanations explain. This idea seems to me a radical misconception of the sort of explanation a reason explanation is; but it is not my present concern.

A different justification for the second premiss might seem to be afforded by a line of thought obviously akin to what I have been considering; one might put it as follows. The rationality that a reason explanation reveals in the action it explains ought, if the explanation is a good one, to be genuinely there: that is, recognizable from an objective standpoint, conceived (cf. § 3) in terms of the notion of the view from sideways on – from outside any practices or forms of life partly constituted by local or parochial modes of response to the world. This putative requirement is not met if we conceive value judgements in the way I would recommend: the ascription of value that one cites in giving an agent's reason for an action, so far from revealing the rationality in the action to an imagined occupier of the external standpoint, need not even be intelligible from there. By contrast, insistence on the second premiss might seem to ensure that the requirement can be met. For on this view an explanation of an action in terms of a value judgement operates by revealing the action as the outcome of an unproblematically cognitive state plus a non-cognitive state – a desire, in some suitably broad sense[21]; and if we think someone's possession of the desires in question could be recognized from a standpoint external to the agent's moral outlook, then it might seem that those desires would confer an obvious rationality, recognizable from that objective standpoint, on actions undertaken with a view to gratifying them.

I shall make two remarks about this line of thought.

First, I expressed scepticism (in § 2) about the possibility of mastering the extension of a value concept from the external standpoint (so that one could move to understanding the value concept by tacking on an evaluative extra). The scepticism obviously recurs here, about the possibility of grasping, from the external standpoint, the content of the envisaged desires. On this view there is a set of desires, a propensity to which constitutes the embracing of a particular moral outlook; if the content of this set can be grasped from the external standpoint, then the actions required by that moral stance are in theory classifiable as such by a sheer outsider. This amounts to the assumption that a moral stance can be captured in a set of externally formulable principles – principles such that there could in principle be a mechanical (non-comprehending) application of them which would duplicate the actions of someone who puts the moral stance into practice. This assumption strikes me as merely fantastic.[22]

Second, the underlying line of thought inherits whatever dubiousness is possessed by its relatives in, say, the philosophy of mathematics. (See § 3, but I shall add a little here.)

Consider the hardness of the logical 'must'. One is apt to suppose that the only options are, on the one hand, to conceive the hardness platonistically (as something to be found in the world as it is anyway: that is, the world as characterized from a standpoint external to our mathematical practices); or, on the other (if one recoils from platonism), to confine oneself to a catalogue of how human beings act and feel when they engage in deductive reasoning. (Taking this second option, one might encourage oneself with the thought: at least all of this is objectively there.) On the second option, the hardness of the logical 'must' has no place in one's account of how things really are; and there must be a problem about making room for genuine rationality in deductive practice, since we conceive that as a matter of conforming our thought and action to the dictates of the logical 'must'. If one recoils from platonism into this second position, one has passed over a fully satisfying intermediate position, according to which the logical 'must' is indeed hard (in the only sense we can give to that idea), and the ordinary conception of deductive rationality is perfectly acceptable; it is simply that we must avoid a mistake about the perspective from which the demands of the logical 'must' are perceptible. (As long as the mistake is definitely avoided, there is something to be said for calling the intermediate position a species of platonism.)[23]

Now it is an analogue to this intermediate position that seems to me to be most satisfying in the case of ethics. The analogue involves insisting that moral values are there in the world, and make demands on our reason. This is not a platonism about values (except in a sense analogous to that in which the intermediate position about the logical 'must' might be called a species of platonism); the world in which moral values are said to be is not the externally characterizable world that a moral platonism would envisage.[24] Non-cognitivism and descriptivism appear, from this point of view, as different ways of succumbing to a quite dubious demand for a more objective conception of rationality. If we accept the demand, then they will indeed seem the only alternatives to a full-blown moral platonism. But in the logical case, we should not suppose that recoiling from platonism commits us to some kind of reduction of the felt hardness of the logical 'must' to the urging of our own desires.[25] In the ethical case too, we should not allow the different option that the intermediate position affords to disappear.[26]

5 Non-cognitivism, as I see it, invites us to be exercised over the question how value experience relates to the world, with the world conceived as how things are anyway – independently, at least, of our value experience being as it is. The non-cognitivism I have been concerned with assumes that evaluative classifications correspond to kinds into which things can in principle be seen to fall independently of an evaluative outlook, and thereby permits itself to return an answer to the question which clearly does not undermine the appearance that evaluative thinking is a matter of the genuine application of concepts. As one's use of an evaluative term unfolds through time, one is genuinely (by the non-cognitivist's lights) going on in the same way. Admittedly, the non-cognitive ingredient in what happens makes the case more complex than our usual paradigms of concept-application. But the non-cognitive extra, repeated as the practice unfolds, is seen as a repeated response to some genuinely same thing (something capturable in a paradigmatic concept-application): namely, membership in some genuine kind. To put it picturesquely, the non-cognitive ingredient (an attitude, say) can, without illusion by the non-cognitivist's lights, see itself as going on in the same way. Given that, the whole picture looks sufficiently close to the usual paradigms of concept-application to count as a complex variant of them. But I have suggested that the assumption on which the possibility of this partial assimilation depends is a prejudice, without intrinsic plausibility.

Might non-cognitivism simply disown the assumption?[27] If what I have just written is on the right track, it can do so only at a price: that of making it problematic whether evaluative language is close enough to the usual paradigms of concept-application to count as expressive of judgements at all (as opposed to a kind of sounding off). Failing the assumption, there need be no genuine same thing (by the non-cognitivist's lights) to which the successive occurrences of the non-cognitive extra are responses. Of course the items to which the term in question is applied have, as something genuinely in common, the fact that they elicit the non-cognitive extra (the attitude, if that is what it is). But that is not a property to which the attitude can coherently be seen as a response. The attitude can see itself as going on in the same way, then, only by falling into a peculiarly grotesque form of the alleged illusion: projecting itself on to the objects, and then mistaking the projection for something it finds and responds to in them. So it seems that, if it disowns the assumption, non-cognitivism must regard the attitude as something which is simply felt (causally, perhaps, but not rationally explicable); and uses of evaluative language seem appropriately assimilated to certain sorts of exclamation, rather than to the paradigm cases of concept-application.

Of course there are some who will not find this conclusion awkward.[28] But anyone who finds it unacceptable, and is sympathetic to the suggestion that the disputed assumption is only a prejudice, has reason to suspect that the non-cognitivist is not asking the right question. It is not that we cannot make sense of the non-cognitivist's conception of a value-free world; nor that we cannot find plausible some account of how value experience relates to it (causally, no doubt). But if we resist both the disputed assumption and the irrationalistic upshot of trying to read an account of the relation between value experience and the world so conceived, not based on the disputed assumption, as an account of the real truth about the conceptual content of the experience, then we must wonder about the credentials of the non-cognitivist's question. If we continue to find it plausible that asking how value experience relates to the world should yield a palatable account of the content of value experience, we must wonder whether the world that figures in the right construal of the question should not be differently conceived, without the non-cognitivist's insistence on independence from evaluative outlooks.[29] In that case the non-cognitivist's anxiety to maintain that value judgements are not descriptive of *his* world will seem, not wrong indeed, but curiously beside the point.

NOTES

1 There is an excellent discussion of this line of thought (though more sympathetic to it than I should want to be myself) in Bernard Williams, *Descartes: The Project of Pure Enquiry*, Penguin, Harmondsworth, 1978, Chapter 8. (I shall not pause to criticize the application to secondary qualities.)

2 The parallel is suggested by Williams, *ibid.*, when (p. 245) he writes of 'concepts . . . which reflect merely a local interest, taste or sensory peculiarity'.

3 Cf. J. L. Mackie, *Ethics: Inventing Right and Wrong*, Penguin, Harmondsworth, 1977, p. 22.

4 Cf. Mackie, *ibid.*, pp. 40–1.

5 The non-cognitivist's conception of the world is not exhausted by primary-quality characterizations. (See David Wiggins, 'Truth, invention, and the meaning of life', *Proceedings of the British Academy*, 62 (1976), pp. 361–3.) So his notion of the world as it is anyway is not the one that figures in the argument about secondary qualities. What is wanted, and what my parenthesis is intended to suggest, is an analogy, rather than an addition, to the secondary-quality argument.

6 This formulation fits Mackie's error theory, rather than the different sort of non-cognitivism exemplified by R. M. Hare's prescriptivism (see, e.g., *Freedom and Reason*, Clarendon Press, Oxford, 1963), in which ordinary evaluative thinking has enough philosophical sophistication not to be enticed into the projective error of which Mackie accuses it. But the idea could easily be reformulated to suit Hare's position; this difference between Hare and Mackie is not relevant to my concerns in this paper.

7 Cf. Hare, *ibid.*, p. 33 (on the thesis of universalizability): 'What the thesis does forbid us to do is to make different moral judgements about actions which we admit to be exactly or relevantly similar'. In Chapter 2, Hare claims that this thesis of universalizability just is the thesis that evaluative concepts have 'descriptive' meaning (which is Hare's version of the thesis I am sceptical about): see p. 15. The identification is undermined by my remarks about supervenience.

8 The point is not merely that the language may lack such a term: a gap that might perhaps be filled by coining one. (See Hare, 'Descriptivism', *Proceedings of the British Academy*, 49 (1963).) What I am suggesting is that such a coinage might not be learnable except parasitically upon a mastery of the full-blown evaluative expression.

9 See Hare, *op. cit.*, Chapter 2. Mackie (*op. cit.*, p. 86) objects to the

idea that a corresponding value-neutral classification is (as in Hare's position) part of the meaning of an evaluative term, but evidently in the context of an assumption that there must be such a corresponding classification.

10 Nor even that we really understand the supposition that such a thing might happen; see Barry Stroud, 'Wittgenstein and logical necessity', *Philosophical Review*, 74 (1965), pp. 504–18.

11 In the context of a physicalistic conception of mind, this paragraph will be quite unconvincing; this is one of the points at which a great deal more argument is necessary.

12 *Must We Mean What We Say?*, Charles Scribner's Sons, New York, 1969, p. 52.

13 See Michael Dummett, 'Wittgenstein's philosophy of mathematics', *Philosophical Review*, 68 (1959), pp. 324–48. (For a corrective, see Stroud, *op. cit.*)

14 Simon Blackburn objected that the central 'rule-following' passages in Wittgenstein discuss cases where following the rule is a matter of course. (There are no hard cases in mathematics.) In the end I do not mind if my remarks about hard cases correspond to nothing in Wittgenstein; they indicate (at least) a natural way to extend some of Wittgenstein's thoughts. (Where hard cases occur, the agreement that constitutes the background against which we can see what happens as, e.g., disputes about genuine questions cannot be agreement in judgements as to the application of the concepts themselves: cf. § 242. What matters is, for instance, agreement about what counts as a reasonable argument; consider how lawyers recognize competence in their fellows, in spite of disagreement over hard cases.)

15 This is not an easy recipe. Perhaps finding out how to stop being tempted by the picture of the external standpoint would be the discovery that enables one to stop doing philosophy when one wants to (cf. § 133).

16 The idea of rules as rails seems to pervade Chapter 2 of Hare's *Freedom and Reason* (cf. notes 7 and 9 above). Hare argues there that evaluative words, if used with 'that consistency of practice in the use of an expression which is the condition of its intelligibility' (p. 7), must be governed by principles connecting their correct application to features of value-independent reality (that which can be 'descriptively' characterized, in Hare's sense of 'descriptively'). Hare mentions Wittgenstein, but only as having introduced ' "family resemblance" and "open texture" and all that' (p. 26) into 'the patter of the up-to-date philosophical conjurer' (p. 7). It is hard to resist the impression that Hare thinks we can respect everything useful that Wittgenstein said, even while retaining the essentials of the picture of rules as rails, simply by thinking of the mechanism as incompletely rigid and difficult to characterize in precise terms.

17 I distinguish opposition to the realism that involves the idea of the external standpoint from anti-realism in the sense of Michael Dummett (see, e.g., *Truth and Other Enigmas*, Duckworth, London, 1978,

passim), which is the positive doctrine that linguistic competence consists in dispositions to respond to circumstances recognizable whenever they obtain. (See my 'Anti-realism and the epistemology of understanding', in Jacques Bouveresse and Herman Parret (eds), *Meaning and Understanding*, De Gruyter, Berlin and New York, 1981.)

18 See *A Treatise of Human Nature*, III. I. I, in the edition of L. A. Selby-Bigge, Clarendon Press, Oxford, 1896, p. 457.

19 As Hare uses the word 'descriptive', a descriptive judgement is, by definition, not action-guiding. Hare does not consider a resistance to non-cognitivism that accepts the first premiss of the Humean argument.

20 See especially *Virtues and Vices*, Blackwell, Oxford, 1978, p. 156. From the point of view of a resistance to non-cognitivism that accepts the first premiss of the Humean argument, the difference between non-cognitivism and descriptivism tends to pale into insignificance, by comparison with the striking fact that they share the disputable conception of the world as such that knowing how things are in it cannot by itself move us to moral action.

21 Either, as in non-cognitivism, acceptance of a moral judgement really is a composite state including a desire; or, as in descriptivism, the moral judgement is itself strictly cognitive, but it makes the behaviour intelligible only in conjunction with a desire.

22 See my 'Virtue and reason' (cited in the footnote to the title of this paper).

23 The following passage seems to be an expression of the intermediate position:

> What you say seems to amount to this, that logic belongs to the natural history of man. And that is not combinable with the hardness of the logical 'must'.
>
> But the logical 'must' is a component part of the propositions of logic, and these are not propositions of human natural history (RFM VI, 49).

24 Hence Mackie's error is not committed. (It is a fascinating question whether Plato himself was a moral platonist in the sense here envisaged: I am myself inclined to think he was not.)

25 On these lines: to 'perceive' that a proposition is, say, a conclusion by *modus ponens* from premisses one has already accepted, since it constitutes having a reason to accept the proposition, is really an amalgam of a neutral perception and a desire (cf. non-cognitivism); or the perception constitutes having a reason only in conjunction with a desire (cf. descriptivism). I am indebted to Susan Hurley here.

26 For the suggestion that Wittgenstein's philosophy of mathematics yields a model for a satisfactory conception of the metaphysics of value, see Wiggins, *op. cit.*, pp. 369–71.

27 Simon Blackburn pressed this question, and what follows corresponds to nothing in the paper I read at the conference.

28 I mean those who are content with a view of values on the lines of, e.g., A. J. Ayer, *Language, Truth and Logic*, Gollancz, London, 1936, Chapter VI.

29 The pressure towards a conception of reality as objective, transcending how things appear to particular points of view, is not something to which it is clearly compulsory to succumb in all contexts, for all its necessity in the natural sciences. See Thomas Nagel, 'Subjective and objective', in his *Mortal Questions*, Cambridge University Press, 1979.

VI

REPLY: RULE-FOLLOWING AND MORAL REALISM

Simon Blackburn

Hume wrote, of reason and taste:

> The one discovers objects as they really stand in nature,
> without addition or diminution: the other has a productive
> faculty, and gilding or staining all natural objects with the
> colours, borrowed from internal sentiment, raises in a manner
> a new creation (Appendix 1 of the *Enquiry Concerning the
> Principles of Morals*).

The focus of our problem is the way in which his theory of the
productive or projective power of the mind should be defined and
debated. His idea is that the world proper, the sum totality of
facts, impinges upon us. In straightforward judgment we describe
the facts that do so. But in addition to judging the states of affairs
the world contains, we may react to them. We form habits; we
become committed to patterns of inference; we become affected,
and form desires, attitudes and sentiments. Such a reaction is
'spread on' the world, as Hume puts it in the *Treatise*, by talking
and thinking as though the world contains states of affairs answering to such reactions. The important thing about a part of
discourse to which this theory is appropriate is that it serves
primarily as an expression of the habits and sentiments of the
people using it.

There seem to be three possible reactions to a projective picture
about some area of discourse. One might say that it is not really
assessable, marking no genuine alternative to a straightforward
acceptance of the judgments in question as descriptions of a larger

reality. The world, on this view, could not be partitioned so as to contain some states of affairs (e.g. physical ones) but not others (e.g. moral, or counter-factual, or causal ones). Or, one might say that there is a debate and that a realist (as I shall call one who opposes Hume's picture) wins it; finally one might hold, as I do, that there is a debate, and the Humean wins it. In denying the existence of a perspective from which one could, as it were, take an entirely neutral peek at the contents of reality, and find that values are or are not among them, John McDowell seems to embrace the first view. Perhaps it is only from this mythical perspective that we can accept any explanation of our evaluations: to philosophize at all is to step to a place that does not exist. Myself I see the boot on the other foot: we will be able to give sense to the perspective if we can see how to conduct the debate. By so doing we construct our right to talk of the God's-eye view. But McDowell seems to veer towards the second view, that realism wins, both in his belief that there are specific arguments against projective theories, and in his embrace of the idea that our affective natures expand our sensitivity to how things are, on the lines of any mode of perception. Perhaps he feels he is allowed to sympathize with both because he thinks the burden of defining the debate falls entirely upon the projectivist: it is he who has 'to explain what it is that value judgments are being said not to be'. But the questions about the existence of the debate affect both the parties to it. A projectivist must focus sharply enough on notions like description, truth, the world, to explain what he thinks moral judgments are *not*; a realist must focus sharply enough to explain what he thinks they *are*. My own view is that this is very hard for him. When, in part III of this paper, I describe the programme which I have called 'quasi-realism', which shows how far a projectivist may adopt the intellectual practices supposedly definitive of realism, it becomes hard to see what else a realist can want – what point *he* can be making in opposition to projectivism.

But surely we do have a serviceable way of describing the debate, at least as far as it concerns evaluations and morals. It is about explanation. The projectivist holds that our nature as moralists is well explained by regarding us as reacting to a reality which contains nothing in the way of values, duties, rights and so forth; a realist thinks it is well explained only by seeing us as able to perceive, cognize, intuit, an independent moral reality. He holds that the moral features of things are the parents of our sentiments, whereas the Humean holds that they are their children. Each side will then attempt to belittle the other's explanation, and remove whatever obstacles are presented to his own, and this is exactly what McDowell does, both by alleging various difficulties for the projectivist, and by trying to rebut the association with Platonism, which is naturally (and I think rightly) worrying to anyone who believes that it is a causal, or at least explanatory, process, starting with the goodness of a thing, which ends with our approving of it.

Since we have this way of placing projectivism, I find it hard to sympathize with McDowell's propensity to hint that it is pointless. It has as much point as any attempt to understand ourselves. But of course it is true that we will need some way of evaluating the competing explanations, and it is theoretically possible that we come to regard their difference as illusory. But I see little danger of that. It is quite different if we generalize projective theory. It is undoubtedly tempting to apply Hume's mechanism not only to such things as gods and values but also, as he did, to causes, and (once we are in the swing of it) to conditionals, generalizations, other minds or even our spatial and temporal descriptions of the world. To stem the tide we might indeed become sceptical about whether in some of these applications we have a distinct theory, or only a notational difference from simple realism.[1] But the main reason why projectivism might turn out to be no real rival to realism about, say, our description of the world as containing causally interacting particulars in space and time, is that we may lack a conception of the reality upon which this creation is raised; hence we could have no explanation of how this thin reality works on an imaginative mind to give us our thoughts. This difficulty does not afflict the evaluative case, and whatever view we take about a global theory of truth, the question of whether we are to see values as things to which we respond or as things which we spread on the world will remain. And as McDowell's own paper shows, people will certainly believe that they have arguments for one side or the other.

In the next section I turn to McDowell's specific argument against a projective theory. In the subsequent section I turn to the positive theory of objectivity in moral judgment, derived from his interpretation of Wittgenstein, and argue that it is badly mistaken, both giving us no conception of moral truth in many places when we need it, and giving an entirely spurious authority to majority consensus. I then try to earn, on behalf of the projectivist, a right to use the concepts of truth and objectivity which delude people into realism.

I

McDowell's main argument against the projectivist raises the problem of disentangling the objective (by the non-cognitivist's standards) from the appetitive or projected:

> 'Now it seems reasonable to be sceptical about whether . . .
> corresponding to any value concept, one can always isolate a
> genuine feature of the world . . . to be that to which
> competent users of the concept are to be regarded as
> responding when they use it. . . . If the disentangling
> manoeuvre is always possible, that implies that the extension
> of the associated term, as it would be used by someone who
> belonged to the community, could be mastered [by an
> outsider]' (p. 144).

The outsider is someone who has no tendency to share the community's reaction, nor has he even embarked on an attempt to make sense of it. The point is that to him the class of things eliciting the admiration, or whatever other reaction is in question, may have no shape. He cannot see why one thing or another belongs to it, and cannot reliably go on to classify new cases. But the projectivist is supposed to be claiming that in principle he could still lack any understanding of the reaction, yet come to understand the *kind* of thing eliciting it. He could come to see the things which the community reacts to as genuinely forming a kind.

At the symposium from which these papers grew I expressed scepticism about whether a projectivist is committed to this, and McDowell now admits the possibility that he need not be. (He takes it up in his § 5.) However, I think it is still worth going through the argument I used, since the point has some intrinsic interest, and since the option McDowell considers in § 5 is one against which he finds objection (I come to that later).

Let us suppose for a moment that some group of human beings does share a genuine tendency to some reaction in the face of some perceived properties or kinds of thing. Surely it need not surprise us *at all* that they should know of no description of what unifies the class of objects eliciting the reaction, except of course the fact that it does so. We are complicated beings, and understand our own reactions only poorly. Now suppose the outsider, who fails either to share or to understand the reactive tendency, cannot perceive any such unifying feature either. Then he will be at a loss to extend the associated term to new cases, and there will be no method of teaching him how to do so. To take a very plausible candidate, it is notoriously difficult or impossible to circumscribe exactly all those things which a member of our culture finds comic. Any description is likely to have a partial and disjunctive air which would make it a poor guide to someone who does not share our sense of humour, if he is trying to predict those things which we will and will not find funny. This may not be a merely practical matter: there is no *a priori* reason to expect there to really *be* a unifying feature. Let us describe this by saying that the grouping of things which is made by projecting our reactive tendency onto the world is *shapeless* with respect to other features. The puzzle then is why McDowell sees shapelessness as a problem for a projective theory. The necessary premise must be that a reactive tendency cannot be shapeless with respect to those other features which trigger it off, whereas a further cognitive ability can pick up features which are shapeless with respect to others. But why? Do we really support a realist theory of the comic by pointing out the complexity and shapeless nature of the class of things we laugh at? On the contrary, there is no reason to expect our reactions to the world simply to fall into patterns which we or anyone else can describe. So the plight of the outsider affords no argument against a Humean theory.

Now even if our sense of humour is in my sense shapeless, this does not entail the lack, on any particular occasion of humour, of an objective feature to which we are reacting. We might want to regard it as true that on any occasion the comic reaction is a reaction to some perceived set of features. It is just that all these sets form a class which independently of our tendency to find them funny, has no shape. It may on occasion be hard to say quite which features were the funny ones (the twitch of the eyebrow, the timing of the remark), and of course there is no presumption that the humorist or his audience knows which features they are. But on occasion we might do: for instance I tell a joke just by enumerating certain features of a situation. I don't in addition tell you that the feature of being really comic was also present. But in this case the implication said to hold in the passage I have quoted does not hold. For we may know to which features a person reacts on particular occasions yet still have a disjunctive and partial class which could not enable the outsider to predict the comic effect of new occasions.

Of course, it *is* hard to tell just what was so funny about some occasion for humour. But McDowell admits some form of supervenience (p. 144), and supervenience is only a requirement because things are funny (or admirable, or whatever) in virtue of their other properties. But once this is said the difficulty of coming to understand just what it is in virtue of which something is funny or good is a universal difficulty for anyone interested in humour or value. It is no harder for the projectivist, seeking to detect what shape he can in our reactions than it is for the realist, seeking what shape he can in the world we describe as funny and good.

So I conclude that the belief that we had here an especial difficulty for the projective theory was erroneous.

It is not clear to me that anything in the attack on projectivism which, I hope, I have just deflected, connects with the use of Wittgenstein in McDowell's paper. The connection he alleges is that projectivists refuse to take my way out – that of being unconcerned by the shapeless nature of our attitudes – because, in a pre-Wittgensteinian muddle about 'following a rule' they think that there *must* be an 'authentic' property (at the objective level) corresponding to the extension of the projected property – a real 'kind' to which all and only comic or good things belong (p. 145). I think I can see two different thoughts here, but I am not sure that either of them would arise only from a pre-Wittgensteinian muddle, or desire for an illusory security. The first thought a projectivist might have is this. Since we are after all only animals in a natural world, whose reactions, however complex, are elicited by the things we come across, surely there must be some explanation possible of why we react as we do. This explanation must proceed by trying to find common elements in the things eliciting the reactions. I cannot see that Wittgenstein has shown this thought to be mistaken. It certainly expresses no desire for an illusory *security*. It expresses the desire for further understanding of ourselves, and on the whole I think we ought to approve of it, whether it is in principle satisfiable or not.

The other thought which might lead a projectivist to suppose that there has to be an 'authentic' property shared by all and only the things to which he reacts in some way is this. He worries: 'Unless the things to which I react alike fall into "kinds", then when I approve of some new thing I cannot regard myself as "going on in the same way"; and if someone fails to approve of it, I cannot criticize him on the grounds that his reaction is inconsistent with his previous practice. But we need this concept of consistency in moral practice. Hence the things to which we react must fall into kinds'.

I don't think this is a very impressive argument (see section III, part 5). But in any case on p. 145 McDowell looks set to rescue the non-cognitivist from it. It afflicts him only if he forgets how all cases of going on in the same way are founded on nothing but shared human responses. Once he realizes this he will demand no further classification into kinds, to reassure him about the consistency of his tendency to respond to things in the same or different ways. This kind of tendency is all that you could ever have anyway, so even if things did divide into kinds at the natural, pre-evaluative level, so that we could see ourselves as having only shapely reactions, this offers no superior account of consistency – no underpinning for it, leaving it untainted by our bare natures.

But this cannot be McDowell's point! He cannot believe that Wittgenstein delivers one from the threat which shapelessness poses to a respectable notion of consistency. For in § 5 he presses exactly the same attack: he urges that a projective theory which tolerates shapelessness cannot regard evaluative assertions as making genuine judgment, because new evaluations could only be seen as 'going on in the same way' by a 'grotesque' error (p. 158). So although on p. 145 he writes as though it is pre-Wittgensteinian illusion which leads the unwary projectivist into thinking that attitudes must be shapely, throughout § 5 be himself endorses this thought. I suppose that he must have had some other problem for the projectivist in mind, but I do not know what it is. It would need to claim a projectivist cannot accept the Wittgensteinian thoughts about the sources of consistency lying in our own natures, whereas a realist can accept those thoughts. But there is no reason to believe this.

Myself, I believe that we do require a conception of 'going on in the same way' in ethics, not in the sense that we demand that all the things to which we have a given attitude form one kind, but in the sense that it worries us if we cannot draw distinctions when we react differently. I later give my own explanation of why this thought is proper to a Humean. But in any case I doubt whether the 'whirl of organism' explanation is at all adequate, because, as I argue in the next section, we can well fear that although we all naturally and unhesitatingly react alike to case A and case B, still we might be wrong to do so. This brings us to the positive theory which McDowell builds upon Wittgenstein's work.

II

When I was asked to reply in this symposium, I was aware of the colonial ambitions of the rule-following considerations, but I had thought that the territory of ethics was safe from annexation, for two important reasons. One is that the passages in Wittgenstein explicitly concern only cases where 'everything is a matter of course'; where 'disputes do not break out' (§ 240); where there is no element of inspiration or any 'hearkening' or special sensitivity. By contrast ethical evaluations or descriptions, and in particular 'hard cases', are often not at all a matter of course, do provoke disputes, and do involve questions of special sensitivity; indeed the hard cases in question could be defined as ones in which this is especially so. The whole stress in Wittgenstein is on the automatic and compelling nature of rule-following. The mental life of one who refuses to compute as we do after a standard training in arithmetic may be indescribable, and it may be quite literally unimaginable. But the mental life of one who parts company on a hard ethical case is usually all too imaginable, or at least we fail to imagine it only if we have had part of our natures amputated.

McDowell concedes that his application marks an extension of Wittgenstein's cases (note 14) – an extension from cases where we cannot really understand the hypothesis of a divergent practice to cases where we can. But this marks an extremely important divide. For it could be that we have some title to regard ourselves as thinking the truth when (as when we accept a proof) we can form no conception of what it would be to think differently. But it would not follow at all that we have the same title when we are all too aware of the possibility of thinking differently. I believe that some of John McDowell's views on virtue suggest that with increasing virtue comes an increasing approximation to the mathematical case, so that the virtuous man is eventually distinguished by a certain inability to see how reasonable men can differ. This, I must say, represents a value over which I find it hard to enthuse (Edward Heath is not everyone's cup of tea); but in any case, however it is with the virtuous man, with us who are less exalted there exists a lively sense of the objectivity of ethics alongside a lively awareness of alternative points of view. And this is not the case in Wittgenstein's examples.

Second, one of the essential possibilities for a moral thinker is that of self-criticism, and of the thought that our own culture and way of life leads us to corrupted judgment. We can think that evaluations which to us are routine and matter-of-course might be in principle capable of improvement. And it is not easy to see how this thought is to be construed if objectivity is somehow 'based on' consonance in a form of life. Wittgenstein's work has often been charged with leading to a kind of relativism (if it's your game then it's right for you), and especially if we extend his work to cases where we actually know of different systems of thought, it will be important to avoid the trap. I do not think this has been done: it seems to me that in McDowell's development there is no room for a concept of moral truth which allows that a man who dissents from the herd may yet be right.

We can come to see the difficulty by following McDowell's treatment of our thoughts about 'hard cases', where we have a conviction that we are right, and they are wrong, about some fine or disputed evaluation. I believe that it is fair to represent his views like this. There is a dilemma which is apt to grip us when we think about such cases. The dilemma is that either there must be a hard proof, forcing everyone to concede the correctness of one side and incorrectness of the other, or there can only be 'free creative decision'. However, this dilemma should only grip us if we fail to profit from Wittgenstein's rule-following considerations. These show us the way in which any rule-following has a consensual origin: they wean us from the idea that there are Platonic rails in the mind, laying down the way in which new cases must be described, and show us how simple consensus in new applications of terms amounts to the only or the fundamental reality underlying any process of judgment. Once this is appreciated we can see how to retain the conviction that, in a disputed case, just one side is right and the other wrong. In this way Wittgenstein can be used to give a foundation to a notion of ethical objectivity.

This is highly mysterious. Let us imagine a 'hard case': two groups (them and us) apparently use an expression with some evaluative component in fair agreement. But a case arises in which we are adamant that the word applies, and they are equally adamant that it does not. All efforts to find a hard proof, making them see that they must agree with us, or vice versa, fail. The problem is to avoid the conclusion that the matter is one of free creative decision. To put the same problem equivalently, it is to license the thought, which each group is likely to have, that there is a real truth of the matter – that they are wrong and we are right. I quite agree that this problem is fundamental to the metaphysics of ethics. I give my own solution of it below. But far from helping us towards a solution Wittgenstein's considerations point quite the other way. In so far as they are relevant, they provide reason for quite dismissing talk of one side being right and the other wrong; they force us to impale ourselves on McDowell's dilemma.

For Wittgenstein is taken to teach us that the judgment of inconsistency or blindness, which we each want to make of the other group, is really, somehow, consensual. Coming adrift, that is going wrong in a new application of an old term, is not a matter of jumping pre-existent Platonic rails determining which way one ought to go, for there can be no such things. It is a matter of getting out of step, of having an organism that whirls differently from the others. Suppose this is true. If that is the kind of way to see judgments of inconsistency and blindness, then it follows that they cannot be made when, as in the hard cases, there is no consensus to serve as a background upon which they are based. To take an analogy, being 'in step' in a marching body without an instructor is a matter of consensus: somebody can be judged out of step only in relation to a consensus stepping the other way. For just this reason it follows that there could be no sense to a dispute between two divergent halves of a body as to which one is really in step. Similarly an anthropocentric consensus founds judgments of consistency only if it exists, and *ex hypothesi* in the hard cases it does not: there are simply organisms which whirl one way and ones which whirl the other.

To put the point another way, suppose we grant that judgment grounded on the success of the appeal 'But don't you see?' is genuine judgment. Nothing *more grand* than this ever exists as a foundation for a notion of correctness in judgment. McDowell wishes to infer that something *less grand* does just as well – for in the hard cases the appeal is, *ex hypothesi*, not successful. But unfortunately it is wrong to infer, from the proposition that routine consensus is sufficient to justify the notion of correctness in new application of a term, the startling conclusion that correctness may exist even when consensus does not. Instead, as the anti-private-language use of his ideas shows, Wittgenstein regarded consensus as a necessary as well as perhaps sufficient foundation for the notion of correctness. So the only proper use of his teaching would conclude that it is an illusion that there is a real right or wrong answer when groups of organisms whirl differently. He drives us on to the first horn of the dilemma, since finding a hard proof would exactly be finding something which precludes anyone from whirling the other way, and only then does objective correctness make sense. If Wittgenstein leads us this way, however, he fails to allow for the possibility that goose-stepping along with everyone else can yet lead to moral error.

I can think of only two replies to this. One could be to deny the possibility of persistently hard cases. McDowell talks of us appealing to 'a hoped-for community of human response'. Now the open-ended nature of moral argument means that this hope is never entirely extinguished. But it can become quite unrealistic. The moral half-nelson forcing convergence on some issue may always be just around the corner, but experience teaches us that there are people who will just never see moral or aesthetic questions the way we do. Yet still we may properly retain the conviction that we are right and they are wrong. A related idea would be that the consensus on the *previous* judgments made with the disputed term is all that is needed for the generation of the idea of correctness. The lack of consensus on the new case does not undermine the notion of the objective correctness of just one side, because that notion is somehow extended on to it from our agreement in preceding or central cases. I get a vague sense that McDowell is manoeuvring towards this position from the end of his note 14. In any case, it will not do, for it amounts to saying that where there is correctness there is really a proof: there is no way of reconciling the divergence at this case with the practice exhibited in previous cases. If there is no such proof either way, then to see the previous practice as yet determining correctness for just one side, would be like seeing the practice of golf as determining the rules of tennis. In a hard case we come up against the fact that our form of life, our practices or whirls of organism, are flexible enough to be extended in either of two directions. Reference to their preceding shape is not enough for human beings to see only one way to extend them. It is precisely here that it is difficult, and essential, to give some sense to the thought that nevertheless one judgment may be right and the other wrong. But it is precisely this that Wittgenstein's discussion, taken in McDowell's way, forbids us to do.

III

I should now like to say how I think we should approach the issue of assessing a projective picture of morality. We should say: let us suppose that the picture is correct. Then how far can it go to capture the elements in our thinking about morality which at first sight seem explicable only on a realist metaphysic? The same question, it should be noticed, can be put for anti-realism about many other kinds of discourse, and the results achieved in one area (e.g. morality) can often be applied to others (e.g. the use of counterfactuals, or judgments of chance or cause). I now list a number of problems often alleged for the projective picture, and show how the 'quasi-realist' copes with them. I shall start with the problem which has loomed so large in the preceding section.

1   Moral judgments are not based on consensus in such a way that they cannot be turned on that consensus, and find it lacking. In this they differ from judgments of secondary properties, with which they are sometimes compared. If most of us come to taste phenol-thio-urea as bitter, then that is *what it is* for the stuff to

become bitter.[2] If most of us come to find wanton violence admirable, that is not what it is for wanton violence to become admirable: it is what it is for most of us to deteriorate, in a familiar and fearful way. How can we account for this notion of fallibility, on a projective picture?

On that picture a moral disposition or sensibility is a tendency to seek, wish for, admire, emulate, desire, things according to some other features which one believes them to possess. Such dispositions vary. Some, one admires. Some, one does not. One's own may well contain elements which seen in the open one would not admire. We don't *have* to be smug. We could learn that we come to admire things too often because of propensities which we regard as inferior: insensitivities, fears, blind traditions, failures of knowledge, imagination, sympathy. In this way we can turn our judgments on our own appetitive construction, and may find it lacking. The projection of this possibility is simply the expression of fallibility: I think that X is good, but I may be wrong. Thus a projectivist can go beyond saying of our moral sensibility that it might change, to saying that it might improve, and not only because of improving knowledge, but also because of improving reactions to whatever information we have.

The solution of McDowell's dilemma is then immediate. A decision in a hard case need never present itself as a free creative decision. For one may feel, and often should feel, that in letting a verdict fall some way one might be falling victim to an inferior determination of attitude – giving rein to tendencies which one would disavow, could one see them for what they are. Equally, even if the consensus of opinion agrees, we may all be treating alike the very cases which we should not: the herd may fail to mark the very divisions which it should.

This only comes as a surprise if people feel: surely the projectivist denies that there is a right and wrong way to 'spread' attitudes on the world – no ('real') truth or falsity to generate a standard of correctness. But the fallacy is clear. The projective theory indeed denies that the standard of correctness derives from conformity to an antecedent reality. It does not follow that there is no other source for it. And there is: to moralize at all involves commitment to some way of using an input of information to determine an output of reaction. And we are extremely sensitive (and surprisingly unanimous: the general character of the wise man is usually painted in the same way) to the features in such dispositions which we count as flaws and excellences. But we often do not know how much our own sensibilities betray such weaknesses, and how much our age and culture encourages dispositions which, could we see them, or could we improve upon them, we would be unable to endorse.

Of course, these evaluations of dispositions are themselves 'subjective': they are ours. But there is no circularity in using our own evaluations to enable us to assess, refine, improve upon, our own evaluations, any more than there is in rebuilding Neurath's boat at sea. Nor is anything given an axiomatic status (although, as I have remarked, our beliefs about what makes a good sensibility are often very firm): relying upon other planks we can criticize each plank in turn. A critic might say: 'But can you really say that someone who is satisfied with a differently shaped sensibility, giving him different evaluations, is *wrong*, on this theory?' The answer, of course, is that indeed I can. If his system is inferior, I will call it wrong, but not, of course, mean that it fails to conform to a cognized reality. But it ought to be changed, for the better.

Notice, too, how simply this theory explains the way in which other projections become objectified. We can say 'I fear that some of the things I (or we) find funny, are not really all that funny'. This need mark no error, no involvement with a prehistoric metaphysic of a world containing one real distribution of comedy.[3] It expresses a worry whether our reaction is a function of things we could endorse if we knew them, and we are often right to be so disturbed.

2   The next problem which threatens is indeterminacy. We have just seen the projectivist able to give sense to notions of improvement, refinement, and progress towards correct opinion. He can rule out some moral opinion as just wrong. But there is no particular reason for him to think that the core of attitudes which any admirable human being must share is sufficient to force improvement to tend towards just one limit. So aren't we really denying that there is a moral truth after all?

The problem was to give an account of those of our operations with a concept of moral truth which we cannot do without. But the idea that in the end of progress there should be just one package of attitudes and dispositions possible for the virtuous man is one which we can well do without. When there arise cases in which, in Hume's phrase, there is such divergence of opinion as is *'blameless on both sides'* we have indeterminacy. As we have seen, it is not inevitable that I immediately classify the man who diverges from me as victim of an inferior sensibility. For I may doubt my own, and I may be impressed by other evidence that his is as good as mine; experience may teach me that his is better, since as I improve I may find my judgment tending towards the ones he made all along. Such occasions give us opportunities for learning, whereas the existence of coarse or horrendous moral dispositions (the Nazi of endless examination papers) is philosophically quite uninteresting. This is also independent of the question which Williams takes to be important when we consider our reaction to a rival sensibility, namely whether it is a live option for *us* to actually come to share *their* views.[4] But I learn about, say, aesthetic truth when I learn that someone whose ear I cannot despise, whose discriminations are as fine as mine in other cases, whose acquaintance with music is as large or larger, actually likes Wagner, even if experience shows that it is not a live option for me to come to share his passion.

The image, then, is of a tree where the trunk represents a core of attitude which we regard as beyond discussion. To lack it is to be beyond the moral pale. The branching represents such divergence of opinion as is blameless on both sides. But in the actual practice of moral dispute, there is no decision procedure for telling whether one is at a node. In practice we must proceed as though there is a right answer (this is why 'relativism' is so grotesque), and often there will be one, for it will turn out that branching one way was inferior after all.

3   We now need to consider whether the theory of meaning to be associated with projections is adequate to the ways we actually use sentences expressing our opinions. In particular, we use them in indirect contexts, where they do not function to commit us to any attitude. When I say 'If kicking dogs is wrong, so is kicking cats' I do not express an attitude towards kicking dogs. So what is the sentence 'kicking dogs is wrong' doing in this context?

This popular problem has in fact an easy answer. Let us call sentences used as a projective theory claims ones which express *commitments*, as opposed to ones for which a simple realist theory of truth is appropriate, which we say express *judgments*. Now in using a conditional form we work out the implications of a certain supposition: we imagine a supposition added to our other stock of judgments and commitments (with minimum appropriate change) and express ourselves on the other changes it implies. So the question is whether the relevant notion of making a supposition is capacious enough to embrace both judgments and commitments. The idea that it is not arises from thinking of us as hypostatizing a state of affairs – the one making the antecedent true – and since the projectivist is supposed to be denying the existence of such a thing, he cannot cope. But there is no need for this picture. When we are committed to a notion of moralizing well or badly, as I have shown us to be, we need to work out the implications of commitments just as much as of judgments. In other words, we want to express ourselves on what else is involved if we make a certain commitment – we want to say things like 'You cannot commit yourself to that (have that attitude) without committing yourself to this other, or making this other judgment'. The hypothetical form shows us doing this. Often, but not always, it will itself show another moral commitment, because only from some moral perspective is it accepted that one attitude or commitment involves another. I agree that if kicking dogs is wrong, then so is kicking cats, because my attitude is that cats deserve as well as dogs. This means that we can smoothly explain how one conditional may embed in another, since in exactly the same way we might want to explore the implications of *that* commitment: 'If that's right', you might argumentatively challenge, 'stamping on ants must be wrong too'.[5]

Because I believe that quasi-realism is perfectly able to cope with indirect contexts, I don't wholly approve of the label 'non-cognitivism' for the metaphysics of the projectivist. Among the contexts which are explicable are 'I don't just believe that kicking dogs is wrong, I know it', or 'I believe that . . . but it would be presumptuous to claim to know it', or 'The trouble with moralists like them is that they treat all their opinions as knowledge'. We do not have to link the concept of knowledge with only those judgments which are read off from the world. We can quite well separate out, among our commitments, those of which we hold that no improved perspective yielding a revision is possible, from others. The former are those which we regard as being in the trunk of the tree: that kicking dogs is wrong is there, but that the government ought to spend more on philosophy is more marginal, while the trouble with lots of moralists is that they do indeed see all their opinions as immune to any possibility of improvement.

4   Delicacy in treating indirect contexts is also essential to handling the issue of the 'mind-dependence' of commitments on a projective picture. Thus, suppose a projective theory must involve us in believing things like 'If we had different attitudes it would not be wrong to kick dogs', or 'If we did not have the habits and expectations we do, trees would not cause shade'. Then clearly it is refuted, because these things are absurd. Fortunately, however, the projective account of indirect contexts shows quite clearly how to avoid them. The counterfactual 'If we had different attitudes it would not be wrong to kick dogs' expresses the moral view that the feature which makes it wrong to kick dogs is our reaction. But this is an absurd moral view, and not one to which a projectivist has the least inclination. Like anyone else he thinks that what makes it wrong to kick dogs is that it causes them pain. To put it another way: he approves of a moral disposition which, given this belief as an input, yields the reaction of disapproval as an output; he does not approve of one which needs belief about our attitudes as an input in order to yield the same output, and this is all that gets expression in the counterfactual.

A projectivist is only tangled in these unlovely counterfactuals if he makes the mistake of thinking that after all there is a state of affairs making the projected commitment true, only one about *us*. He must not think this, nor is there any reason for him to do so, provided he has a proper appreciation of the theory of meaning which must be attached to his metaphysic. To make an evaluative remark is to commit yourself, not to describe yourself, and to use an indirect context to describe the commitment is often to reveal further beliefs and commitments – such as the one about kicking dogs.

For semantics, it is going to be important to use the notions of truth and falsity in assessing commitments. Otherwise such things as a conjunction of which one part is moral and the other descriptive will not be understood as using the normal truth-functional conjunction, and this would be disastrous. But if we are wedded to the idea that interpretations should be specified for sentences, in a recursive theory of meaning, by describing situations in which the sentence is true, then quasi-realism offers no obstacle. The sentence '*a* is good' is indeed true, in English, if and only if *a* is good. That is, if and only if we are committed to the goodness of *a* will we allow that the English sentence is true. That is its rule of use. But saying this tells us nothing about the kind of commitment it is: it is quite irrelevant to the metaphysics.[6] The important task for the projectivist is to license the operations with the concept of truth which we go in for, and this I have tried to show him doing. He must also show how his conception of what is done by the sentences in question explains what is done when they are embedded, and this I have tried to start upon. The main problem recedes when we see that new sentences, resulting from putting evaluative sentences in conditionals, counterfactuals and so on, themselves express new commitments of the same sort (or of familiar sorts – they might be logically true or factually true) so that multiple embeddings will provide no problem.[7]

5 A final remark about consistency and shapelessness might help, if only to show how far we are from regarding uses of evaluative language as 'sorts of exclamation' or 'sounding off'. Why should a projective theory expect us to be worried if, for all we can show, we are reacting to like cases very differently? Shouldn't it be perfectly happy if our responses are not only rich and complicated, but also, for all we can tell, fickle? The answer to this takes us back to the first part of this section. I there pointed out our ability to step back from our moral sensibilities, to see whether we can endorse them or not and to worry about the kinds of function from belief to reaction that describes us. Now it is not at all surprising that a fickle function – one which has an apparently random element through time, or across similar cases – is one which we cannot readily endorse or identify with. Partly this is a question of the purpose of moralizing, which must at least partly be social. A fickle sensibility is going to be difficult to teach, and since it matters to me that others can come to share and endorse my moral outlook, I shall seek to render it consistent. But partly it arises simply from the value of justice. When I react to like cases differently I risk doing an injustice to the one which is admired the least, and one of our common values is that we should be able to defend ourselves against such a charge. This

requires an ability to mark the divisions. On the other hand, when we are rightly regarded as just 'sounding off' I take it that we don't much care about getting social agreement, and we might not much care about doing injustice ('I know I am being frightfully unjust but . . .'). We can do this, but we do not have to, and in serious evaluative practice we do not.

Of course, it is true that our reactions are 'simply felt' and, in a sense, not rationally explicable. But we should not be too worried about reason here. In general, reason follows where truth leads. Once we happily categorize certain moral judgments as true, we will conform to our general usage of the word 'reason' if we classify dispositions which tend to their acceptance as reasonable. A quasi-realist need not be frightened of the concept. He might, like Hume, prefer to reserve the term for dispositions to genuine, non-projected, judgment, and there would be a point in doing this, since we have quite enough invective at our disposal for people with horrid or queer desires. The areas where we are certain of our ways of achieving the truth are ones where we want to condemn variations as unreasonable and we are not often so certain in our evaluations. But I do not think there is any good way of defining a projectivist-descriptivist debate by calling on the concept of rationality or reason. The difficult concept for the projectivist to master is that of truth, and once that is done reason looks after itself.

IV

The successes of quasi-realism leave us with an acute problem of deciding whether there is a debate between realist and projective theories in an area, or whether we have no debate, but only pictures and metaphors, from which we can profit as we please. The most depressing conclusion (for surely it would be depressing to find that such a great and persistent debate has no method of conducting itself; that the philosophies of, say, Hume, or Kant, or Peirce, are not real philosophies at all) would be to see the debate as entirely empty. Someone with realist sentiments makes the world rich, and the interpreting mind lazy; someone with the opposite instincts makes the world poor, and the interpreting mind busy. The only sure way to decide would be to discover that our conception of a fact or state of affairs puts constraints upon judgment. If we could be sure that there could be no such thing as a moral, or conditional, or causal, or whatever, fact, then projectivism wins. Thus, I have argued elsewhere that it is difficult to give a satisfactory conception of a moral state of affairs, enabling it to relate in the right way to those natural facts upon which it is logically supervenient.[8] If such a kind of argument is possible, then one side may win. It is however here that the later Wittgenstein provides an obstacle, and I shall end by saying a little about how I regard the problem he seems to raise.

The debate between a realist and his opponent must arm itself with a conception of a fact or state of affairs which makes it significant to ask whether such things could exist, to make true the statements from some part of our discourse. But the later Wittgenstein must surely counsel us *not* to come to issues in philosophy with a preconception of some kind of thing which a fact must be, then to debate whether there are any of a certain sort. Rather, you look at the discourse first, and tailor the concept of truth to fit it afterwards. The mistake of the *Tractatus* is to insist *a priori* that the only states of affairs are arrangements of objects in a space – leaving no room for facts about agency, or the self, or morality, and so on. Seen in this spirit, the later Wittgenstein must lead us to conclude that there is no debate (and there may be other themes in his thought which tend to this conclusion too).[9]

But I was very struck, on reading McDowell's persuasive exposition of the 'rule-following considerations', by the extent to which they illustrate precisely the kind of argument which, on the above account, Wittgenstein would have us avoid. In fact, they conform very closely to a paradigm of that kind of argument, namely Hume's treatment of the concept of cause.[10] Causal powers were supposed to be items which relieve the vertigo we feel when we contemplate the continued order of the physical world. They are items which existing at one time yet cast their straightjacket over other times, guaranteeing continuation and order. According to Hume we cannot conceive of a state of affairs with this potency. This is not primarily an epistemological point, although he can add that the 'ground and nature' of confidence in powers is nothing else than confidence in the continued order of nature anyhow. But the primary worry is metaphysical, about the kind of fact we can conceive there to be, and the projective theory is a metaphysical solution to it. In Wittgenstein there can be no fact, such as the fact that a man has understood a term, or is obeying a rule, which relieves the vertigo we feel when we contemplate the continued order of his classifications. There is no fact which exists to make true any description of his past understanding or intentions, and which provides a logical standard of correctness for his future sayings. The only fact there turns out to be is one of a consensus in behaviour, and this is not quite what we expected. We wanted an 'act of meaning' which can anticipate reality (§ 188) just as before Hume we might have wanted a power to do so. But 'you have no model of this superlative fact' (§ 192). Furthermore the consequence is exceedingly close to Hume : 'it is not possible that there should have been only one occasion on which someone obeyed a rule' (§ 199). We were seduced into thinking that there was a 'superlative fact' of some sort, and there is none.

Now I do not primarily want to discuss whether Wittgenstein is right about this. But I do want to make two points. The first is that *if* he is right about it then he faces the paradox that language itself becomes impossible. In other words, we can become gripped by what I call a *wooden* picture of the use of language, according to which the only fact of the matter is that in certain situations people use words, perhaps with various feeling like 'that fits', and so on. This wooden picture makes no room for the further fact that in applying or witholding a word people may be conforming to a pre-existent rule. But just because of this, it seems to make no room for the idea that in using their words they are expressing judgments. Wittgenstein must have felt that publicity, the fact that others do just the same, was the magic ingredient turning the wooden picture into the full one. It is most obscure to me that it fills this role: a lot of wooden persons with propensities to make noises is just more of whatever one of them is. (Notice that Hume would have been quite happy with the parallel point about causes.)

Be that as it may, the more immediate point is that Wittgenstein is here quite blatantly doing what the official picture has him avoiding. He is attacking a certain conception of a fact: the fact that lies behind our use of words and directs it; the one which makes true the proposition that a man understands a word; the one which points beyond the present and constrains future applications; the essential thing which is only indicated by success with a word, and only 'guessed at' when we teach someone to understand a word (§ 210). So Wittgenstein cannot be hostile to a certain kind of anti-realism, or, at any rate, he cannot be hostile to a certain way of conducting the debate, for it is that which he himself is using. The anti-realist, too, charges his opponent with inventing a 'superlative fact' with various extravagant powers. He alleges that the realist conception of a moral fact, or causal fact, or whatever, is false, for the world could contain no such thing, just as Wittgenstein is arguing that the world could contain no such thing as a piece of understanding, on a traditional interpretation of it.

Still, it may be replied, Wittgenstein is not so much attacking the existence of certain facts – for otherwise he would be stuck with the consequence of the wooden picture, that judgment is impossible – but he is teaching us to see them rightly. Of course people follow rules, have flashes of understanding, and so on, and of course a man can go wrong in his applications of a term. It is just that the kind of fact which makes these things true is not what we thought it was, but is something to do with his agreement with social practice. So Wittgenstein must allow one kind of metaphysics – that which reinterprets the kind of state of affairs making certain judgments true or false – but it does not follow that he is ever sympathetic to a realist/anti-realist debate.

This is right, so far as it goes. But it means that Wittgenstein is a poor ally. For the kind of critique that he mounts, in favour of a reinterpretation of the kind of fact making a judgment true, might easily be powerful enough to make us think that no such reinterpretation could be successful: there will be nothing deserving the name of a fact or state of affairs which could do the job (if I am right that a lot of wooden people is just more of whatever one of them is, rule-following will be a case in point). In that case anti-realism will offer the only salvation. In fact, I am not sure that Wittgenstein would have denied this. For example, when he discusses the first-person he urges the view that sentences which certainly seem to be used to describe states of affairs are not to be regarded as doing so, but are really expressive in function. Thus 'I am in pain' should be seen as an utterance which expresses pain, rather than describes myself (I do not think this is plausible, actually). Again, he remarks 'My attitude towards him is an atti-

tude towards a soul. I am not of the *opinion* that he has a soul'
(p. 178). In such cases the fact that we have no 'model' for the
truth conditions of some remark is a sufficient motive for an
expressive or projective theory of it. So it is hard to see Wittgenstein as consistently hostile to the kind of debate we want.

If quasi-realism is successful, a projectivist has the right to think
of moral judgments as true or false, as reasonable or unreasonable, and so on. He can use the same evaluations of them that we
use of ordinary judgment, even saying that some of them correspond to the facts, represent how things are, accord with the
world – for all these are ways of endorsing such judgments. His
achievement was to derive our right to think of moral judgments
in this way, by showing how, in 'objectifying' our sentiments, we
commit no mistake but merely adopt a needed intellectual orien-
tation towards them. By expressing them in the same way that we
express ordinary beliefs we can reflect on our judgments and
conduct our debates, and there is no question in doing this of
succumbing to any illusion. I think this, too, is a conclusion broadly consonant with Wittgenstein's later thought. At least some of
his efforts seem to have been aimed at rescuing our right to think
of such things as truth, certainty and proof, whilst facing up to
the anthropocentric sources of our thought; the trouble is that he
never seems to have really dispelled the relativistic and sceptical
implications of this thought. But a more sympathetic reading
might well identify him as a protagonist of quasi-realism.

If there is no illusion in kidnapping 'cognitivist' terminology for
projected qualities, how should we think of the old debate? It
needs a shared conception of genuine judgment, genuine truth,
accessible to proof and understanding, so that intuitionists or
realists can say that evaluations fall within that area, and senti-
mentalists or projectivists can deny it. But if, without error, we
can see the notions as capacious enough to cover projections of
sentiment, then to whom should we award victory? It seems that
we could, after all, say that evaluations are judgments, are true
and false and rational, so that intuitionists won – yet it seems hard
to use the very successes of projectivists against it.

But this is too hasty. Although we have given the projectivist
the riches of ordinary evaluations of judgment, it does not follow
that all the attributes of traditional truths or states of affairs are
given to moral facts. Moral 'states of affairs', above all, play no

role in causing or explaining our attitudes, their convergences, their importance to us. They are constructs from our procedures, not their originators, their children, not their parents. The objectivist illusion was (and I fear still is) to think that mentioning a moral reality, and flattering our understandings of it, affords some explanation of our practices in evaluation and judgment. The realist has no explanation of our evaluations, and he has no explanation of the structure of moral truth – such things as supervenience simply become brute mysteries. His illusion was to think that he had a theory, that by citing moral reality he could do away with the need to earn the concepts associated with objectivity.

Morally I think we profit from the sentimentalist tradition by realizing that a training of the feelings rather than a cultivation of a mysterious ability to spot the immutable fittingnesses of things is the foundation of knowing how to live. Metaphysically we profit by seeing how much of the apparatus of objectivity can be acquired on slender means, by earning what is otherwise just handed out. There is virtue in this; one appreciates it more. One is less easily deluded about its relation to other things, such as consensuses of opinion. And one is less inclined to the guilt about possessing it, which issues in scepticism.

NOTES

1 I have tried to come at the theme in two other papers: 'Opinions and chances', in D. H. Mellor (ed.), *Prospects for Pragmatism, Essays in Honour of F. P. Ramsey*, Cambridge University Press, 1980; and 'Truth, realism and the regulation of theory', in *Midwest Studies in Philosophy, vol. V (Epistemology)*, Minnesota University Press, Morris, 1980.

2 The example is Jonathan Bennett's: 'Substance, reality and primary qualities', in C. B. Martin and D. M. Armstrong (eds), *Locke and Berkeley*, Macmillan, London, 1966.

3 I here dissent from John Mackie, who takes this kind of fact to indicate a mistaken metaphysics in ordinary thought. Cf. his *Ethics: Inventing Right and Wrong*, Penguin, Harmondsworth, 1977, pp. 30–5.

4 Bernard Williams, 'The truth in relativism', *Proceedings of the Aristotelian Society* (1974–5), p. 221ff.

5 I first gave this answer in 'Moral realism', in John Casey (ed.), *Morality and Moral Reasoning*, Methuen, London, 1971.

6 I have the impression that the opposite view is held by some of the followers of Tarski, but I do not know why.

7 In the background for this section is the theory of conditionals in general put forward by Ernest Adams and Stalnaker. The strictures of David Lewis ('Probabilities of conditionals and conditional probabilities', *Philosophical Review* (1976) can be met by prohibiting needless embeddings, I think. See Bas van Fraassen, 'Probabilities of conditionals', *Foundations of Probability Theory etc.*, 1 (1976). Stalnaker's theory is in 'Probability and conditionals', *Philosophy of Science* (1970); Adams's is in *The Logic of Conditionals*, Reidel, Dordrecht, 1975.

8 'Moral realism', *op. cit.*, part II.

9 Derek Bolton, *An Approach to Wittgenstein's Philosophy*, MacMillan, London, 1979, brings out this aspect of the difference between the early and late philosophies.

10 After I had noticed this and talked about it at the symposium, it was brought to my attention that Saul Kripke had drawn exactly the same parallel, in a lecture given in Ontario (1976) and Cambridge (1978). Rogert Fogelin also notices the parallel, in *Wittgenstein*, Arguments of the Philosophers, Routledge & Kegan Paul, London, 1976.

FOLLOWING A RULE AND THE SOCIAL SCIENCES

PART FOUR

FOLLOWING A RULE AND
THE SOCIAL SCIENCES

VII

UNDERSTANDING AND EXPLANATION IN THE *GEISTESWISSENSCHAFTEN*

Charles Taylor

The issue about rule-following and explanation in the sciences of man comes down, I think, to a question about the kind of understanding which is required for an adequate explanatory account. Winch[1] has used a Wittgensteinian 'rule-following' approach in order to plead for a social science which takes the descriptions of the actors themselves seriously. And this has been thought by critics to lead to a hopeless impasse, where we might be expected to frame our explanatory accounts in the language of the society we are studying – in the case of a primitive society, who have nothing like our practice of social explanation, this would be a near impossibility.

The issue that arises out of this, therefore, is whether or to what degree an insistence on our understanding what the actors are doing in their own terms must lead us to this impasse, which can be characterized by two related demands: (1) that the language of social explanation be, or at least include, that of the agents themselves, and (2) that the agents' self-understanding be regarded as incorrigible.

It is by no means clear that Winch himself lands in the impasse which accepting these two requirements constitutes. I think a careful analysis of what he writes leaves at least an open question. But this is the position which has come to be associated with his name in the discussion. In order to avoid invidious attributions, I'd like to call the position defined by accepting requirements 1 and 2 'vulgar Wittgensteinian' (or VW for short). This is also meant to duck the issue whether VW can properly be attributed to Ludwig Wittgenstein himself.

I

First, let's look at the case for demanding that we take account of the agents' own description. The issue could be put in this way: there is a kind of understanding which we could call 'human understanding', and which we invoke when we say things like: 'I find him incomprehensible'; 'At last I understand what makes him tick'; 'Now we understand each other'.[2] This is the kind of understanding which we have, or think we have, when we believe we understand someone as a human being.

We can perhaps get closer to seeing what is involved here if we reflect that understanding someone, in so far as we take it beyond the stage of pre-understanding, where we just know how to be on the same wavelength with him, in so far then as we try to formulate this understanding, involves being able to apply the desirability characterizations which define his world. I come to understand someone when I understand his emotions, his aspirations, what he finds admirable and contemptible, in himself and others, what he yearns for, what he loathes, etc. Being able to formulate this understanding is being able to apply correctly the desirability characterizations which he applies in the way that he applies them. If he admires integrated people, then understanding him requires that I be able to apply this concept 'integrated' in the sense it has for him.

I am talking here about explicit understanding, and therefore have been a bit too quick in the above paragraph. It could be that I understand him in the sense of pre-understanding, that is, I have a sense of what makes him tick, and he and I sense ourselves to be 'on the same wavelength' (*nous nous entendons*), although neither of us may have formulated some of the loves and hates, aspirations, admirabilia, etc., which are the basis for our mutual understanding. My claim is, however, that the explicit formulation of what I understand when I understand you requires my grasping the desirability characterizations that you self-clairvoyantly use, or else those which you would use if you had arrived at a more reflective formulation of your loves, hates, aspirations, admirabilia, etc.

Now thereby hangs a problem for science. The desirability characterizations we attach to actions to make ourselves more understandable, such as 'just', 'charitable', 'generous'; and those we apply to ways of life, such as 'integrated', 'fulfilled', 'dedicated', 'free from illusion'; and also negative ones, like 'fragmented', 'false', 'hollow', 'shallow', etc.; all of these pose two problems as candidates for scientific discourse as this is usually conceived.

First, they cannot be intersubjectively validated in an unproblematic way. Whether a way of life is truly integrated, or free from illusion, is a matter of potentially endless interpretive dispute. Moreover, we tend to believe that there are or may be certain moral pre-conditions, certain pre-conditions of character, for the successful discernment of these properties. We don't expect callow youth to have as good an eye for the life free from illusion as those who have grown wiser with age (a class which is not, of course, co-extensional with those who have aged). When it comes to understanding what a life of fine sensibility is, some people are distressingly philistine. And so on. Using this kind of concept, one cannot hope for replicable findings on the part of any scientifically competent observer. Or put another way, 'scientific competence' for terms of this kind would have to include certain developments of character and sensibility which themselves are only recognizable as such from the standpoint of those who have acquired them.

Closely connected with this vulnerability to interpretive challenge is a second feature: these terms are inextricable evaluative; and, what is more, they are what one could call strongly evaluative. I want to speak of strong evaluation when the goods putatively identified are not seen as constituted as good by the fact that we desire them, but rather are seen as normative for desire. That is, they are seen as goods which we ought to desire, even if we do not, goods such that we show ourselves up as inferior or bad by our not desiring them. Now along with unambiguous application, it is usually thought that the terms of a scientific discourse should offer a value-free account. And thus in this respect, too, the desirability characterizations whereby we understand people seem inappropriate for a science of society.

But then this brings us up against the issue usually associated with Winch. Suppose we are trying to give an account of a society very different from our own, say a primitive society. The society has (what we call) religious and magical practices. To understand them in the strong sense discussed above would require that we come to grasp how they use the key words in which they praise and blame, describe what they yearn for or seek, what they abhor and fear, etc. Understanding their religious practices would require that we come to understand what they see themselves as doing when they are carrying out the ritual we have provisionally identified as a 'sacrifice', what they seek after in the state we may provisionally identify as 'blessedness' or 'union with the spirits'. (Our provisional identifications, of course, just place their actions/ states in relation to our religious tradition, or ones familiar to us. If we stick with these, we may fall into the most distorted ethnocentric readings.) We have no way of knowing that we have managed to penetrate this world in this way short of finding that we are able to use their key words in the same way they do, and that means that we grasp their desirability characterizations.

But because applying any desirability characterizations has the twin difficulties mentioned above, it is naturally tempting to try to finesse this understanding. We can see this temptation at work in many of the theories adopted in social science. For instance, a case like the one we are examining here might tempt us to finesse understanding with a functionalist theory. We come at the society in question with some general thesis about religion, that religious practices perform certain functions in society, e.g. that they contribute to social integration. On the strength of this principle, we can perhaps dispense with an understanding of what the priest or medicine man is doing in the terms of his own society. One identification we have of this ritual activity is that it is part of a process which contributes to social integration. This may allow us to explain what is going on, for instance why rituals happen when they do, at the times of the year they do, or more frequently in periods of stress, etc. We may perhaps thus hope to dispense altogether with an understanding of ritual action in the agents' own terms.

This will seem the more plausible if we argue that the significance of a great many actions of people in any society escape their full consciousness or understanding. We cannot expect that the members of the tribe will have a clear grasp of the socially integrative nature of their religion as we do. Their understanding of this is, on the contrary, almost bound to be distorted, fragmentary, 'ideological'. Why should we pay any special attention to it, once we are on to a more satisfactory account of what is going on, which we now have, thanks to our functional theory? This course seems all the more evidently superior, since our theory is in a language of science, whereas the discourse of the tribe's self-understanding manifestly is not.

Now the Winch thesis is that the attempt to finesse understanding in this way is futile. It can only lead to sterility. I think this thesis is right. Perhaps the most economical way to present, or at least hint at, the argument for it is to look at the question of the validation of a functional theory. I want to follow the above example and discuss a functional theory, but I hope that it will appear that the argument applies to any attempt to finesse understanding through a putatively 'scientific' identification of the action of the subjects under study, where this be on the individual or the social level.

Consider the problem of validating a functional theory. Here a great many of the criticisms made of functionalism, even by other mainstream social scientists, can be shown, I think, to demonstrate rather the indispensability of understanding. Take the question of knowing how much you have explained. Even if a functional theory could get over the challenge of showing how it could be positively established, that is, of what can be said to make us believe it – and this is no small issue, because brute induction will not be decisive in this kind of case – the question can arise of how much we have explained. Let us say there is some truth in the claim that religions generally contribute to social integration; and that we can establish this. The question still arises of the significance of this finding. How much can we explain of the actual shape of the religious practice in this society by this functional theory?

It could be, for instance, that although religions are generally integrative, a very large number of possible religious practices could have done the job equally well in this society. In this case, our functional theory would do nothing to explain the kind of religion we see here, why there is this kind of ritual, that form of hierarchy, that type of fervour, those modes of blessedness, etc. In short, most of what we want to explain in a given society may lie outside the scope of the explanation; which may at the limit sink to the marginal significance of the background observation that disruptive religions tend to destroy the societies in which they take root, and hence flourishing religions tend not to be disruptive.

Even though we may show our theory to be true, in some senses, we may be challenged to show that it is significant. Does it explain something substantive about the religious forms of the society, or is it rather in the nature of a banal observation about the poor long-term prospects of disruptive religions?

The only way to meet this challenge is to take up the attempt to show how the detail of the religious form – the kind of ritual, the form of hierarchy, etc. – can be explained by the functional theory. We have a closely analogous case if we take historical materialism, which is very much like a functional theory – and indeed, is a functional theory, if we agree with G. A. Cohen's interpretation.[3] Historical materialism claims to be able to explain the evolution of the 'superstructure' of society, e.g. the political and religious forms, in terms of the evolution of the 'base', i.e. the relations of production. Sceptics of historical materialism have doubts precisely about the scope of what is to be explained by the relations of production. Can we really account for political and religious change in these terms? Marxists are thus challenged to explain precisely the detail of political and religious development: can one explain the rise of Protestantism? the differential spread of Lutheran and Calvinist theologies? and so on.

The challenge to explain detail is essential to the validation of this kind of theory. But it is a challenge which cannot be met, except by acquiring an adequate understanding (in our strong sense) of the actions, theologies, ideals, etc., which we are trying to explain. There is no way to finesse the requirement of understanding. Our Marxist or other historian convinces us he has explained the detail when he can give a convincing interpretation of it in his canonical terms. But to give a convincing interpretation, one has to show that one has understood what the agent is doing, feeling here. His action/feeling/aspirations/outlook in his terms constitutes our *explanandum*.

In the end, there is no way to finesse understanding if we are to give a convincing account of the explanatory significance of our theory. I hope it will be evident that this applies not only to functionalist theories, but to any attempt to identify what agents

are doing in 'scientific' language, be it that of holistic functionalism, or of individual utility-maximization, or whatever.

II

So the attempt to finesse understanding is futile. This is the Winch
thesis. Does it then land us in the VW? I believe not. But here is
where the issue has become bedevilled by multiple confusions,
and becomes difficult to disentangle. Certainly, if you ask most
graduate students (not to say teachers) working in the social
sciences or interested in its philosophy, you get a fairly widespread
consensus on what the options are (but disagreement on which to
take): either you buy a *Verstehen* approach at the cost of relativism
of the VW kind; or else you escape relativism by cleaving to
objective science at the expense of *Verstehen*.

I want to plead for a third approach. What this approach is
comes out best if we try to ask why pleading the importance of
understanding is widely thought to lead one inescapably into the
VW. This latter, it will be recalled, was characterized by two
claims:

1 The language of social explanation must be or include that
   of the agents themselves;
2 The agents' self-understanding is incorrigible.

Why should this be thought to follow from the thesis that the
agents' understanding cannot be finessed? Just because we cannot
do without their self-understanding, why do we have to give it the
centrality and incorrigibility that 1 and 2 demand?

This is the more surprising if we think of the argument sketched
in the previous section. There we came to the conclusion that we
have to master the agents' language of self-description and desirability characterization in order to identify the *explananda* that
our theory has to give an account of. Any functional theory, for
instance, can only demonstrate its scope by its explanation of the
detail of social practices, beliefs, etc.; and we need understanding
in order to identify what needs to be explained. But there is no
implication in this argument that the language of the agents' understanding must be part of the *explanans*, only that it is basis to

the *explanandum*. Why then see a plea for *Verstehen* as a plea for 1, which formulates precisely this implication?

I think the answer is something like this: the language of agents' understanding frequently has a number of embarrassing commitments implicit in it. The problem is how to use this language seriously, i.e. not just in an 'inverted commas' use, even if only to classify *explananda*, while remaining free of the commitments.

What are these commitments? A crucial part of the agents' language of self-understanding is his vocabulary of desirability characterizations, which he applies to actions, ways of life, situations, etc., in his world. These involve strong evaluations; that is, these evaluations are inextricably involved in the vocabulary. When I say 'inextricably involved' I mean that this vocabulary resists the kind of canonical transposition which a non-naturalist theory tries to put all value vocabulary through, where its 'descriptive' and 'evaluative' components are supposedly separated; so that we end up identifying neutral criteria for the application of the term, to which we have to add a colourless pro- or con-attitude in order to get the full sense of the term.

For when we look at the desirability characterizations of almost anyone's language, we see that this kind of split cannot be effected without distortion. Evaluation cannot be separated from description, because evaluations are criterially involved in the application of the important classificatory terms. An act isn't really an act of courage, unless the motive is not totally despicable. A life isn't integrated, unless there is some scope and larger purpose incorporated in it. We cannot hold that satisfying a given goal or aspiration is humanly fulfilling unless we defend the view that this goal or aspiration is of fundamental importance to us as humans. And so on.

The very application of this language involves thus assessing things by the standards of the implicit evaluations. The canonical transposition of non-naturalism can never pose as a translation of our ordinary language of desirability characterizations. Rather it is a revision, in the interests of a certain metaphysical view. The classificatory criteria for actions, feelings, etc., shorn of their evaluative force, are not the same criteria.

The language, then, has certain evaluative commitments. But these are in turn inseparable from certain ontological commitments. These will always typically concern the nature of human

motivation. For instance, when we hold a certain aspiration fulfilling, and thus defend the view that it is of fundamental importance for human beings, we are committing ourselves to an implied
hierarchical classification of human motivations; we are saying
something about what human beings are like. And this ought to
have repercussions on the way we attempt to explain what they
do.

But the commitments may also go beyond human motivation.
Say we are studying a religious way of life, in which there are
desirability characterizations like 'blessed', or 'close to God'.
These too will be applied on the basis of evaluations; and these
evaluations will carry ontological commitments. But they will include things beyond human nature; in this case, the existence of
God, or some gods.

Now if the language of self-understanding carries these commitments, then what are we meant to make of them when we use
this language to identify our *explananda*? What does the atheist
do in his study of the religious life-form? Now there is an unso-
phisticatedly realist answer to this question: the atheist doesn't
believe that there is a God; he therefore treats the agent's religious
activity as based on a misapprehension. But this doesn't make his
understanding of the agent's own language any the less vital to
the enterprise. On the contrary, to the extent that we see people's
behaviour as minimally rational, in one common sense of this
word 'rational', viz. as responding appropriately to what surrounds
them as they understand it, identifying the shape of their erroneous views is obviously essential to the task of explanation. A
trivial example should illustrate this general principle. I am throw-
ing a stick so that my dog will fetch it. I see him as seeking the
stick in order to retrieve it. The whereabouts of the stick play an
important role in controlling his behaviour; hence reference to
them plays a role in explaining this behaviour. Let's say by some
sleight of hand, I make him think I have thrown the stick over
the fence; he goes tearing around behind. Just to the extent that
his behaviour is to be explained in terms of the stick-whereabouts,
I cannot explain what he does on this occasion without identifying
the nature of his error.

Similarly when we explain the actions of people whose ontology
we do not share. Their language is full of value/ontological commitments which we consider wrong, or confused, or distorted, or

inadequate in some way. The world we see them acting in, the human nature they share with us, we see as different from how they conceive them. But in order to understand what they are doing, we have to get a grasp on their misapprehension, and thus we have to understand their language of self-understanding.

This simple realist construal gives an idea of how we can be committed strongly to the thesis that understanding is necessary for explanation, without in any way being involved in the VW position. For clearly, on this construal, we accept neither 1 or 2. The actual account of what they do will be in terms of our ontology, and we are precisely treating their understanding as highly corrigible; for we are claiming that it is wrong.

But we tend to be uncomfortable in this realist construal. It seems to involve us in saying that we are right and others are wrong. And quite apart from any such sin of arrogance, the implication of realism is that concerning strong evaluations, there is a fact of the matter. We are invited to take the language of people's desirability characterizations seriously, at least in this sense, that they are portrayals (or imply portrayals) of how things are with us (and possibly also with the universe, God, etc.). If the portrayals are wrong, then this will figure in our account as well. Thus we had our atheist student of the religious form treating the agents' belief in God as a misapprehension. The student who is a believer will treat it very differently; and he will return the compliment when studying the atheist's way of life.

On this view, the sciences of man are up to their neck in the business of adjudicating different conceptions of human nature (not to speak of the universe, God, etc.) which are bound up with different evaluations. This science would be anything but *wertfrei*. But the dominating scientific tradition of our civilization recoils away from such an adjudicating science; science is supposed to be *wertfrei*. There must thus be an alternative way of dealing with the value/ontological commitments of our languages of understanding.

The dominating approach takes as its principle:
3 Concerning strong evaluations, there is no truth of the matter.

It applies to the language of understanding the canonical transposition of non-naturalism; and sees the terms as applied on the basis of neutral, 'purely descriptive' criteria, while their application is accompanied by a pro-attitude. The pro-attitude, being just a stance towards the things in question, cannot be either true or false. In using the language to identify our *explananda*, we are in no way committed to the pro-attitudes which accompany this language in the agent's discourse. We are applying the terms by the underlying neutral criteria.

Science thus treats the evaluations as something irrelevant, concerning which it doesn't have to adjudicate. Adjudication by science isn't possible, since there is no truth of the matter. We neither have to affirm nor deny the ontological/value commitments of a given discourse of understanding, its evaluative construal of human nature, for instance. Rather, we treat these commitments as based on a confusion. There are in fact no commitments of this kind; rather the evaluative language expresses certain pro-attitudes, which are then confusedly reified as ontological commitments. And pro-attitudes are the kind of thing that we neither have to affirm or to deny *qua* scientists, however we may feel as human beings. Science can remain neutral on these matters.

In terms of our analogy of the dog chasing the stick, we say that the dog's erroneous views on the whereabouts of the stick were explanatorily crucial because the whereabouts of the stick is crucial. If we hold, as the realist view seems to, that there is such a thing as the correct evaluative construal of human nature, then we have to understand the erroneous views about it in order to explain what the agents holding them do. We have to take these views seriously as claims about what is. But if we hold that there is no truth of this matter, then we can ignore all such construals. Or rather, we shall see them as operative in our lives not as construals (as the dog's view on the whereabouts of the stick was operative precisely as a view on the whereabouts of the stick), i.e. not as views which can be true or false, but rather as pro-attitudes, self-given injunctions, emotive reactions, or whatever. We see them not as cognitions but as conations.

Let's call this approach the neutralist one. It corresponds to the mainstream scientific approach of our civilization. But it is incompatible with understanding. This for the reason mentioned above. The non-naturalist transposition is not a translation of the language of understanding, but a revision of it. If understanding people humanly is, or at least involves, coming to be able to apply

201

their language of self-understanding, including their desirability characterizations, then applying some canonically transposed language in which all the criteria of application of terms are neutral, i.e. don't involve evaluation, cannot amount to understanding. The 'cleaned-up', descriptive terms are not the same as those of the original, undivided language. They cannot even claim to offer us extensional equivalents, and they certainly don't carry the sense of the originals.

Thus this way of avoiding the value/ontological commitments of languages of understanding carries the price that we have to avoid languages of understanding as well. It's incompatible with the *Verstehen* thesis defended in the previous section. Those who espouse *Verstehen* and want to espouse 3 must look for another solution.

That is where, I suggest, the VW comes in. It offers such a solution. Unlike neutralism, it doesn't propose a canonical transposition of the language of understanding. We are able to take it with all its value implications, and its seeming commitments. It is essential for explaining what people are doing. But using this language doesn't for all that require that we take a stand on the implied value/ontological commitments; for once again there turn out not to be such commitments; or rather they do not take a form such that there could be controversy about them.

This is because the evaluations of a given language must be seen in the context of a form of life. And forms of life are not candidates for affirmation or denial; they are just how people in fact live. We can, of course, (sometimes) choose to live in this way or not. But forms of life are not the kinds of thing which can be right or wrong, veridical or illusory. Recognizing two mutually incompatible forms of life (that is, two forms which you couldn't live at the same time) is not the same as making two mutually incompatible affirmations.

Thus if we return to our example of the atheist studying the religious form of life, we can once more deny that this requires him to take a stand on the (apparent) value/ontological commitments of the language of understanding of the agents he is studying. They will understand themselves and others in such assertions as 'He is close to God', 'She is blessed'. Now if we take these as flatfooted assertions implying some disposition of things in the supernatural, as remarks like 'He is in bed', or 'She is at table', imply some disposition of furniture in the natural world, then we will be worried about whether things in the supernatural are really so or not. But this is the wrong way to take them, so the argument goes.

Rather we should see them as utterances which play an essential role in this way of life. We can see them as utterances which do something, produce some effect, e.g. like the conversation-opener: 'Fine weather we're having'. The truth value of this utterance is irrelevant; indeed, it often functions best when used ironically. It is one of the things we say in the course of a way of life in which we regularly relate through what we call conversation. Or again, we can see these as analogous to ritual utterances, like the performative: 'I give you the Queen', said by the toastmaster after the banquet. We would be very far from understanding this if we asked sceptical questions about what was said here, like 'Just how did he give her?' Once again, the point of this analogy is to focus our attention on what is being done with the words; what is being brought about inter- and intra-personally by asserting things like 'He is close to God'. Once we grasp this fully, we understand what this religious way of life is all about.

And once we have done this, it is alleged, the question about the truth or falsity of the implied ontological claims is somehow defused. They turn out not to be the point of this language. Asking after them shows a misunderstanding, analogous to that of our sceptic at the banquet who wondered how the Queen was given. We can't abstract ontological commitments from given utterances; we can only understand these utterances in the context of the whole form of life. The unit of judgment is thus the form of life. But a form of life is not something which can be veridical or illusory. It is just what we do (or they do).

Now the atheist by definition isn't living the religious life form. He can however come to understand it. This requires that he master the language through which it is carried on; that he learn how to apply such utterances as 'He is close to God'. But this doesn't require that he take a stand on some ontological/value commitments, that he judge them true or false. For a form of life can't be judged this way. It can be lived or not, but not affirmed true or denounced as false.

Now this is a *Verstehen* thesis which nevertheless accepts 3. It is a *Verstehen* thesis because it makes grasping the language of self-understanding essential for grasping a form of life. But at the same time, it defuses the issue of endorsing or rejecting the seeming ontological/value commitments; not in the way that the neutralist approach did, by offering a supposed translation into a neutral language. On the contrary, we cannot transpose the language of understanding into another medium; understanding a society requires that we understand the members' language. But we defuse the issue by seeing all the utterances as making sense only within the total form of life; and this we see as something on which we are not called upon to, indeed, cannot take a stand. The basic thesis underlying this view is:

4 Forms of life are incorrigible.

But this lands us in VW. From 4, follows 2. Individual agents may make a mistake in their self-understanding in the terms of their own society; but the language of self-understanding of a society must be understood as the way they sustain a form of life, which itself is incorrigible. So then is this language. Then 1 seems in danger of following too, since each society which has a different language will have a different form of life. These societies will be incomparable. We will not be able to understand them in some common explanatory language. Each will have to be understood in its own terms.

III

We are now perhaps in a position to answer the question posed at the beginning of the previous section: why do people think that accepting the *Verstehen* thesis lands you in VW? And the answer perhaps comes to light if we see the VW thesis as partly an attempt to combine *Verstehen* with 3. This 3 is a principle shared by both neutralism and VW. It is a very deeply held principle in our civilization. It fits with certain subjectivist views about ethics which are for many the easiest way of accounting for ethical pluralism; and it seems to avoid the kind of arrogance which claims that other views are misguided. VW fully satisfies this latter motive: it gives each way of life the legitimacy of the incorrigible. It is what (some) people do. So it is natural to assume that if the

Verstehen thesis is true, it must be true in the form which respects 3, viz. VW.

But this is a severe drawback for the *Verstehen* thesis, since 1 and 2 are hard to accept. The first seems to make scientific explanation very hard indeed; and leaves one quite unclear what to do when faced with a primitive society which hasn't yet developed a practice of explanation in anything like our sense. One needs to be able to draw relations of correspondence between descriptions in the agents' language of acts, feelings, beliefs, etc., and descriptions in ours, if we are ever to have a science of another society, and especially of a primitive society. But the principle that each form of life is *sui generis* seems to forbid this re-description in our terms. But being *sui generis* seems to be involved in the forms of life being incorrigible; for if we could re-describe what they are doing in our terms, then might we not have a case for saying that our description was more perspicuous, or more adequate than theirs? Then 2 would be breached, and, one could argue, 4 as well.

And 2 is pretty hard to believe as well. It seems to espouse an almost mind-numbing relativism.

So the *Verstehen* thesis defended in section I is in trouble. Because of its allegiance to 3, it finds itself taking the form of VW, and this is unacceptable. The solution is obviously, to drop 3, and hence escape from VW; to accept some variant of what I described as the realist position.

This doesn't need to be an arrogant and ethnocentric procedure. On the contrary, there is a form of realism which has learnt from VW, or perhaps from non-vulgar Wittgensteinianism. Because we take languages of understanding seriously in regard to their value/ontological commitments, we don't need automatically to assume that ours is correct in its commitments and that foreign languages are wrong. We can, on the contrary, start with the assumption that we may learn something more about ourselves as well in coming to understand another society.

Following this form of realism, the adequate language in which we can understand another society is not our language of understanding, or theirs, but rather what one could call a language of perspicuous contrast. This would be a language in which we could formulate both their way of life and ours as alternative possibilities in relation to some human constants at work in both. It would be a language in which the possible human variations would be so formulated that both our form of life and theirs could be perspicuously described as alternative such variations. Such a language of contrast might show their language of understanding to be distorted or inadequate in some respects, or it might show ours to be so (in which case, we might find that understanding them leads to an alteration of our self-understanding, and hence our form of life – a far from unknown process in history); or it might show both to be so.

This notion of a language of perspicuous contrast is obviously very close to Gadamer's conception of the 'fusion of horizons' and owes a great deal to it. An excellent example of an illuminating theory in comparative politics which uses such a language (or languages) is Montesquieu's. The contrast with despotism was, of course, not an unqualified success, because it wasn't based on a real understanding of the alien (Turkish or Persian) society. But Montesquieu's contrast between monarchy and republic brought about a great deal of understanding of modern society precisely by placing it relative to (at least the traditional image of) republican society in a language of perspicuous contrast.

This kind of realism clearly avoids the pitfalls of VW. Our account doesn't have to be in the language of understanding of the agents' society, but rather in the language of contrast. And the agents' language clearly is not taken as incorrigible. At the same time, we aren't committed to an ethnocentric course. This much has been learned from VW, that the other society may be incomprehensible in our terms, that is, in terms of our self-understanding.

This realism is superior also to neutralism. For it can accept the validity of the *Verstehen* thesis. In fact, neutralism, by claiming to avoid understanding, always ends up being unwittingly ethnocentric. The supposedly neutral terms in which other people's actions are identified – the functions of functional theory, or the maximization-descriptions of various consequentialist accounts of individual action – these all reflect the stress on instrumental reason in our civilization since the seventeenth century. To see them everywhere is really to distort the action, beliefs, etc., of alien societies in an ethnocentric way. A good example is the theory of development dominant until recently in American political science. This was based on the notion that certain functions were being performed by all political systems, only in different ways by different structures. But these functions, e.g. interest-aggregation and -articulation, are only clearly identifiable in our kind of society, where the political process is played out through the articulation of individual and group interests. This identification of functions presupposes a degree of individuation which is not present everywhere. The importance of understanding another people's language of self-understanding is precisely that it can protect us against this kind of ethnocentric projection.

We can see how the three approaches – neutralist, VW and realist – relate if we take a well-discussed example. This is the question of how to account for the exotic practices of primitive societies; for instance their magic. This is the issue taken up by Winch in his 'Understanding a primitive society'.[4]

Very crudely put, there are two families of positions on this issue. The traditional view of earlier Western anthropology, going back to Frazer, is to see magic as a kind of proto-science/technology, an attempt by primitive people to master their environment, to do what we do better by modern science and technology. This view naturally gave grounds for criticizing the factual views seen as implicit in the magical practices, the belief in magical powers and spirits. But, of course, the criticism was only of the factual claims; there was no claim to have disproved the values of these societies.

This view is naturally congenial to neutralists. It allows us a way of identifying what these people are doing, at least what general category their actions fit in, transculturally. At least to get this far we don't need to grasp their self-understanding in all its peculiarity.

In contrast to this, the rival view is influenced by VW or by other similar doctrines. It holds that identifying these practices as a proto-technology is an ethnocentric howler. Rather we have to understand what is going on here as a quite different practice, which may have no corresponding activity in our society. The various rituals of magic are thought to have a 'symbolic' or 'expressive' function, rather than being intended to get things done in the world. The tribe dances to recover its sense of the important meanings it lives by in face of the challenge of drought, rather than seeing the dance as a mechanism to bring on rain – the way we see seeding clouds for instance.

We can see that this view puts the magical practices beyond the strictures of modern science and technology. The tribe is not making a factual error about what causes precipitation, they are doing something quite different which cannot be judged in these terms; indeed, should not be judged at all, since this is just their form of life, the way that they face the human constants of birth, death, marriage, drought, plenty, etc. There may be nothing quite corresponding to it in our society. We have to understand it in its own terms; and it is the height of ethnocentric gaucherie to judge it in terms of one of our practices, which are all quite incommensurable with it. To come to grips with it we need understanding.

Now the realist view I'm defending here would disagree with both these approaches. Perhaps somewhat paradoxically, it would accuse both of them of sharing an ethnocentric assumption: that the tribe's practice must be *either* proto-science/technology *or* the integration of meaning through symbolism. For it is a signal feature of our civilization that we have separated these two, and sorted them out. Even our pre-modern forbears of four centuries ago might have found this a little difficult to understand. If we examine the dominant pre-seventeenth century world-views, such as the conceptions of the correspondences that were so important in the High Renaissance, it is clear that what we would consider two quite independent goals – understanding what reality is like, and putting ourselves in tune with it – were not separated, nor separable. For us, these are goals which we pursue respectively through science, and (for some of us perhaps) poetry, or music, or flights into the wilderness, or whatever.

But if you have a conception of man as rational animal as a being who can understand the rational order of things, and if (following Plato) we hold that understanding this order is necessarily loving it, hence being in tune with it; then it is not so clear how understanding the world and getting in tune with it can be separated. For the terms in which we get in tune with it, lay bare the meaning of things, must be those in which we understand it as rational order. And since it is rational order, these will be the most perspicuous terms of understanding. On the other side, to step beyond the conceptual limits of attunement to the world, to cease to see it as a rational order, to adopt, say, a Democritan perspective on it, must be to step beyond the conceptual limits of perspicuous understanding.

I am reminding us of this bit of our past only to illustrate what it can be like not to have sorted out two goals which we now consider quite distinct and incombinable. We do this because the seventeenth-century revolution in science involved, *inter alia*, sorting these out and rigorously separating them. This has been the basis for our spectacular progress in natural science of the last three centuries.

So a realist hypothesis I put forward is that the way to understand the magical practices of some primitive societies might be to see them not through the disjunction, either proto-technology or expressive activity, but rather as partaking of a mode of activity in which this kind of clear separation and segregation is not yet made. Now identifying these two possibilities: respectively, the fusion and the segregation of the cognitive-manipulative and the symbolic-integrative (to give them sonorous names), is an example of the finding of a language of perspicuous contrast. It is a language which enables us to give an account of the procedures of both societies in terms of the same cluster of possibilities.

Unlike the neutralist account, it doesn't involve projecting our own gamut of activities on to the agents of the other society. It allows for the fact that their range of activities may be crucially different from ours, that they may have activities which have no correspondent in ours; which in fact they turn out to do. But unlike the VW view, it doesn't just accept that their particular activities will be incommensurable with ours, and must somehow be understood on their own terms or not at all. On the contrary, it searches for a language of perspicuous contrast in which we can understand their practices in relation to ours.

This means that their self-understanding is not incorrigible. We avoid criticizing them on irrelevant grounds. We don't see them as just making a set of scientific/technological errors. But we can criticize them. For the separation perspective has *in certain respects* shown its undoubted superiority over the fusion perspective. It is infinitely superior for the understanding of the natural world. Our immense technological success is proof of this.[5] It may be that we are inferior to the primitives in other respects, e.g. our integration with our world, as some contemporaries would hold. But this is something which the language of contrast should help us to assess more clear-headedly. It certainly contributes to our understanding, whatever the verdict, because we can see how the modern scientific perspective is a historic achievement and not the perennial human mode of thought.

This example illustrates well how the *Verstehen* perspective, far from landing us in VW, necessarily pushes us on to a new form of realism. You haven't really understood a primitive society until you've understood yourself better as well, through a language of perspicuous contrast.

NOTES

1 Cf. Peter Winch, *The Idea of a Social Science*, Routledge & Kegan Paul, London, 1958.
2 The use is even more prominent in other languages: 'maintenant on s'entend' gives just the sense I'm getting at here.
3 *Karl Marx's Theory of History*, Oxford University Press, 1978.
4 *American Philosophical Quarterly*, 1 (1964).
5 I haven't got space here to answer the (ultimately misguided) Feyerabendian objections to this claim.

VIII

REPLY: EVALUATIVE 'REALISM' AND INTERPRETATION[1]

Philip Pettit

In his paper on 'Understanding and Explanation in the *Geistes-wissenschaften*' Charles Taylor is principally concerned to argue that if one is a non-relativist, and what I call a humanist, then one must adopt a realist position on values. Taylor takes his claim to be important in the philosophy of social science because he has a subsidiary argument to the effect that if one adopts a realist position on values then one must view social science, so far as it is concerned with explaining what people do and say, as value-laden. Being himself a non-relativist and a humanist he espouses a realism about values and embraces a conception of social science as evaluatively committed and critical.

In this response to Taylor I wish mainly to play analyst, looking at realism about values and its connection to value-ladenness, but also to play ally, drawing out some implications of a value-laden picture of social science, specifically in regard to cross-cultural understanding. In the first section I offer a general account of realism and anti-realism, distinguishing between the different interpretative strategies recommended by anti-realism. In the second I describe how the issue between realism and anti-realism arises in connection with values and I draw a distinction between what I call prescriptive realism and evaluative realism; I suggest that our concern is with evaluative realism, presenting and endorsing Taylor's subsidiary argument to the effect that such realism would entail value-ladenness. In the third section I characterize evaluative anti-realism and I work out the sense which ought to be given to the opposed doctrine of evaluative realism. In the fourth section I turn to the claim in Taylor's principal argument, that humanism and non-relativism jointly entail evaluative realism, and I try to show that while it needs strengthening and supplementation the argument is not without plausibility. Finally in the fifth section I speculate on the concrete significance of evaluative realism for social science, and in particular for cross-cultural understanding; my remarks on this matter will suffer from lack of detail but I hope that their drift will not be unclear.

I

The issue between realism and anti-realism is whether or not it is epistemologically scandalous so to interpret a class of assertions that something like the following result goes through: that an assertion is capable of being true or false even when the appropriate evidence for or against it is unavailable in principle. (This has to be slightly qualified to cover the redescriptivism discussed later.) The realist, to put the matter intuitively, is not averse to ascribing to the assertions a subject-matter of such a relatively inaccessible kind that the result follows. The subject-matter is thought of as capable of determining the truth-value of an assertion, even if evidence is lacking to determine its assertibility value. If the subject-matter is identified with the truth-condition of the statement, then the truth-condition is represented as something which is capable of obtaining (not obtaining), even when we cannot tell that it obtains (does not obtain): that is to say, even when the assertibility condition is not realized (even when the counter-assertibility condition is not realized). The realist may stop short of proclaiming the principle of bivalence according to which, however things stand with its assertibility, every statement is true or false. But what he does say is something closely connected, being a claim which the principle would support.[2]

Understood in this way, the issue between realism and anti-realism is primarily an epistemological one. Specifically, it has to do with whether in interpreting assertions, and in particular in assigning a subject matter to them, one may neglect a strong verificationist constraint. The realist will naturally admit certain epistemological constraints on interpretation. He will be as ready as anyone, for example, to ridicule an account of what speakers say that depicts them as holding forth on matters with which the evidence prompting their utterances has no connection. Again he will be as liable as anyone to insist that speakers must be acquainted with some instances, or at least analogues, of what it is for those things to obtain which they are interpreted as asserting to obtain. Where he breaks with the anti-realist is in rejecting the verificationist constraint, that assertions should not be so interpreted that the capacity of a statement to be true or false comes apart from our ability to judge which it is.

It is worth commenting, in parenthesis, on why the constraint mentions 'our ability', rather than 'the ability of the speakers'. A constraint involving the latter phrase might seem to outlaw an interpretation according to which members of a geographically isolated tribe were speaking in certain utterances of places that they imagined to exist far away: it would be beyond their ability to judge whether any such assertions were true or false. Typically however the anti-realist would not wish to proscribe a construal of this kind, since geographical isolation is a contingent fact about the speakers. What he is anxious to rule out are interpretations which sever truth-conditions from assertibility conditions on the basis of less changeable characteristics. Thus, whereas he could tolerate the idea that the subject-matter of certain assertions was geographically beyond the ken of the speakers, he might baulk at the thought that it was historically inaccessible, being in the remote past, or psychologically inaccessible, being in another mind. The disposition of the anti-realist in these regards is usefully marked by speaking of our ability rather than that of the speakers in formulating his preferred constraint. What the anti-realist wishes to rule out is this possibility: that even if we were in the position of the speakers, and were possessed of as much evidence as is compatible with that position, we should not be able to tell whether those truth-conditions obtain that are ascribed to the speakers' assertions. And how is the position of the speakers identified? That depends on the sort of assertions in question. It is identified by reference to historical position for statements about the past, by reference to psychological position for statements about other minds, and so on for the other kinds of assertion which typically engage anti-realists.[3]

As we understand it, the issue between realism and anti-realism

213

is a general epistemological one. However it is with respect to specific classes of assertion that battle is usually joined between the doctrines. They engage with one another for example over statements about the past, statements about other minds, physical object statements, theoretical statements in science, unrestricted generalizations, modal statements and statements ascribing values. The realist who defends his general position in respect of any such specific body of discourse will argue for a line of interpretation which entails that truth value may be determinate when assertibility value is not. The anti-realist will argue in every case for a pattern of interpretation which evades this result. Where the realist is drawn into dispute, the reason will be that he regards the line of interpretation which he favours, offensive though it may be to a verificationist mentality, as the only faithful rendering of what speakers say in making the statements in question. Thus his line of interpretation will be what we might call a literal or standard one. On the other hand the pattern of construal which the anti-realist urges will be more or less revisionary or non-standard being motivated by epistemological scruple rather than concern for accurate representation of what, intuitively, is said in the statements.

What sorts of interpretation are available to the anti-realist in dealing with those classes of statement which can be construed in a standard manner only at the cost of breaking the verificationist constraint? We can distinguish three main varieties of interpretation to which he may help himself, though the list is not necessarily exhaustive. These I describe respectively as instrumentalism, reductivism and redescriptivism. The three patterns of construal are in some degree non-standard, though the first is probably more so than the second and both the first and second are certainly more so than the third.[4]

With any problematic set of assertions the instrumentalist says that they are not to be seen as answerable either to truth-conditions or to assertibility conditions. Far from the assertions' having an offensively inaccessible subject-matter such as the standard interpretation would ascribe, the instrumentalist denies that they have any subject-matter at all. He says that each assertion in the class or at least each troublesome assertion, should be interpreted as an utterance the significance of which has in no way to do with anything that is said to be so, but consists exclusively in the effect with which the utterance is typically made. Thus the assertions are assimilated to non-assertoric speech-acts such as questions, commands, wishes, and the like. There may be standards determining when they are rightly or wrongly made – assertibility conditions, in a loose sense of the phrase – but these are not evidential constraints: they are like the standards by which a command is judged to be acceptable or a question is judged to be relevant.

On at least one version of the approach, someone who says that theoretical statements are merely engines of prediction, or that laws are merely inference tickets, is cleaving to an instrumentalist line, representing such assertions as akin to 'Expect or infer such and such in situations so-and-so'. So also perhaps is someone who is of a more fictionalist bent, and takes theoretical statements to be as-if assertions which do not say that such-and-such, but rather that it is as if such-and-such. Again someone who takes a so-called ascriptivist view of psychological statements is an instrumentalist in our sense. He says that to assert that a person acted voluntarily, for example, is not to report on any condition in the world, whether a condition of truth or an assertibility condition, but merely to effect something: to make an utterance akin to 'Let him be held praiseworthy or blameworthy for what he did, depending on how his action is viewed'.[5] Finally a certain sort of language-game enthusiast may be represented as an instrumentalist. He says of a problematic set of assertions, and perhaps of all assertions, that their significance is summed up in the use that they have in various language-games: and this in a way that renders vain the idea that there is anything which the statements assert to be so. (This line is close to what Charles Taylor calls 'vulgar Wittgensteinianism'.)

The second variety of interpretation available to the anti-realist is a reductivist one, although reductivism, like instrumentalism, may be defended for other than anti-realist reasons. The reductivist agrees with the realist that the statements with which he is concerned have a subject-matter; indeed he takes this feature to be part of what distinguishes assertoric utterances from non-assertoric ones. What he argues is that the subject-matter is not offensively inaccessible. He holds that, however the subject-matter is read, each assertion in the relevant class that is true (false) reduces to an appropriately assessable statement, or set of statements, of evidence. More specifically, each such assertion is said to be true (false) if and only if a corresponding statement of evidence can be defended; or, more simply, is true.

A reductivist interpretation may or may not be definitional: it may or may not claim that what is meant by the original statements is what is meant by the corresponding statements of evidence. Whether or not it is definitional, it may or may not be exhaustive. It is exhaustive if all the original assertions are held to be true or false, so that they each reduce to a statement of evidence. It is non-exhaustive if some statements are held not to be reducible to statements of evidence, and are not said either to be true or to be false: in this case they may be held to be meaningless, as logical positivists would have had them; they may be said not to have any truth-value; or judgment may simply be suspended in their regard. Examples of reductivism abound in the philosophical literature. Phenomenalism offers a reductivist thesis in respect of physical object statements, positivism (of the non-instrumentalistic sort) in respect of theoretical statements, and behaviourism in respect of statements of psychology.[6]

The third pattern of interpretation to which the anti-realist may have recourse is what I call the redescriptivist one. Redescriptivism rejects the reductivist claim that for every assertion in a problematic set, which has a determinate truth-value, there is a statement or set of statements of evidence with which it stands or falls: that is, to which it is bound by a formula of the kind ' "S" is true (false) if and only if E', where 'S' is the original assertion and 'E' is the evidence statement. On the other hand redescriptivism insists against realism that for every such assertion, it must at least be the case that we can say what a grasp of the truth-condition consists in. What is required is that for every problematic assertion there should be 'criteria' of truth and falsity, in what is often said to be Wittgenstein's sense of that term. The criteria are not linked to the assertion as tightly as the reductivist's statement or set of statements of evidence, since they are defeasible: they are allowed not to be sure-fire guarantees of truth and falsity. However, they are held to be intimately connected with the assertion, for it is in an understanding of them that a grasp of the assertion's truth-condition is said to consist.[7]

It may be useful to put rediscriptivism on a map of anti-realist options. Faced with assertions whose literal construal would offend against the constraint to which he is committed, the anti-realist may deny that they have any truth-conditions (instrumentalism), or he may deny that the truth-conditions of the determinate assertions among them are inaccessible, reducing the assertions to statements of evidence (reductivism). What now appears is that there is at least one further option available: the anti-realist may ascribe truth-conditions to some or all of the assertions, and he may admit that they are strictly inaccessible, revealing his anti-realism only in the insistence that for any such assertion it must be clear what it is that counts as seeing that the truth-condition is realized or not realized. This further option is redescriptivism. It means redescribing what it is to assent to, or dissent from, any statement which is judged to have an inaccessible truth-condition; hence the name that I give to it. With an assertion such as 'John is in pain' the redescriptivist who takes this to be true, and who sees it as involving an inaccessible truth-condition, will feel obliged to characterize what it is, in practical terms, to believe such a proposition: what attitudes it is to strike, what expectations it is to form, what commitments it is to make, and so on.

Redescriptivism marks a nice middle position between instrumentalism and reductivism. The redescription which it counsels may be expected to look very like the account offered by one sort of instrumentalist, the language-game enthusiast, of what it is to understand a problematic statement. On the other hand the redescription is meant to serve the role for which the reductivist's reduction was designed; it is meant to show why it is reasonable to ascribe a determinate truth-value to an assertion which on a standard reading would break the verificationist constraint. Like reductivism, redescriptivism may be definitional or not: it may or it may not claim that in explicating what it is to grasp the truth-condition of an assertion it is setting out what the assertion means. Again the redescriptivism may or may not be exhaustive. It is exhaustive if it takes every statement in a problematic set to be subject to an appropraite redescription, and to be capable therefore of having a truth-value. It is non-exhaustive if it says that some statements resist redescription and refuses to assume that they are true or false.

We have seen that the issue between realism and anti-realism has to do with the appropriateness of imposing a certain verificationist constraint on the interpretation of assertions, and that, where realism would counsel a standard line of interpretation in defiance of the constraint, anti-realism would prescribe a non-standard pattern of construal, whether instrumentalist, reductivist or redescriptivist. At this point we are ready to turn to the question of what it means to be realist or anti-realist about ascriptions of value. Before we do so, however, it may be worthwhile mentioning that to be a realist in the sense characterized here is not necessarily to be a realist in either of two other common uses of the term.

On the first of these uses, to be a realist is to believe that a theory within a given body of discourse might uniquely satisfy all the evidential constraints conceivable and yet fail to be true; it is to hold that the connection between assertibility and truth is entirely contingent.[8] A realist in our sense need have no truck with this doctrine since he is free to say that although certain assertions do not reduce to, or are not redescriptively responsive to, corresponding statements of evidence, their being interpreted as they are presupposes that those statements express the appropriate evidential constraints. We need not seriously entertain the possibility that one might interpret a theory in a manner linked with the assumption that certain evidential constraints are appropriate, and yet in face of the perfect fulfilment of those constraints consider that the theory might be false; to consider that the theory might be false in such a case would be by the same stroke to put in doubt the assumed interpretation of the theory: that, or to evince standard sceptical misgivings. Thus if our realist has the interpretation of a class of assertions turn on the assumption that certain evidential constraints are appropriate, he need not be drawn into realism in the further sense envisaged here. It may be noticed in passing that when we spoke earlier of the epistemological constraints which the realist is likely to acknowledge, we suggested that he would have interpretation turn on just such an assumption. The thought was put negatively and minimally when we said that the realist is as liable as anyone to ridicule an account of what speakers say that depicts them as holding forth on matters with which the evidence prompting their utterances has no connection.

On a second common use of the term, over and beyond the use to which we have put it, to be a realist is to claim that if certain statements are true in the strict sense then the entities to which they refer and the properties which they ascribe are discernible from points of view other than that of a person making the statements. This claim would restrict the items about which it made sense to be realist to purely objective ones; it would close the possibility that they might yet be subjective, in the sense of being available to view only from a particular perspective.[9] Once isolated, the thesis can be seen to be nothing more than a dogma, since while we must naturally require that what is acknowledged from any point of view should be compatible with what is acknowledged from others, there is no reason why it should have to be capable of being discerned from other points of view. We must be careful not to burden our realist with an unnecessary and undefended proposition.

II

Let us turn then to what realism about the ascription of values would mean. The first question to ask is: what body of statements is encompassed in the class of value-ascriptions? If we restrict ourselves to statements bearing more or less directly on action it appears that we are concerned with judgments on particular classes or instances of action which are non-contingently reason-giving. Each judgment has the characteristic that if it is accepted by an agent in a circumstance where it bears on an option before him then it gives him a reason for taking or rejecting that option: and this, not just contingently on other things being true of the agent such as that he has some specific desires. That the judgment gives the agent a reason for acting in a certain way does not mean that he inevitably acts in that way of course; other judgments that he also accepts may counsel a different line. The only test that the judgment provides the appropriate reason is that the agent's accepting it would be taken as an intelligible explanation of his acting appropriately: and this, without the postulation of special desires or whatever in the agent.[10]

By the account just offered the value ascriptions with which we are concerned apparently cover judgments like the following:

A 1 What John did was kind (cruel);
   2 James's offer was thoughtful (thoughtless);

3 That was a generous (mean) thing to do;
4 The swim was enjoyable (unenjoyable);
5 What Mary did was what was (less than) best;

These are value ascriptions in respect of actual instances of action which seem to be such that had the agent accepted that they would be true before acting in his chosen fashion, he would have had reason to act or not to act as he did: and this, independently of what else was true of him.

At the other end of the spectrum from particular to general, our value ascriptions must cover judgments such as:

B 1 Helping others is fulfilling (frustrating);
  2 Squash is fun (a bore);
  3 One ought (not) to take regular exercise;
  4 It is (not) good to spend some time alone each day;
  5 Abortion on request must (not) be allowed under any circumstances.

These value ascriptions bear on classes rather than instances of action, but they appear to share the characteristic of being non-contingently reason-giving with our earlier examples.

Finally we have equal reason to count as value ascriptions judgments which are made from the agent's point of view prior to acting and which, although they seem at first sight to bear on particular actions, must actually be construed as being about classes. The agent reflects positively or negatively on his doing such-and-such where that to which he is ascribing value is not a particular action – none has yet occurred to have value ascribed to it – but any action contemplated by him which will be a case of his doing such-and-such. Thus we have:

C 1 Going for a walk will relieve (worsen) my distress;
  2 Speaking to John will clear the air (only confuse things);
  3 I ought (not) to answer Mary's letter;
  4 It would (not) be pleasant to have a chat with James;
  5 I must (not) do such a thing.

Do the statements exemplified in our three lists constitute a sufficiently homogeneous class for us sensibly to raise the realism versus anti-realism issue in their regard? I do not think so, for the reason that they contain two relevantly distinct sub-classes, the one of which I will describe as evaluations, the other as prescriptions. The first four examples in each list may be taken as evaluations; the last in each list is a prescription. The difference between the two classes of value statement is that whereas prescriptions present the courses of action on which they bear as, all things considered, what must be done or avoided, evaluations depict the corresponding projects only as *prima facie* desirable or undesirable. The prescription depicts a particular action, or any action of a certain class, as good or bad *simpliciter*, the evaluation pictures it as good or bad *secundum quid*, good or bad in a certain respect.[11]

Whether a value statement is an evaluation or a prescription is sometimes, but not always, clear from its linguistic form. Statements which employ concepts such as 'is kind', 'is generous', 'is fun', are reasonably taken as always just evaluations: they specify a respect in which an action is desirable or undesirable without suggesting that the action is so *simpliciter*. On the other hand statements which say that an action represents the best course possible, that it is absolutely obligatory, or that it must be done, certainly have the force of prescriptions: the comment they make on the action is not relative to a particular respect but is taken to carry under any description of the behaviour. However between these two clear-cut classes we find value ascriptions which do not show in their linguistic form whether they are evaluations or prescriptions. These are statements which use such evaluative notions as 'good' and 'bad', 'right' and 'wrong', 'ought', and 'ought not', and so on. The trouble with them is that it is not clear just from the words used whether what is characterized in one of these terms is said to be unconditionally desirable or undesirable, or desirable or undesirable only in a certain respect. 'Good' may mean 'good absolutely' or only 'good as such', and so on for the other terms.[12]

There are two useful tests for deciding whether an ambiguous value ascription is a prescription or an evaluation. The first has to do with the connection between the ascription and action. With a prescription the failure of an agent to act in accordance with it counts as powerful evidence against his having endorsed the judgment in the first place. Even if he publicly claimed to endorse the judgment, his behavioural failure will give us reason to think that he was insincere or self-deceived; if it does not lead us to that conclusion, this will be because we accept some special explanation of the failure in terms of weakness of the will or psychological incapacity. With an evaluation, on the other hand, it is more or less unsurprising that an agent who accepts it should still fail to act accordingly. Since the evaluation bears on an action only under a particular aspect, we can understand why it should fail to move the agent: we naturally take it that other aspects of the action engaged contrary evaluations in the agent and that these prevailed over the original one in question.

The second test for whether an ambiguous value statement is a prescription or an evaluation has to do with the effect of what we may call internal negation: this involves putting a 'not' before a value predicate such as 'good' or after a value expression such as 'ought', as distinct from negating the statement as a whole, say by the use of a prefix such as 'It is not the case that . . .'. To negate a proposition as a whole is always to produce a statement which is inconsistent with it, assuming that the meaning of the terms within the proposition remains the same. The difference in the effect of internal negation on prescriptive and evaluative statements using ambiguous value concepts is that in the first case it produces an incompatible statement, in the second it does not. The reason for the difference is that if the prescription says that an action is good *simpliciter* then a statement which says that it is not good *simpliciter* is bound to be incompatible with the original, whereas if the evaluation says that it is good *secundum quid*, i.e. in a certain respect, then a statement which says that it is not good *secundum quid* need not conflict with the first claim, the respect in which it is said not to be good being a different one. Thus it cannot be at once that I must take a certain line of action and that I must not take it, while it may be that one and the same project can be said to be good and not good, something that I ought to do and something I ought not to do.[13]

Because of the deep-running difference between them there is no reason to think that the realism debate must be settled in a similar fashion for evaluations and prescriptions. There is a parallel between evaluations and prescriptions on the one hand and singular perceptual reports and lawlike generalizations on the other, a parallel which suggests that one may be a realist on evaluations without being a realist on prescriptions, even if the converse is not true. As evaluations provide the agent with

222

grounds for making a prescription and acting in accordance with it, so singular perceptual reports supply the theorist with grounds for forming a lawlike generalization and predicting along the lines that it suggests. Of course the prescription may not be made explicitly, the evaluations leading directly to action, but something similar holds here too, since perceptual reports may lead directly to prediction, the appropriate generalization not being explicitly spelled out. The importance of the parallel is the suggestion it encourages: that where reports underdetermine the generalization that is extracted from them, so evaluations may underdetermine the prescription that they are invoked to support. If the suggestion goes through then it will follow that as it would make sense to be a realist about perceptual reports while going for anti-realism on laws, so it would be coherent to be a realist on evaluations while espousing anti-realism on prescriptions.

Which sort of realism about values are we concerned with in our debate? If the parallel just drawn is valid, this question comes down to the following. Would evaluative realism be sufficient to entail the value-ladenness of social science, or is prescriptive realism also required? My answer is that evaluative realism would indeed be sufficient for the job. A reason for saying so is provided by Charles Taylor in his argument that if one adopts a realist position on values, then one must view social science as evaluatively committed.

The first and crucial premise of Taylor's argument is summed up in this passage:

> understanding someone, in so far as we take it beyond the
> stage of pre-understanding, where we just know how to be on
> the same wavelength with him, in so far then as we try to
> formulate this understanding, involves being able to apply the
> desirability characterizations which define his world. I come to
> understand someone when I understand his emotions, his
> aspirations, what he finds admirable and contemptible, in
> himself and others, what he yearns for, what he loathes, etc.
> Being able to formulate this understanding is being able to
> apply correctly the desirability characterizations which he
> applies in the way that he applies them. If he admires
> integrated people, then understanding him requires that I be

able to apply this concept 'integrated' in the sense it has for him (p. 192).

The desirability characterization is a value ascription in respect of an instance or class of action such that we do not have to be told other facts about an agent in order to understand why he finds it reason-giving, granted that he takes it to bear on an option before him. More specifically, since this is only to say that it belongs with our three lists of examples, the desirability characterization is an evaluative, as distinct from prescriptive, pronouncement. It ascribes a *prima facie* value to a course of action which would make it intelligible that someone would follow that course but which is consistent with his not doing so, since other *prima facie* values may outweigh its effect.

The other premises in Taylor's argument may be set out more briefly:

2 Social science involves such understanding as is mentioned in premise 1;
3 Evaluative realism would mean that in seeking this understanding of others one should be prepared to discover that their desirability characterizations are false;
4 Evaluative realism would therefore mean that in pursuing social science one should be prepared to assess one's subjects' evaluations negatively;
5 To be thus prepared would be to renounce one aspect of the value-freedom of social science: specifically, its neutrality (see section V below);
6 Evaluative realism therefore would make social science value-laden.

Of the premises in the argument only the first and second require any defence: the others merely spell out what evaluative realism and value-ladenness mean. The second premise will be considered later in another connection, and may be allowed to pass. The first premise, on the other hand, is an empirically plausible claim. It appears that we do indeed rely on desirability characterizations in coming to a certain sort of understanding of other people, and even of ourselves. We may therefore embrace the conclusion that evaluative realism would make it impossible to hold that social science was value-free.

The immediate relevance of Taylor's argument for us is that it yields an answer to the question posed a little while ago. We asked whether evaluative realism was sufficient to make social science value-laden or whether prescriptive realism was also necessary. We now have our answer. In what follows we need concern ourselves only with the case for evaluative realism since our focus is the value-ladenness thesis. What we shall do in the final two sections is first to look at the argument for evaluative realism, considering in particular the case made for it by Charles Taylor, and then to tease out some implications of evaluative realism for social science, especially cross-cultural understanding. Before coming to those sections, however, it will be useful to look in some detail at what it may mean to be an evaluative realist or anti-realist.

III

In order to be an evaluative anti-realist one has to be disposed to give positive answers to the following four questions:

1 Construed standardly, are utterances such as A 1–4, B 1–4 and C 1–4 evaluations? In particular, are they non-contingently reason-giving when understood in the ordinary way: do they offer grounds for action independently of any contingent facts about the agent who is guided by them?

2 Construed standardly, are such evaluations assertions? That is to say, are they appropriate subjects for the ascription of truth and falsehood, or do they resist such ascription in the manner of questions and commands?

3 Construed standardly, do such evaluative assertions offend against the verificationist constraint which the anti-realist wishes to impose on interpretation? In other words, does the standard construal assign such evidence and truth-conditions to them that we must countenance the possibility that an evaluation is true (false), even when we cannot tell whether the truth condition obtains (does not obtain), the evidence pro (con) being unavailable?

4 Does the offence mentioned under 3 count as an objection against the literal construal of evaluative utterances? Does

it counsel the need for a revisionary interpretation which will not transgress against the verificationist constraint?

One can readily understand why the evaluative anti-realist answers questions 1 and 2 affirmatively: in our ordinary practice, where we display the construals that we spontaneously make, we do treat evaluations as reason-giving for anyone, regardless of the contingencies of his desires or needs or whatever; and we do take evaluations as the sort of utterances that may be true or false. It is not so clear on the other hand why the anti-realist should give a positive answer to question 3. Why should anyone think that judgments about generosity or kindness, or about goodness or rightness in some respect, should ever elude us, the appropriate evidence pro or con not always being available? The case contrasts with that of judgments about the past or about other minds, judgments which are often implicated in evaluative ones, where we can see how the notion of inaccessibility gets a grip. Indeed it contrasts also with that of prescriptive value judgments, since the evaluative evidence underlying prescriptions is sometimes conflicting and indecisive.[14] Perhaps the only reason why one might be tempted to give an affirmative answer to the third question is that one thinks that no judgment with a reason-giving force, other than a judgment about states of desire or need, or about the prospects of satisfying those states, can be empirically supported: the thought is not particularly intuitive but it does connect with the common prejudice that values are not facts, or at least not empirical facts. But in any case, granted that the evaluative anti-realist answers question 3 affirmatively, it will be clear why he also gives a positive response to question 4, demanding that a revisionary analysis be found for evaluative utterances. Here at last his verificationist constraint is engaged and it forces him to reject the standard construals described in his answers to the first three questions.

So much for the motivation of evaluative anti-realism.[15] But what now are the strategies of interpretation that the anti-realist may recommend in place of the literal one? The established alternatives, as we have seen, are instrumentalism, reductivism and redescriptivism. All of these, applied to evaluations, are premised on the assumption that on the matter raised in the first question the standard construal is right: the examples we gave are indeed cases of evaluations, in particular cases of non-contingently reason-giving utterances. The instrumentalist line would break with the standard construal on the matter raised in the second question: it would deny to evaluations the status of assertions. The reductivist and redescriptivist approaches would delay the break until the matter raised in the third question comes up: they would allow that evaluations are assertions but would take them in such a way that the verificationist constraint is not offended.

A quick review of these strategies may be useful. An instrumentalist theory of evaluative assertions would assimilate them to non-assertoric speech-acts, denying any subject-matter or truth-value to them. It would characterize the assertions as linguistic acts whose whole significance is to be analysed in terms of the effects they are typically used to bring about. It might take an emotivist or a prescriptivist form, or the form of a language-game thesis associated with what Taylor describes as vulgar Wittgensteinianism. Thus 'Squash is fun' might be represented suggestively as 'Squash: wow!' or 'Play squash!' or 'Squash-is-fun', where the latter is a move in a language game which puts the utterer in the position of having to explain himself if he fails to play squash himself, or at least to enthuse over it.

The second established strategy available to the evaluative anti-realist is the reductivist one. A reductivist approach would characterize a set of evidence statements suitable for evaluations and would say that any evaluation that is strictly assessable reduces to a corresponding evidence statement. What examples can be given of such a reductivist analysis? Subjectivism is one form, or cluster of forms, that the doctrine might take: it would say that to evaluate is always in some manner to record an attitude, positive or negative, which is felt in respect of the item evaluated. Another form is the variety of utilitarianism which would reduce every assessable evaluation to a report on the felicific or non-felicific tendency of the matter under discussion. And still other examples can be constructed out of the many traditional equations that have been imposed on the concept of goodness: the equation with what is willed by the majority, the equation with what is in the public interest, the equation with what is laid down by some authority, and so on.[16]

The third established strategy available to the evaluative anti-realist would seem to be the redescriptivist one. To be a redescriptivist with respect to a class of assertions is to deny that the truth-condition of each assessable assertion can be reduced to a statement or statements of evidence but to hold by the weaker claim that for every assessable assertion there must be a set of defeasible criteria, such that a grasp of the truth-condition of that assertion can be identified with an understanding of those criteria. The redescriptivist option is designed for assertions whose truth-conditions, standardly construed, clearly transcend available evidence, as do the standard truth-conditions of many statements about the past and many statements about other minds. That being so, the option does not fit evaluative statements in any natural fashion, for as between those who dispute the interpretation of such assertions there is insufficient agreement on the relevant truth-conditions and evidence to make it the case that the truth-conditions, standardly construed, clearly transcend available evidence. Thus it is not surprising to find that none of the established non-standard analyses of evaluative statements fits the bill for a redescriptivist construal.

Of the established strategies of revisionary interpretation it would seem then that the evaluative anti-realist may adopt either instrumentalism or reductivism. But we said earlier that each of these is premised on the assumption that our examples of evaluations really are such, in particular that they are non-contingently reason-giving utterances. Instrumentalism and reductivism agree with the standard construal on this issue, which is raised in the first of our questions above; instrumentalism then breaks with the standard line of construal on the matter raised in the second question, reductivism on the matter raised in the third. What we now have to recognize is that the evaluative anti-realist may break with the standard construal on the issue raised in the first question, thus opening up another possibility of revisionary analysis. Such an anti-realist will deny that utterances like those in our examples are reason-giving on their own; he will say that they are so only when supplemented with appropriate injunctions or only when understood on the assumption of certain desires or needs.

This possibility of interpretation can be developed in various forms, but we may consider just one central paradigm: the form it takes in the two-components analysis of R. M. Hare.[17] According to this theory, which we might call reductivism-cum-instrumentalism, every evaluation should be broken down into two components: the one component is a descriptive statement assigning the item evaluated to some readily detectable class; the other is a prescription in respect of that item: a recommendation that it be embraced or eschewed. Thus 'Squash is fun' would break down into a statement assigning squash to the class of activities which are fun and a positive prescription in respect of the game. This doctrine involves the claim that an evaluative predicate such as 'is fun' works at one level in a purely descriptive fashion, so that in principle it might be reduced to a non-evaluative correlate, while serving at a second level to express a prescriptive intention on the part of the utterer.

We have seen that the evaluative anti-realist may adopt an instrumentalist, a reductivist or an instrumentalist-cum-reductivist line of analysis with evaluations. These interpretations may be adopted for reasons other than the anti-realist's concern, but such a concern is standardly satisfied by recourse to one of them. In conclusion it may be worth commenting on what it means to be an evaluative realist. In the strict sense of the term it would be to adopt a position contrary to that of the anti-realist, giving a positive answer to each of the first three questions and a negative answer to the fourth. However that position is scarcely a fetching one since if the third question is answered positively on the grounds that there is no empirical evidence available for or against evaluations, it is hard to see how the standard construal can be upheld: that construal would now seem to break not just the verificationist constraint but also the less contentious condition that speakers should be acquainted with some instances, or at least analogues, of what it is for those things to obtain which they are construed as asserting to obtain. The only recourse for the strict realist would be to involve non-empirical intuition as a source of evidence or evaluative matters but he would have to deny that such intuition works in every case since otherwise one may wonder why the third question is answered affirmatively.

In established usage, as it happens, and certainly in the usage adopted by Charles Taylor, evaluative realism has come to have a looser sense: a sense in which it is a rather more plausible doctrine. The term has come to denote, not a doctrine opposed to anti-realism by virtue of its answer to the fourth question, but one opposed to it at the next possible juncture: that is, by virtue of its answer to the third question. In this loose sense, the evaluative realist is someone who maintains that, standardly construed, evaluations are non-contingently reason-giving; that they are assertions capable of being true or false; but that they are bound by such ubiquitous evidential constraints that the possibility does not arise that their truth-conditions should come apart from their assertibility conditions. Maintaining this, of course, it is also assumed that the evaluative realist sees no reason to revise the standard construal of evaluations and that he takes this pattern of construal to differ from analyses such as the instrumentalist, the reductivist and the instrumentalist-cum-reductivist.

In what follows evaluative realism is understood in the sense just characterized, and not in the stricter sense that it ought to have. The point should be emphasized, for otherwise misunderstanding is inevitable. It should be noted in particular that someone who is an anti-realist on the general epistemological principle, and who embraces the verificationist constraint on interpretation, can still endorse the sort of evaluative realism in question. The doctrine is not so much contrary to evaluative anti-realism as contradictory of it: what it involves is the denial of the anti-realist doctrine rather than the devising of an alternative. In contradicting evaluative anti-realism it does so by arguing that the verificationist constraint is not engaged by evaluations, thus allowing someone to maintain allegiance to that constraint in other contexts. Properly speaking we should not refer to it as evaluative realism but rather as a sort of evaluative anti-anti-realism. However we may be pardoned an ambiguity which allows us to avoid such a barbarism.[18]

IV

In this section our concern is with the case that can be made for evaluative realism, in particular the case which Charles Taylor makes for it. As summarized in my introduction, Taylor's argument is that if one is a non-relativist and a humanist, then one is bound in consistency to adopt a realist position on evaluations. The evaluations that he has in mind are desirability characterizations: these are action relevant evaluations of just the kind that we focused on in the last section. In order to understand the argument we must see what is claimed in the non-relativist and humanist premises, and we must be shown how those premises work to rule out the possibility of evaluative anti-realism, whether in the form of instrumentalism, reductivism or reductivism-cum-instrumentalism. What follows is a charitable charting of the argument, something which should not be mistaken for a whole-hearted endorsement.

'Humanism' is my term, not Taylor's; he speaks instead of the *Verstehen* thesis. What it comes to is the claim (a) that there is something distinctive about the form of understanding that we seek with human beings, a form of understanding that involves us in seeing things from their point of view; and (b) that this form of understanding is indispensable in the sense that it cannot be displaced by a supposedly scientific account of the things that people do. This doctrine is one for which I have argued elsewhere and I will not go through my defence of it here.[19] However, we may just mention the grounds cited in its support by Taylor.

What makes orthodox agent understanding distinctive in his view is first that it resists easy intersubjective validation, and second that it employs inextricably evaluative terminology, making sense of action by depicting it as the pursuit of something that we acknowledge to be desirable (pp. 192–5). He argues on the other hand that the reason this understanding is indispensable is that it cannot be bypassed by a supposedly scientific account, since any such account must rely on it for a characterization of what it seeks to explain (pp. 193–7). Thus in order for a functionalist account of a religious practice to get going it must assume an interpretation, in orthodox terms, of what it is that the people are doing in conforming with that practice.

Non-relativism, Taylor's other premise, is roughly the doctrine that across societies we can still manage to make some assessments of rationality and truth. Many refinements are needed in the proper formulation of the theory but they are not material to our concerns in this paper. Taylor envisages the theory as the negation of the extreme position that he describes in this passage:

Individual agents may make a mistake in their self-understanding in the terms of their own society; but the language of self-understanding of a society must be understood as the way they sustain a form of life, which itself is incorrigible. So then is this language . . . These societies

231

will be incomparable. We will not be able to understand them in some common explanatory language. Each will have to be understood in its own terms (p. 204).

And what has Taylor to say in defence of his non-relativism? He does not provide an argument in its support, and neither will we try to fill the gap. However, he offers the observation which we may well share, that the relativism he means to reject is 'mind-numbing' (p. 205).

Suppose then that we accept both non-relativism and humanism. How are these doctrines meant to force us towards what we describe as evaluative realism? Taylor's line, which is not altogether explicit, is to take the various forms of evaluative anti-realism and to show that each of them is incompatible with one or other of the doctrines. He uses non-relativism to dispense with instrumentalism, or at least with one form of instrumentalism, and he invokes humanism to dismiss reductivism and reductivism-cum-instrumentalism. Thus he argues by elimination for the literal analysis that realism would uphold, though he does nothing to make this analysis proof against objections.

To take instrumentalism first, Taylor considers this theory in its vulgar Wittgensteinian form, as the claim that evaluations are moves in a certain sort of language-game, which do not raise any issue of truth or falsity. His objection to the approach is that in relativizing evaluations to the language-game, and ultimately the form of life, within which they are enunciated, this sort of instrumentalism leads directly to the relativism that he describes as mind-numbing.

> Forms of life are not candidates for affirmation or denial; they are just how people in fact live. We can, of course, (sometimes) choose to live in this way or not. But forms of life are not the kinds of thing which can be right or wrong, veridical or illusory. Recognizing two incompatible forms of life (that is, two forms which you couldn't live at the same time) is not the same as making two mutually incompatible affirmations (p. 202).

We may reasonably complain that Taylor's charge of relativism is aimed only at one form of evaluative instrumentalism, and that it is not in any case very effective, since no argument has been provided to show that relativism is untenable. Both complaints can be stilled, even if full satisfaction is not yet obtained, by the observation that Taylor's line of attack is but a particular instance of a familiar and not disreputable argument against certain ethical theories. The argument is that people dispute about evaluations and that any analysis which would make evaluative disputes unintelligible is obviously inadequate.[20] This argument may be detected in the background of Taylor's charge, since the problem with relativism is precisely that it undermines the possibility of rational agreement or disagreement. Unlike the relativism charge, however, it clearly applies not just to vulgar Wittgensteinianism, but to any form of evaluative instrumentalism. If evaluations fail of being true or false and come out as being merely prescriptions, or expressions of feeling, or moves in a language-game, then the instrumentalist does indeed have to explain what it is that people do when they dispute about them. I do not say that there is no response that the instrumentalist can make to this challenge but I do think that the challenge identifies a *prima facie* difficulty for his analysis.

So much for the argument against evaluative instrumentalism. As for Taylor's line against reductivism and reductivism-cum-instrumentalism, here he invokes his humanism to do the work which he used his non-relativism to do in the earlier case. He does not distinguish explicitly between the pure and mixed varieties of evaluative reductivism, and what he says in criticism of them is sometimes said with one doctrine in mind, and sometimes with another. The criticism is summed up in the following passage in which he rails against the project of reducing the evaluative predicates of a language to non-evaluative ones for which the rules of application are clear and uncontentious.

> If understanding people humanly is, or at least involves, coming to be able to apply their language of self-understanding, including their desirability characterizations, then applying some canonically transposed language in which all the criteria of application of terms are neutral, i.e. don't involve evaluation, cannot amount to understanding. The 'cleaned up', descriptive terms are not the same as those of the original, undivided language. They cannot even claim to

offer us extensional equivalents, and they certainly don't carry the sense of the originals (pp. 201–2).

There are probably two distinct lines of thought in this passage, and more generally in Taylor's article. The first, less obvious one is that a reduction of evaluative predicates to non-evaluative ones is bound to prevent our understanding the behaviour of the person using the evaluative ones, since it will not let us see why the agent pursues things he evaluates in one way, and avoids things he evaluates in another. Here the idea is that any attempt to represent evaluative pronouncements as merely descriptive ones is certain to block the orthodox understanding of the speaker, hiding as it must the connection between those pronouncements and the actions he undertakes.

The other, more central line of thought in Taylor's passage is expressed elsewhere in his paper as follows:

> Evaluation cannot be separated from description, because evaluations are criterially involved in the application of the important classificatory terms. Any act isn't really an act of courage, unless the motive is not totally despicable. A life isn't really integrated, unless there is some scope and larger purpose incorporated in it (p. 198).

What is suggested now is that a reduction of evaluative predicates to non-evaluative ones is bound to prevent our understanding why a speaker applies the terms to such-and-such things, and not to others. The idea is that an essential component in grasping where the predicates should be applied is an insight into the evaluative or reason-giving significance of the terms. The thought is one which John McDowell endorses when he dismisses the following possibility, in which an outside interpreter is envisaged as understanding in reductive fashion a term of moral approval used by the community he is studying:

> one could know which actions the term would be applied to, so as to be able to predict applications and withholdings of it in new cases, not merely without oneself sharing the community's admiration (there need be no difficulty about that) but without even embarking on an attempt to make sense of their admiration.[21]

234

What scope do Taylor's lines of thought have as criticisms of evaluative anti-realism? The first line has very little scope, since the predicates to which anti-realists try to reduce evaluative predicates are usually such as to let us understand the responses of speakers to the things of which they use them. Pure reductivism typically casts positively evaluative terms as ways of reporting states of desire or need, or prospects of satisfying such states, and it is quite intelligible that speakers should respond positively to things of which such reducing correlates hold; this is so whether the states are their own, or their community's, or belong to some authority that they acknowledge. Mixed reductivism on the other hand evades altogether the criticism in the first line of thought: it is guaranteed that speakers will respond appropriately to what they evaluate, since the evaluations are depicted as being not just descriptive of the things evaluated, but also as being prescriptive of the corresponding responses. Probably the only doctrine which would fall to the criticism in question is one that reduced evaluative predicates to descriptive terms lacking all reason-giving character.

Taylor's second line of thought, and that which he more clearly wishes to sponsor, does better than the first in engaging the two sorts of evaluative reductivism. A mixed reductivism is committed to the idea that we should be able to understand where a speaker applies a certain evaluative predicate just by associating with the predicate a term with no reason-giving significance. Equally, a pure reductivism claims that we can grasp the speaker's pattern of application of the predicate by seeing that he uses it of all those things, and only those things, of which he registers approval, or in which he sees the prospect of happiness, or which he takes to be authoritatively prescribed, or whatever.

How persuasive then is the charge brought against the reductivist doctrines? Well, so far as some instances of reductivism are concerned, it is certainly not implausible. The onus would seem to be on the reductivist to show that the possibility described in the quotation from McDowell is a real one. Moreover, the work required of him would seem to be overwhelming in the case of the reductions envisaged by the mixed reductivist, or by the reductivist who makes some sort of authority the touchstone of evaluation. The claim that we can grasp the pattern in a speaker's use of an evaluative predicate just by reference to such reductions

235

is a very strong thesis, and at first glance an extremely suspect one. Short of the claim's being substantiated in detailed examples, we must surely see little reason to believe that it is true. Thus so far as the forms of reductivism in question go, we may reasonably rest unpersuaded.

Does Taylor's line of thought carry against such forms of pure reductivism as reduce evaluations to reports of subjective attitude, or expressions of felicific tendency? It would seem to be more reasonable to hold that reductions of this kind might faithfully represent a speaker's pattern of use with an evaluative predicate. While we might expect the application of an evaluative term to come apart from the application of a purely descriptive one, it is not implausible that it should keep in line with the application of a term recording subjective attitude or felicific tendency. The reason, intuitively, is that what we feel subjectively approved or disapproved, what we find productive or disruptive of happiness, is just what we evaluate positively or negatively.

This comment however reveals the weakness in any reductivism of the kind in question. If we cannot establish what someone feels approval of, or finds the prospect of happiness in, independently of seeing that he attaches a certain positively evaluative predicate to it, then we cannot hope usefully to reduce the predicate to a term recording the attitude or the prospect. Perhaps the only reason that the reductions under discussion are resistant to Taylor's charge is that they are not really reductions, but merely reformulations, of the terms they bear on. An anti-realist is free to claim that in principle an independent characterization is available of what it is for an action to be approved of, or to be productive of happiness, and that such a characterization would rescue the corresponding reduction from triviality. That claim must appear to us as a dogma however; certainly it offers slender ground for thinking that the literal interpretation of evaluations is misconceived.[22]

This completes our consideration of what there is to be said in favour of evaluative realism. Appropriately strengthened and supplemented, it seems that Taylor's argument against the three forms of evaluative anti-realism is not without a certain weight. When we remember that evaluations have the appearance of assertions which are capable of being true or false, and of being true or false in a way that does not obviously reduce to the truth or

236

falsity of putative statements of evidence, we realize that the onus is on the anti-realist to show that some non-literal reading of the utterances is the compelling one. That being where the burden of proof lies, Taylor's argument may reasonably persuade us to remain faithful to the literal interpretation of evaluations, and in that sense to profess evaluative realism.

V

Let us suppose that the case for evaluative realism has been made out. In conclusion I would like to consider where such realism would lead us in the attempt to understand people in other cultures. Taylor's principal claim is that if we are realists then when we find ourselves in conflict with the evaluative characterizations offered or assumed by such agents in legitimation of their actions, we must take a hard line and recognize that there is a fact of the matter at issue; we must refuse the easy relativist option of rendering the conflict as a difference of taste or style. This does not mean for Taylor that we must end up denying everything asserted by the agents that is incompatible with our evaluative beliefs. He has interesting and persuasive things to say, in the spirit of Gadamer's 'fusion of horizons', about the extent to which our own beliefs may be seen in different perspective, and even altered, by the experience of the conflict. What I would like to examine in this final section is precisely the sort of evaluative conflict that is liable to arise in cross-cultural interpretation, and the extent to which it is sharpened by realism; the conflict is of a kind that is not unknown in interpretation within our own culture, but it is more pervasive and problematic in the cross-cultural case.

As evaluative realists, we would naturally take that line with evaluative beliefs which is already found natural with non-evaluative ones. To the extent that we find ourselves able to ascribe divergent non-evaluative beliefs to people in another culture, we may expect also to be able to ascribe divergent evaluative ones. And how far does this ability go? Considered abstractly, it might seem that there is no limit, but limits quickly loom when the question is posed in the context of interpretation. It is now a commonplace that in order to get going in the interpretation of the noises, marks and movements of aliens, we have to assume that what they do is behaviourally rational, issuing from a pattern of beliefs in the light of which it is an intelligible choice, and that the beliefs ascribed on the basis of the first assumption are attitudinally rational, being appropriately responsive to such factors as perceived counter-examples and inconsistencies.[23] This means, so far as language goes, that the natural strategy in assigning reference and extension to subject and predicate terms, and truth-conditions to sentences, is to present the aliens as having such beliefs as we would have found it rational to form in their circumstances, and such beliefs as help to make sense of their non-linguistic behaviour.

Granted such constraints on interpretation, how far as evaluative realists may we expect to be able – perhaps we should say, to be forced – to ascribe to aliens evaluative beliefs which diverge from ours? There are two important sorts of divergence which it will be useful to consider. The one would consist in the aliens' acknowledging a value of a sort that we do not recognize: they have an evaluative predicate in their language which cannot be aligned with any evaluative term or set of terms in ours. The other sort of divergence is less radical. It would involve the aliens' recognizing a value recognized by us but taking it to be realized in cases where we do not think that it is present: they have an evaluative predicate in their language which it is natural to translate into a certain evaluative term in ours, but they apply the predicate in some instances where we would not naturally apply its counterpart.[24]

Is it likely as evaluative realists that we would countenance the radical sort of divergence in construing the evaluative beliefs of aliens? Let us consider first of all the possibility of ascribing to them a radical evaluative mistake: the recognition of a non-existent value, the application of an evaluative predicate which we take to have empty extension. Such a mistake on the part of aliens would correspond to the non-evaluative mistake that we attribute to eighteenth-century chemists when we render what they say in such a way as to attribute to them a belief in phlogiston. If we find it interpretatively sensible to ascribe a radical error in non-evaluative matters, perhaps we should also be open to the prospect of attributing such error in evaluative concerns.

In principle I think that we should indeed be open to this prospect, but something needs to be said on an important difference between the non-evaluative and evaluative cases. Granted the constraints which we mentioned on interpretation, it is sensible to render assertions in such a way as to attribute a radical mistake to the speakers only if we can understand how they came to make the mistake in question. With theoretical scientific beliefs, or for that matter with metaphysical religious ones, it is relatively easy to see how people can come to have what we regard as radically erroneous beliefs: we make sense of their mistake by reference to the lack of evidence at their disposal, the inaccessibility of the alternative view by which we hold, the difficulty of the matter, or whatever. By contrast, it does not seem to be so easy to explain how people can come to have radically erroneous evaluative beliefs: that is, beliefs in values which we regard as non-existent. The theoretical or metaphysical entities about which we readily ascribe error in the other case are items which, if realistically construed, must be recognized to be beyond the immediate cognitive reach of those who speak of them, and this makes radical error understandable. The values about which we take people to be debating in our rendering of their evaluative utterances are not similarly transcendent, and so it appears to be more surprising that people should be radically misled in this area.

While the difference mentioned is undoubtedly a real one, and is likely to mark a difference in our dispositions to ascribe radical non-evaluative and evaluative mistakes, it must none the less be admitted that radical error in the recognition of values cannot be entirely ruled out. What values one countenances is determined at a certain level by the metaphysical beliefs one holds, and error in the latter area may well transmit itself into error in the former. Furthermore, what values one countenances is bound to be influenced by one's natural desire to legitimate the actions of which one is author, and the systems of which one is beneficiary. Finally, even if one is not metaphysically misled or complacently self-deceived, one may have one's perceptions of values radically warped by the effect of received ideology. These possible sources of error might be invoked at the extreme to make sense of the claim that certain aliens hold by a value which to us is non-existent.

This said, however, my inclination is to return to emphasis on the difference between the non-evaluative and evaluative cases, stressing the unlikelihood of ascribing radical misperception in evaluative matters. A further factor which supports that unlikelihood is that in our language we have available such a battery of evaluative terms that it is difficult to envisage being unable to find a term or set of terms among them to correlate with an evaluative predicate in an alien language. We may at first be puzzled at what aliens find motivating in a given property, as Malinowski was puzzled at the excitement occasioned among his argonauts when they were given a 'kula' object for safe-keeping. However, a little imagination should enable us in most cases to give a plausible evaluative rendering of the predicate in question, as Malinowski rendered receipt of the kula object as a mix between winning a trophy and taking possession of an heirloom.[25]

Ascribing radical error is one way of admitting radical divergence. The other way is ascribing radical insight or discovery, taking the natives to recognize a real value in a case where we have not hitherto acknowledged a value, or have perhaps denied that there is any. Were we to attribute such divergence, the result would not be criticism of the natives, as in the error case, but correction of ourselves. How likely is it that we should be persuaded that people in another culture have evaluative insights which radically outstrip our own?

Curiously the likelihood is greater than that of ascribing radical error. In attributing error, we have to explain how the aliens come to countenance a value which we take to be non-existent. In attributing insight, we have to explain how it is that we have not recognized the value in question. Our not recognizing a real value, however, need not mean our denying the value, and so it need not mean holding ourselves to have been in error; it may merely mean taking ourselves to have been in ignorance. It seems less likely that people should be in error about values than that they should merely be in ignorance of them. Thus we may think it not improbable that the attempt to interpret the evaluative utterances of aliens will lead us to ascribe radical insight, and to involve ourselves in self-correction. The linguistic consequence of the ascription of such insight would presumably be the admission that it is impossible to translate a certain term of the alien language into any term of ours, and the introduction of the term as a neologism in our own language.

So much for the possibility of acknowledging radical divergence of evaluative beliefs in interpreting across cultures. What then of the possibility of acknowledging moderate divergence: that is, divergence in respect of the range of instantiation of a value, not in respect of its reality? Here there are fewer problems than in the radical case. To take the error possibility first of all, it is plausible that aliens should often diverge from us in their judgments of the presence of a value that we also recognize. The sources of evaluative error mentioned earlier will make such divergence readily intelligible. Thus we can imagine a circumstance where it is natural to translate a certain alien predicate as 'is glorious', consistently with attributing to the aliens beliefs formulated in terms of the predicate, which we would regard as simply false. Examples of such beliefs might be 'It is glorious for a wife to be burned on her husband's funeral pyre', 'It is glorious to give obedience to one's religious leaders' and 'It is glorious to die for one's country'.

Equally with ascribing moderate error in evaluative beliefs, we are likely to find ourselves ascribing moderate insight, learning to see a certain value realized in a sort of action where we would not have recognized it before. The possibility in question here is one of coming to see something that we had overlooked before, or even coming to see something that we had explicitly denied before. One can imagine the possibility's being realized as we express a dawning recognition with words such as 'Yes, there is something glorious in. . .'. This sort of event is what Taylor envisages happening when, in dealing with an alien magic-religious view, we are struck by the fact that, contrary to our established scientific outlook, there is something attractive about a system which attunes one to the world at the same time that it informs one about it.

The remarks in this final section are designed to show, in support of Taylor's claim, that adopting evaluative realism introduces a dimension of critical interaction to cross-cultural interpretation. So long as we think realistically of values, we must be prepared to find ourselves morally as well as theoretically engaged by the enterprise of interpretation. We must be ready to see ourselves involved alternatively in criticism, in self-correction, and, perhaps more satisfyingly, in self-congratulation. As Taylor himself puts it, evaluative realism destroys the illusion that interpretation across cultures might be pursued in the manner of a value-free enquiry.

In conclusion it may be useful to silence a query which has been suppressed up to now. Someone may say: as an evaluative realist one may be inclined to assess the evaluations ascribed to people in another culture, but as a social scientist one has no reason to indulge that inclination; thus evaluative realism need not undermine the value-freedom of social science. What we have seen in this section enables us to respond to this objection. If one is an evaluative realist then one's ascriptions of evaluative beliefs will not be independent of one's assessments of those beliefs: this, because one will not normally want to ascribe beliefs which, on one's own assessment, there is no reason to maintain. Thus how one explains what people say and do, and how in general one makes sense of their response to their environment, will be crucially affected by what values one recognizes oneself. In this respect, as perhaps in others too, the explanation of human action will be intimately value-laden.[26]

NOTES

1 'Realism' is put in scare quotes for a reason given towards the end of section III. I am grateful to Simon Blackburn, Graham Macdonald, Ian Macdonald, David Papineau, Charles Taylor and David Wiggins for comments on an earlier draft. I am also grateful for comments received when the first three sections of the paper were read to a meeting of the senior philosophy seminar at the University of Bristol.

2 See John McDowell, 'Bivalence and verificationism' in Evans and McDowell (eds), *Truth and Meaning*, Oxford University Press, 1976.

3 David Wiggins draws attention to the distinction between invoking 'our ability' and 'the ability of speakers' in 'What would be a substantial theory of truth?', forthcoming in a *Festschrift* for Sir Peter Strawson, edited by Zak Van Straaten. At least for his purposes, and they are not quite ours, he is unsympathetic to the mention of 'our ability'. However he understands the phrase differently from us, taking the 'our' to refer to a whole culture or race or species. Notice that on our understanding of the phrase, the constraint invoked by the anti-realist may be taken more or less strictly, depending on what evidence is said to be compatible or incompatible with the position of the speakers.

4 An even weaker pattern of appropriate non-standard construal might be thought to be one which breaks with the standard pattern merely in describing assertions that lack determinate assertibility value as also lacking determinate truth-value. Such an interpretative strategy would need grounding in an account of what is wrong with the idea

242

of an assertion's being determinately true or false when it is not determinately assertible or counter-assertible. When such an account is provided, the strategy is likely to collapse into something like redescriptivism. I am grateful to Graham Macdonald for raising this point with me.

5 For a presentation and critique of ascriptivism see Peter Geach, 'Ascriptivism', in *Logic Matters*, Blackwell, Oxford, 1972.

6 On reductivism see Colin McGinn, 'An *a priori* argument for realism', *Journal of Philosophy*, 76 (1979); McGinn sees reductivism as the only way of being an anti-realist, whereas I think that it is one of a number of ways.

7 See Crispin Wright, 'Strawson on anti-realism', *Synthese*, 40 (1979), p. 294, for an excellent presentation of the redescriptivist line.

8 This is what Hilary Putnam describes as metaphysical realism. See his 'Realism and reason', in *Meaning and the Moral Sciences*, Routledge & Kegan Paul, London, 1978.

9 The relevant distinction between subjective and objective is drawn in the last chapter of Thomas Nagel's *Mortal Questions*, Cambridge University Press, 1979. Objectivist realism, as it might be described, is the doctrine criticized by John McDowell in his paper in this volume. It is the absolute conception of things which Bernard Williams characterizes in his *Descartes*, Penguin, Harmondsworth, 1978.

10 For some comment on the issue involved here see the introduction to J. Raz (ed.), *Practical Reasoning*, Oxford University Press, 1978.

11 The difference between judgments of value *simpliciter* and judgments of value *secundum quid* is discussed in Donald Davidson 'Intending' in Y. Yovel (ed.), *Philosophy of History and Action*, Reidel, Dordrecht, 1978. David Wiggins in 'Truth, invention and the meaning of life', *Proceedings of the British Academy*, 62 (1976), draws a distinction similar to that drawn here between evaluations and prescriptions. Notice that it is often unclear whether 'moral' realism is meant to be evaluative or prescriptive realism.

12 This point is well made in Keith Graham, 'Moral notions and moral misconceptions', *Analysis*, 35 (1975); he distinguishes between an action's being generally right or wrong and its being right or wrong decisively.

Evaluations which use ambiguous notions may be regarded as surrogates for evaluations in which the operative respect is spelled out. Thus the later discussions in this paper are carried on as if there were only evaluations of the latter sort.

13 On the two ways of negating judgments of value see Bernard Williams, 'Consistency and realism' and 'Ethical consistency', reprinted in *Problems of the Self*, Cambridge University Press, 1973. David Wiggins in 'Truth, invention and the meaning of life', *op. cit.*, p. 367, points out that 'must' and 'must not' are incompatible, being contraries.

14 The moral dilemmas emphasized in Bernard Williams, *op. cit.*, testify to this. For recent discussions see Ross Harrison, 'Ethical consistency', in R. Harrison (ed.), *Rational Action*, Cambridge University Press,

1979; Samuel Guttenplan, 'Moral realism and moral dilemmas', *Proceedings of the Aristotelian Society*, 1979–80; R. B. Marcus, 'Moral dilemmas and consistency', *Journal of Philosophy*, 77 (1980).

Notice that if one says that each of the rival prescriptions is rightly denied in a moral dilemma, and takes the decision as a toss of the coin, then such a dilemma does not provide a case where assertibility and truth-conditions come apart. The thought might lead one to say that the only plausible prescriptive realism is realism in a broad sense, such as that characterized at the end of section III for the evaluative case.

Notice that one may take the evaluative conflict in moral dilemmas to be particularly severe, and irresoluble only for that reason. The evaluative realist who is inclined towards prescriptive anti-realism may say that cases of less severe evaluative conflict can be resolved and that determinate prescriptions are forthcoming there.

15 It is not much to offer. For a full and committed account of the motivation to evaluative anti-realism see the first chapter of J. L. Mackie, *Ethics*, Penguin, Harmondsworth, 1977. In presenting the motivation for evaluative anti-realism we are imposing rather bluntly the mould cast in section I; this should not cause any problems, however, and it does make for a unified perspective on the different cases where the debate between realism and anti-realism arises.

16 Notice that because they ascribe truth-values to evaluations, reductivist analyses may seem to have the same result for the value-ladenness of social science as evaluative realism would have. However they will not always do so, since it is a common feature of reductivist analyses that they render evaluative facts as facts about states of desire or need, or about the prospects of satisfying such states; the desires or needs will usually be the evaluator's own, or his community's, or they may belong to some authority he acknowledges. Such facts are not of the kind that would raise the value-ladenness issue sharply: they are facts on which native speakers have a special authority, and as interpreters we would be little inclined to question and criticize the natives' views. Things would only be otherwise if the desires or needs were held to be species-wide, which they may well be held to be.

17 See R. M. Hare, *Freedom and Reason*, Clarendon Press, Oxford, 1963. Notice that many of Hare's descriptivist or naturalistic rivals took the view that evaluations were assertions such as those given in our examples, made in a context where appropriate desires or needs are assumed. In our terms the differences between Hare and those critics are not very significant.

18 It may be a concern about such an ambiguity which leads David Wiggins in 'Truth, invention and the meaning of life' (*op. cit.*) to speak of anti-non-cognitivism. Notice however that evaluative anti-realism in its reductivist form need not be non-cognitivist; there is still truth to be known.

19 See Graham Macdonald and Philip Pettit, *Semantics and Social Science*, Routledge & Kegan Paul, London, forthcoming, Chapter 2.

20 The argument appears in G. E. Moore's *Ethics*. Notice that it might be applied, not just against instrumentalism, but against certain reductivist doctrines, such as the sort of subjectivism which would represent people as each speaking of their own attitudinal states in apparently debating some evaluative topic.

21 'Non-cognitivism and rule-following', this volume p. 144.

22 As a general doctrine, evaluative reductivism might seem to be supported by the fact that whether something is to be evaluated in a certain way or not is clearly determined by how it is non-evaluatively characterized: the fact, in other terms, that evaluation is supervenient on (non-evaluative) description. Here it should be noticed that to deny reductivism need not be to deny supervenience, since while description may determine evaluation, evaluation need not effectively determine, and need not therefore be reducible to, description: there may be an indefinite number of descriptions on which a given evaluation can supervene.

23 This is argued in Graham Macdonald and Philip Pettit, *op. cit.*

24 Notice that we ignore the divergence constituted by the aliens' not recognizing certain values acknowledged by us: the asymmetry of the relationship between interpreter and interpretee makes this case less pressing than those which we consider.

25 See B. Malinowski, *Argonauts of the western Pacific*, Routledge & Kegan Paul, London, 1922.

26 The remarks in this paragraph need elaboration, for it will not be clear how exactly the evaluative realist assumption is likely to affect interpretation, especially when prescriptive realism is not assumed. Such elaboration is attempted in the final chapter of Macdonald and Pettit, *op. cit.*

INDEX

247

Index

existence, mistakes about, 78–9, 82
experiential sentence, 60
explanation, 32, 47, 67–8, 191–210

first-person speech, 11–18
Flew, A. G. N., 70
Fodor, J. A., 137
Fogelin, Rogert, 187
Foot, Philippa, 155
force, 107
Frege, Gottlob, 35, 37–9, 65, 107, 122

Gadamer, H. G., 206
Geach, Peter, 122, 243
Geisteswissenschaffen, understanding and explanation in, 191–210
Graham, Keith, 243
grammar, 19–20, 32, 47, 121–2; *see also* language
Guttenplan, Samuel, 244

Hacker, Peter, 32, 69–71, 95
Hare, R. M., 26–7, 159–61, 228, 244
Harman, G., 136
Harrison, Ross, 243
Hart, H. L. A., 70
Holtzman, Steven, 1
humanism, 230–43
Hume, David, 154, 165, 167, 170, 181
humour, 168
Hurley, Susan, 161

I speech, 11–18
identity and difference, 32
inconsistency, 172
indefiniteness, 74
indeterminacy, 176–7
infinity, 129
institution, rule as, 72, 75
instrumentalism, 59–61, 232–3
interpretation and evaluative realism, 211–45

investigation-independence, 99–106

Jones, O. R., 94
judgments in language, 4–5

Kenny, A. J. P., 86, 93
knowledge, tacit, 110, 118–36
Kripke, Saul, 31, 69, 87, 187
Kuhn, T., 37

Ladefoged, P., 137
language: Augustinian, 37–47; as calculus, 44–7, 52–3, 66–7, 73–4; creativity of, 69, 122–3; descriptive, 15–17, 37–9; first-person, 11–18; judgments in, 4–5; model of, 122–30; natural, 106–37; private, 1–27, 76, 79–82, 93; structure-reflecting, 118–19; *see also* semantic theory
Leich, Christopher, 1
Lewis, David, 187
LFM, 64, 68
logical atomism, 44–5, 68
Luckhardt, C. G., 70

Macdonald, Graham, 242, 244–5
Macdonald, Ian, 242
McDowell, John, 116–17, 141, 164–75, 182, 234
McGinn, Colin, 243
Mackie, J., 159, 161, 186, 244
Malcolm, Norman, 82, 94
Malinowski, B., 240, 245
Martin, C. B., 186
Marx, Karl, 210
mathematics, 21, 26, 50–3; *see also Remarks on the Foundation of Mathematics*
meaning, theory of, 48, 90–137, 177–9
meaninglessness, 14
measurements, 61–4, 75–6
Mellor, D. H., 186
mental processes, 51–2
Merkmal, 47

248

International Library of Philosophy

Editor: Ted Honderich

(Demy 8vo)